Stories, Identities, and Political Change

Stories, Identities, and Political Change

Charles Tilly

ROWMAN & LITTLEFIELD PUBLISHERS, INC.
Lanham • Boulder • New York • Oxford

ROWMAN & LITTLEFIELD PUBLISHERS, INC.

Published in the United States of America
by Rowman & Littlefield Publishers, Inc.
A Member of the Rowman & Littlefield Publishing Group
4720 Boston Way, Lanham, Maryland 20706
www.rowmanlittlefield.com

12 Hid's Copse Road
Cumnor Hill, Oxford OX2 9JJ, England

British Library Cataloguing in Publication Information Available

Library of Congress Cataloging-in-Publication Data
Tilly, Charles.
    Stories, identities, and political change / Charles Tilly.
        p. cm.
    Includes bibliographical references and index.
    ISBN 0-7425-1881-7 (cloth : alk. paper) — ISBN 0-7425-1882-5 (pbk. :
alk. paper)
    1. Social conflict. 2. Social change. 3. Social movements. 4.
Political participation. 5. Storytelling—Social aspects. I. Title.
    HM1121 .T54 2002
    303—dc21

                                                                2002001827

Printed in the United States of America

♾™ The paper used in this publication meets the minimum requirements of
American National Standard for Information Sciences—Permanence of Paper
for Printed Library Materials, ANSI/NISO Z39.48-1992.

Contents

Part IV Political Change

Preface

One lazy afternoon in the summer of 1997, I was scrolling through the Canadian government Web site for information about that great country. To my delight, I came across a link—now, alas, dissolved—to the Comenius Group's program called Fluency Through Fables. "Each month," it announced, "The Comenius Group provides a fable and a variety of exercises to assist students of English." Fortunately, the Comenius Group and the program survived their banishment from the Canadian Web site; through their own Web site, they are still offering services to people who want to learn English. Fluency Through Fables is a fabulous find. The Czech scholar John Amos Comenius (or Komensky), after all, wrote *The Visible World*, reputed to be the first illustrated book for children. More important, the slogan *Fluency Through Fables* vividly labels a paradox that connects knowledge of Canada with pursuit of social science in general.

More on that paradox in a moment. Do you know about the eminent Canadian social scientist Stephen Leacock? You will meet him again in chapter 3. Born in England, Leacock came to a farm in Orillia, Ontario (about 130 kilometers north of Toronto, on Lake Simcoe), in 1876 at the age of seven. By 1887, young Stephen had become Head Boy at Upper Canada College in Toronto before moving on to the University of Toronto. After graduating from the University of Toronto in 1891, he taught at Upper Canada. Looking back decades later, he mused, "Of my pupils, those who seemed the laziest and the least enamoured of books are now rising to eminence at the bar, in business, and in public life; the really promising boys who took all the prizes are now able with difficulty to earn the wages of a clerk in a summer hotel or a deck hand on a canal boat."

The preface adapts "Fluency Through Fables," an address to the Sociological Research Association, Toronto, Ontario, August 1997, hence the focus on Canada. Background: I served on the University of Toronto's faculty from 1965 to 1969.

Recognizing that grim prospect, Leacock had quit his job at Upper Canada in 1899. He then studied political economy with Thorstein Veblen at the University of Chicago, completing a doctorate in four years. Of the Ph.D., Leacock noted, "The meaning of this degree is that the recipient of instruction is examined for the last time in his life, and is pronounced completely full. After this, no new ideas can be imparted to him."

Dr. Leacock returned to Canada, but now to Montreal and McGill University, where he spent most of his career as department chair of economics and political science. (Speaking of eminence, in 1879, when Leacock was ten years old, McGill students invented hockey as we now know it by substituting a flat puck for the ball previously used in team competition on ice. The rest, as they say, is history.) Leacock's textbook, *Elements of Political Science*, became a best-seller. As he grew older and wiser, however, Stephen Leacock turned increasingly from social science to humor—even he said there was a difference!—producing such classics as *Literary Lapses* and *Sunshine Sketches of a Little Town*, a thinly disguised set of fables about Orillia. He called the town Mariposa.

"I don't know whether you know Mariposa," *Sunshine Sketches* begins. "If not, it is of no consequence, for if you know Canada at all, you are probably well acquainted with a dozen towns just like it." Leacock goes on to describe the hubbub of Mariposa, then qualifies:

Of course if you come to the place fresh from New York, you are deceived. Your standard of vision is all astray. You do think the place is quiet. You do imagine that Mr. Smith is asleep merely because he closes his eyes as he stands. But live in Mariposa for six months or a year and then you will begin to understand it better; the buildings get higher and higher; the Mariposa House grows more and more luxurious; McCarthy's Block towers to the sky; the buses roar and hum to the station; the trains shriek; the traffic multiplies; the people move faster and faster; a dense crowd swirls to and fro in the post-office and the five and ten cent store—and amusements! Well, now! lacrosse, baseball, excursions, dances, the Firemen's Ball every winter and the Catholic picnic every summer! and music—the town band in the park every Wednesday evening, and the Oddfellows' brass band on the street every other Friday; the Mariposa Quartette, the Salvation Army—why, after a few months' residence you begin to realize that the place is a mere mad round of gaiety. (Leacock 1970: 1)

Echoing Leacock in 1997, Mayor Clayt French of Orillia actually called the place Sunshine City and declared, "We have much to offer here and I'm certain you will have no difficulty in finding activities in which to participate." As eyes blurred by New York or Toronto regain focus, we see the ferment of small town Ontario. If we are not only sympathetic observers but also reflective social scientists, we eventually recognize the paradox I promised earlier: Stories are crucial to understanding Canadian life and social life in general, but stories hinder our explanation of Canadian life and social life in general.

The Story of Canada, a children's book that Barry Wellman sent to me from Toronto, confronts our paradox without stating it, much less resolving it. Speaking on the book's first page of the period before glaciers began to melt about twenty thousand years ago, the authors remark, "In all those centuries when ice covered the land, no forests, no plants, no animals, and no people could live in the country that is now Canada." By the book's end, they are saying, "But near the end of the 20th century, Canada was still many peoples, many communities." Across the intervening three hundred pages, nevertheless, they have pursued the task of telling a story about something called Canada during two hundred centuries.

What was this Canada? What is it? New Brunswick, Nova Scotia, Québec, and Ontario formed the Dominion of Canada in 1867. After a number of other provinces, Newfoundland and Labrador did not join Confederation until 1949. St. Pierre and Miquelon persist today as French possessions lying between Newfoundland and Nova Scotia. In 1990 representatives of Inuit peoples settled their land claims on the federal government, at least provisionally, with the creation of a 350,000-square-kilometer semiautonomous territory called Nunavut. The secession of Québec remains an ever-present possibility. Yet, authors of *The Story of Canada* have little choice but to take the territory your atlas and mine label "Canada" as a coherent, self-propelling entity.

Stories concerning everything that happens inside such a boundary have peculiar properties:

• Although we tell them forward, their logics run backward, from the present state of affairs to prehistory; they involve a subtle teleology.
• They presume that where state boundaries begin, so does a society; where they end, that society also ends.
• They impute a kind of coherence and self-propulsion, or at least self-motivation, to units ranging from individual Canadians to "peoples" and "communities" within the territory to something called "Canada" as a whole.

I am not complaining about the social scientific simplifications of a great Canadian humorist or the social scientific premises of a very effective Canadian children's book. I want instead to point out that, as Stephen Leacock's stories and *The Story of Canada* illustrate, a certain sort of story prevails in social accounting and remains almost indispensable to it. Yet, that sort of story generally misrepresents the ontology and causal structure of the social processes about whose outcomes people tell such stories. (Chapter 3 takes up the place of stories in social analysis in much more detail, while chapter 6 shows you Jacques Rancière concluding— wrongly, I argue there—that the defects of such stories render historical explanation of social processes impossible.) As a consequence, social scientists confront a series of difficult problems, but also encounter a wonderful opportunity.

Stories intervene at three different points in the work of explaining social processes:

First, in the available evidence about social processes, which commonly arrives in the form of stories people tell about themselves or others and therefore requires unpacking

Second, in the social behavior to be explained, which often features storytelling
and responses to it

Third, in prevailing explanations by participants, observers, and analysts, which
likewise borrow the conventions of storytelling

For integration into effective explanations, all three require the peculiar combination of skepticism about the stories told with close attention to how stories work.
Stories thus present serious problems for social analysts. But they also present an
opportunity. The opportunity is to build systematic explanations of storytelling
into more general accounts of social processes.

This book reports a decade's exploration of these problems and of the opportunity they open. It pivots on (1) stories, (2) collective conversations, (3) political
identities, and (4) large-scale political changes we can better understand if we pay
attention to how stories, conversations, and identities actually work. Between its
introduction and conclusion, the book presents edited versions of a dozen essays
published in widely scattered places from 1992 to 2000. It documents encounters
with the questions raised, but not well answered, by analysts of social construction.
It takes seriously the challenge not only to recognize but also to explain the construction of political entities and identities. It argues repeatedly that stories matter,
but fail dramatically to provide viable explanations; indeed, these stories demand
explanation in their turn.

Seen from behind the backs of raconteurs, most of social life consists of interpersonal transactions whose consequences the participants can neither foresee nor
control. Yet, after the fact, participants in complex social transactions seal them with
stories. Those stories portray the participants as acting with deliberation and fore-
sight. Even more impressive, participants often succeed in producing collective
agreement on what happened. Nationalist leaders, union organizers, and social
movement activists fashion widely accepted stories about who they are, where they
came from, and what they are doing. As he lays out his superb ethnography of daily
life in an Ulster village, Henry Glassie comments on the importance of storytelling:

> It is no falsification to find a fit between the hopes of the angry romantics and the in-
> tentions of Ballymenone's tellers. Their stories exist within two intersecting categories
> of action that compel the creative person into social responsibility. As a heightened
> kind of speech, the story lifts above the "silence" through which individuals sicken into
> themselves. Stories rise above "talk" where words are idle, unconnected, or potentially
> harmful. Stories rise above "chat," where words bring people into engagement, above
> "crack," where engagement becomes amusing. (Glassie 1982, 155)

Ballymenone's stories, with their partial division into Protestant and Catholic stories in this mixed village, provide bolsters for political identity, but they also provide the means of surmounting political barriers.

The prevalence and power of storytelling in political processes set problems of
description, conceptualization, and explanation. *Descriptively,* a large share of all the

evidence available on such political processes arrives packaged in stories: participants' declarations, court proceedings, observers' reports, historians' reconstructions, and more. Analysts must therefore learn enough about the production of such stories to reconstruct both what happened and how the prevailing accounts came to prevail. (I often tell my students they must develop and test two separate, if interdependent, theories: one concerning the processes generating their evidence, the other concerning the processes they are ultimately trying to explain.)

Conceptually, analysts have choices to make concerning the social locations of collective stories: In individual consciousness multiplied? In culture at large? In the voices of leaders and storytelling specialists? In conversations among activists? Elsewhere? From the viewpoint of *explanation,* finally, we face the problems of (1) accounting for the emergence and dominance of certain stories, and (2) tracing the impact of stories on politics. The chapters that follow offer repeated attempts to clarify the explanatory problems.

Stories play significant parts across a wide range of social life. This book, however, concentrates on their place in political mobilization, conflict, and change. It returns over and over again to political identity stories—collective, public replies to the question "Who are you?" It pinpoints political identity stories in nationalism, citizenship, social movements, democratization, and state transformation. It rejects, however, the easy image of storytelling as a monologist speaking to a rapt, silent audience. It insists instead (as chapter 9 states most explicitly) on shared political stories as outcomes of contentious conversation. Its image of storytelling resembles what happens as people caught in a turbulent crowd piece together what is happening, then, after the crowd has dispersed, they compare and reassess their earlier readings of the event.

As the book proceeds, three clusters of ideas repeatedly come into play. The first cluster concerns ontology—what entities we can reasonably assume to exist in social life. I distinguish among utter skepticism, solipsism, holism, methodological individualism, phenomenological individualism, and relational realism, making the case for treating social transactions and relations as the fundamental entities of social life. To put it more ponderously, but also more accurately, social life consists of relationally and culturally channeled, error-filled and error-correcting transactions among social sites that continuously modify the relations and culture within which they occur. Unpacked, this sort of relational realism says the following:

- Social sites consist of loci in which organized human action occurs; they include individuals, aspects of individuals, organizations, networks, and places. (An example from the Indian conflicts of 1990 discussed in chapter 9: Some people in Hyderabad showed up in public as Hindus, others as Muslims, even though they had plenty of other identities at their disposal; in this case, "Hindus" and "Muslims" became distinct social sites.)
- Transactions—transfers of energy organized by people—connect social sites. (Example: Hindus stabbed Muslims, and Muslims stabbed Hindus.)

- Repeated transactions constitute relations among social sites. (Example: A series of well-defined, and hostile relations connected Hindus and Muslims in Hyderabad.)
- Transactions take place within limits set by previous relations among the sites (or types of sites) in question, including culture, the shared understandings and their representations in objects and practices. (Example: Mobilized Hindus and Muslims drew on widely shared beliefs about each other's perfidy.)
- From the perspectives of the sites, transactions ordinarily involve errors and error correction; efficient transactions involve relatively small errors and rapid error correction. (Example: Hyderabad's ten weeks of violence began with a land dispute between two gangs in the course of which two Hindus killed a Muslim, which activated much more general mobilizations on either side of the Hindu–Muslim boundary.)
- However minimally, each transaction modifies relations among sites, including shared understandings and their representations. (Example: Members of the two categories moved from uneasy but peaceful coexistence to street fighting in which more than three hundred people died.)

This ontology differs radically from the assumption of self-maintaining social systems (holism) and from either phenomenological or methodological individualism. Holists might treat Hyderabad's Hindu–Muslim conflict as a product of malfunction in Indian society. Phenomenological individualists might try to plumb Hindu and Muslim mentalities for explanations of their incompatibility. Methodological individualists would most likely try to reconstruct the strategic game pitting Hindus against Muslims. The book's relational realism also rejects solipsism and utter skepticism, claiming that transactions are real and observable. (Chapters 2 and 6 offer the book's most sustained and explicit critiques of solipsism and skepticism, but the entire text battles against them.)

The second cluster of ideas concerns explanation—what we can reasonably take as a valid account of why in some circumstances (or class of circumstances) X happened rather than a possible Y. Distinguishing among covering law, system, purposive, and mechanism-process explanations, I argue for mechanisms and processes as the core of effective social scientific explanation. (Processes are recurrent combinations or sequences of causal mechanisms.) In the Hyderabad case, that program calls for a close look at the mechanisms and processes by which local fights (in this case, between two gangs) activate major boundaries and promote mutual destruction across those boundaries.

Assuming that explanatory strategy, the third cluster concerns identity mechanisms and processes. Chapters to follow examine the interplay among storytelling, conversation, social categories, boundary formation, identity claims, interpersonal solidarity, collective contention, and political change. They treat the construction, challenge, defense, and transformation of collective answers to the questions "Who are you?" "Who are we?" and "Who are they?" as central to a wide range of political contention. (In the Hyderabad events, the crucial answers given certainly include "Hindu" and "Muslim," but they also turn out to include "wrestler" and "political patron.") Thus, the book's overall orientation is relational, mechanism-oriented, and identity-centered.

Rogers Brubaker and Fred Cooper, two students of social processes who have earned great respect, have recently proposed that we expunge *identity* from our analytic lexicon because the term has acquired too many meanings and too few specifications (Brubaker and Cooper 2000). I propose instead that we get identity right. We can, I think, escape the search for inner selves about which Brubaker and Cooper rightly complain by recognizing that people regularly negotiate and deploy socially based answers to the questions "Who are you?" "Who are we?" and "Who are they?" These are identity questions. Their answers are identities—always assertions, always contingent, always negotiable, but also always consequential. Identities are social arrangements reinforced by socially constructed and continuously renegotiated stories.

My view has strong implications for teaching and writing. To the extent that we pursue social science as explanation, we must find ways of constructing and communicating nonstory models. To the extent that we pursue it as enlightenment, however, we must reassemble our results into superior stories that nonspecialists can carry into their own social experiences. We can think of four levels of proximity to standard stories. At the enlightenment end of the scale we purvey *superior stories*. Such stories

- include all the major actors that a valid causal account of the events in question would identify and relate;
- within the social interactions they describe, accurately represent cause-effect relations among actions of participants in the story, even if they neglect indirect, incremental, and other effects that are not visible in the participants' interactions;
- provide effective means of connecting the story with times, places, actors, and actions outside its purview; and
- offer means of relating causes explicitly invoked by the story with other causes that are indirect, incremental, unintended, collective, and/or mediated by the nonhuman environment.

Superior stories, that is, do not identify all the relevant causal mechanisms and processes, but they remain consistent with fuller, more adequate causal accounts. Without the polemics I have deployed elsewhere (e.g., in Tilly 1995d, 18–41), for instance, chapter 7 implicitly challenges a common standard story in British historiography. In that story, the British Ruling Class (or even Britain personified) confronts the People (alias the Unruly Masses) and, motivated either by Fear or by Wisdom, makes gradual Concessions to Democracy.

Chapter 7 proposes a superior story. In its version, political entrepreneurs such as Lord George Gordon, William Pitt, and Daniel O'Connell assemble coalitions whose competition and joint action eventually pressure the British government to enlarge Catholics' political rights. The story is superior because the causes it represents did work more or less as the story says. It nevertheless falls short of a satisfactory explanation because it fails to represent a series of incremental, indirect, unanticipated, and otherwise complex causes such as those by which the Napoleonic Wars increased the House of Commons' powers relative to the royal government and the House of Lords, thus increasing the regime's responsiveness to popular pressure (Tilly 1997a).

One level closer to explanation, we can *contextualize* stories, which means placing crucial stories in their nonstory contexts and seeing what social work they do. In the case of Catholic Emancipation, we can scrutinize the contradictory stories that prevailed among advocates and opponents of the Catholic cause. Still closer to explanation, we can *generate* stories, account deliberately for the form, content, and deployment of the stories that people—now including observers and analysts—create. In the case of Catholic Emancipation, we provide an account of how and why so many ordinary English people accepted the portrayal of Catholics as a menace to the British political system. At that point we come close to integrating standard stories with deep social scientific explanation.

These opening reflections incorporate, of course, some storytelling of their own. I have spoken as though from the earliest writing in the book (in 1990) to the latest (in 2001) I pursued a consistent set of ideas, needing only to fill in blanks and find applications. A contrary reader, however, might well enjoy reading this book in another way—looking for hesitations, contradictions, and blind alleys in the path I have taken. A contrarian might reasonably complain, for example, that I repeatedly point to my one-time collaborator Stein Rokkan as a model for students of political change, yet Rokkan himself generally pursued the sorts of covering law explanations of politics that I reject. Another might rightly point out that the identity mechanisms featured in the book's earlier chapters play no more than bit parts in the analyses of large-scale political change that dominate the book's fourth and final section. Let me admit frankly that the book as a whole represents incomplete and sometimes inconsistent work in progress.

Another confession that sounds a warning: Most of the book works with concrete historical episodes—Zapatista self-presentation in Mexico, political repertoire change in Great Britain, Hindu–Muslim conflicts in India, and more. Those repeated concrete cases can create an illusion of confrontation between arguments and evidence. Elsewhere I have often presented similar material as evidence for one argument and against another. Many of the British episodes, for example, come from a long-term effort to explain how and why the forms of national contentious politics changed in Great Britain between the 1750s and the 1830s. This book, however, deploys the episodes almost exclusively to clarify conceptual and theoretical points. This book does not stand or fall on the adequacy of its evidence. It succeeds or fails to the extent that it produces more adequate theories of political change and identifies new ways of gathering evidence to test those theories.

Let me also warn that assembling a book from a dozen pieces prepared for different audiences leaves not only gaps and badly fitted edges, but also awkward overlaps. If you read this book through to the end, you will hear multiple versions of a sermon on the virtues of relational analysis, repeated definitions of social movements, many statements about the negotiated and interactive character of political identities, several discussions of connections between top-down and bottom-up nationalism, and more than one discourse about conceptions of democratization. In a pessimistic reading, all this redundancy threatens boredom, impatience, and/or resentment. In an optimistic reading, this modus operandi underlines the points of greatest importance. I hope this book attracts quite a few fellow optimists.

My students at the New School and Columbia have paid me the compliment of taking the ideas in this book seriously. Instead of dutifully writing notes or yawning behind their hands, they have energetically demanded clarification, application, and extension of my ideas about stories, identities, and political change. However inadequately, this book replies to their demands.

New York City
August 2001

Part I

STORIES AND EXPLANATIONS

1

Introduction

The next time you compose a letter explaining why you haven't replied to urgent messages recently, hire Subcomandante Marcos of Zapatista fame as your scribe. The self-styled subcomandante led the guerrilla force of Chiapas, Mexico's poorest and southernmost state, that began to attract world attention in January 1994. The *guerrilleros* called themselves EZLN, for Zapatista Army of National Liberation, thus claiming succession from the famed peasant leader of the Mexican Revolution, Emiliano Zapata. Writing to "all the large, medium-sized, small, marginal, pirate, buccaneer, and etcetera presses who are publishing the communiqués and letters of the EZLN and have written asking for a prologue for your respective publications, or have requested an exclusive of some kind or other," he first itemizes the immense difficulties his newly recruited guerrilla band has encountered in the mountains, then tells the following story:

> On one of these days of exploration, we returned to camp, as always, completely wiped out. While the rations of *pinole* and water were being distributed, I turned on the short-wave radio to catch the evening news, but out of the radio came only the strident song of parrots and macaws. . . . But I didn't let such a small incident bother me, as I was accustomed to seeing in these mountains things as apparently absurd as a little deer with a red carnation in its mouth (probably in love, because if not, why a *red* carnation?), a tapir with violet ballet shoes, a herd of wild boar playing cards and, with their teeth and hooves, tapping out the rhythm of "we will break down the house to see Doña Blanca" . . . I wasn't much surprised and I moved the dial looking for another station, but there wasn't anything but the songs of the parrots and macaws.

This chapter adapts "Stories of Social Construction," unpublished lecture, University of Michigan, December 1997.

3

The comandante goes on to tell a colorful tale. He opens the radio, birds galore fly out, and he finds the skeleton of a parrot buried beneath a cross and the inscription *Requiescat in Pace*. Near the tomb he discovers a tiny nest containing a gray egg speckled with green and blue, then a letter containing a story within the comandante's story. The dead parrot's letter describes her love affair with a handsome macaw and asks anyone who finds the letter to take care of their offspring, the speckled egg. The comandante places the egg on his belly, then waits for it to hatch. He reports his surprise

> to see come out of the shell neither a macaw nor a parrot, nor even a little baby chicken or a dove. No, what came out of the shell was—a little tapir! Seriously, it was a little tapir with green and blue feathers. A plumed tapir! In a moment of clarity . . . I understood the true meaning of this sordid little story. . . .
>
> What had happened was the parrot . . . had a liaison with a tapir, they sinned, and she was trying to frame the macaw. But everything had now fallen apart. . . . Having figured out the mystery, the only thing left was to decide what I was going to do with the bastard tapir—and I am still trying to decide. For the time being I carry her hidden in my knapsack and give her a little of my food. I don't deny that we like each other, and my maternal instinct (excuse me, paternal) has given way to an insane passion toward the tapir, who throws me ardent glances which don't have much to do with polite gratefulness but rather with a badly controlled passion. My problem is severe: if I fall into temptation, I will not only commit a crime against nature, but also incest, because, after all, I am her adopted father. I have thought about abandoning her, but I can't, she is more powerful than I. In short, I don't know what the hell to do.
>
> As you can see, I have too many problems here to be able to attend to yours. I hope that now you will understand my continued silence in regard to the questions that you insist on putting before me. . . .
>
> *Salud*, and please send me a veterinary manual for wild animals of the tropics. (Ross et al. 1995, 23–25)

Ever the revolutionary dialectician, Marcos offers his materialist analysis as thesis and the plumed tapir as antithesis, but leaves his synthesis for future work. As this book ends 200-odd pages from now, if you complain that I haven't solved all the problems my topic raises, I will offer my reply in the style of Subcomandante Marcos. Plenty of work remains for all of us.

The *guerrillero's* letter exemplifies, if fancifully, a series of problems that have risen higher and higher on the agendas of historians and social scientists over the last twenty years: When it comes to describing and explaining social processes, do any credible versions of realism remain? If many or all social processes entail discursive construction of the entities within them, must interpretation replace description and explanation as central activities of social science? Is discursive construction itself accessible to systematic description and explanation? Is it possible to make falsifiable statements—descriptive or explanatory—about social processes? Can we incorporate narrative processes into a viable vision of realist social science? Or, in the last analysis, is the effort to explain human storytelling just a tale of macaws and plumed tapirs, another awkward foray into magic realism?

After years of denial, I have come to think that failure to address these pressing questions directly, instead of shrugging them off as impertinent distractions, has cramped the credibility and fruitfulness of what could be a rich renewal of relational realism. It is time to rediscover the centrality of social transactions, ties, and relations to social processes and to investigate connections between social relations, on one side, and social construction, on the other. Structural realism stands as the thesis, social construction as the antithesis—the seductive plumed tapir—and relational realism as the hoped-for synthesis.

I stumbled into these problems myself along two paths that first diverged, then converged again. Both started with participation, beginning in the 1950s, in the Marxist-populist drive to construct a "history from below" that would somehow introduce the vivified voices of ordinary and oppressed people into accounts of political processes. The first path from that starting point was an effort to comprehend and respond to a critique of the structural realism my own work had forwarded for many years. I first heard that critique's muffled drumbeat as rhythms of Habermas, Heidegger, Derrida, and Foucault reached Ann Arbor during the 1970s, then experienced it as roaring tympani at the New School for Social Research during the 1980s.

Although such figures as Albert Soboul, Eric Hobsbawm, E. P. Thompson, and Alberto Caracciolo certainly disagreed sharply about many historical issues, by and large they (and the rest of us populist historians) assumed that popular entities, identities, and interests formed more or less automatically in the course of social change, then constituted observable realities. The chief analytical problem, it then seemed, was to identify processes that promoted shared consciousness of objective interests and organizational capacity to act on those interests. A new generation of analysts, however, challenged that sort of structural realism in the many names of social construction. My first path toward this book's topic, then, took me through consideration of that challenge.

The second path was different. As I finished my youthful analysis of the 1793 counterrevolution in France (Tilly 1964), I took up a longer-range examination of relations between what I then thought of as "social change and political upheaval" in France. Involved in cataloging conflict-filled events, I soon borrowed from Eric Hobsbawm and George Rudé a distinction between prepolitical and political, between traditional and modern, between old and new forms of protest and almost as soon started recognizing inadequacies in my whole formulation of the problem. It took me years to correct those inadequacies—enough years that critics still sometimes identify my work with long-abandoned trichotomies such as primitive-reactionary-modern or competitive-reactive-proactive.

Here we need not retrace that whole tortuous itinerary, but need only pull out two related strands: reformulation of ideas about repertoires of contention and about contentious identities. By a *repertoire of contention* I mean a set of performances by which members of any pair of politically constituted actors make claims on each other, claims that, if realized, would affect their object's interests. By *contentious identities* I mean collective answers to the question "Who are you?" "Who are we?" and "Who are they?" offered by participants in such claim making. Over the years, I have frequently studied repertoires and contentious identities by means of systematic catalogs enumerating strikes, violent incidents, revolutionary situations, contentious gatherings, or other similar sequences of events within well-defined time-place settings. Anyone who tries to relate such events, individually and collectively, to their social contexts eventually recognizes the interactive, negotiated, contingent, culturally shaped character of repertoires and identities—in short, begins to modify the simplest structural realist position in the direction of social construction.

Of course, many historians and social scientists had moved in that direction long before me. They criticized structural realists for reifying social categories, organizations, and interests; for exaggerating the ubiquity, homogeneity, directionality, and power of large-scale change processes; for neglecting cultural variation; for failing to take phenomenology seriously. To the extent that they led to radical phenomenological reductionism or to solipsism, as they often did, these criticisms did not advance our inquiries into social processes. Short of those extremes, however, they identified serious weaknesses of populist history as commonly practiced from the 1950s onward. Intelligent consideration of these weaknesses can produce an effective dialectic. Populist history serves as thesis, constructivist skepticism as antithesis, and relational realism as synthesis.

The problem as a whole requires attention to the interplay between cognitive processes and social transactions; to questions of epistemology and ontology; to the influence of social networks on political action; to the tension between individualistic and collective accounts of social processes; to the relative importance of deliberate means-end action, on one side, and indirect, cumulative, unanticipated, and environmentally mediated causes in social life, on the other. Here I will bypass these issues, which much of my recent writing pursues obsessively, in favor of an illustrative focus on contentious politics. By *contentious politics* I mean collective, public making of claims that, if realized, would affect the interests of those claims' objects. Within that vast zone, furthermore, let us concentrate on just two phenomena that the Zapatista mobilization dramatizes: first, the formation, assertion, and transformation of contentious identities; second, the creation, deployment, and alteration of contentious repertoires.

To see more clearly what is at issue, we can return momentarily to Chiapas. Emerging from the Lacandona jungle in Chiapas on New Year's Day 1994, Subcomandante Marcos and his Zapatistas made their first public declaration from the balcony of the governmental palace in San Cristóbal. In that text, they told a different sort of story from Marcos's yarn about the parrot and the tapir. The story related how a long-suffering people had suffered centuries of oppression and deprivation, but finally *HOY DECIMOS ¡BASTA!*—Today, we say Enough. The text's authors identified themselves variously as follows:

- A product of 500 years of struggle
- Poor people like us

- People used as cannon fodder
- Heirs of our nation's true makers
- Millions of dispossessed
- "The people" as described in Article 39 of the Mexican national constitution
- The Zapatista Army of National Liberation
- Responsible, free men and women
- Patriots

They denied that they were "drug traffickers, or drug guerrillas, or bandits, or whatever other characterization our enemies might use." They opposed themselves explicitly to

- The dictatorship
- The political police
- A coterie (*camarilla*) of traitors who represent the most conservative and anti-national groups
- The Mexican federal army
- The party in power (PRI) with its supreme and illegitimate leader, Carlos Salinas, installed in the federal executive office

For all its splendid eccentricities, notice the classic properties of the Zapatistas' collective self-presentation. Through the mouth, pen, and battered Olivetti portable of Subcomandante Marcos, they declare themselves to be the local manifestation of a popular movement extending back to the Spanish conquest, the enemy of a corrupt national power structure, the worthy, unified, numerous, and committed ally of all Mexicans that corrupt powerholders are oppressing. Their identity resides not in the sum of their common attributes, not in their shared consciousness, but in their collective relation to Mexican power.

Or rather their relations, plural. For they exist as allies of the region's Mayan *campesinos* and of liberation movements elsewhere; as articulate interlocutors of journalists, media personalities, and computer users throughout the world; as military opponents of the current national regime. To each of those relationally defined identities, furthermore, corresponds a distinctive repertoire of claim-making means, ranging from press conferences through land occupations to armed attacks on government buildings.

I will resist the temptation to trace Zapatista politics across the years since the Lacandona Declaration. Their colorful example leads almost without effort to my main arguments. Here is a quick summary: Critics of realistic approaches to social analysis have placed social construction high on the agenda of social science, but have not provided convincing explanations of the social constructions that people actually produce, accept, and use. In the course of social interaction, people produce, negotiate, register, and respond to stories having remarkably uniform logical and ontological structures, a fact that poses serious analytical and pedagogical problems for social science. Reflection on conversation as a model and vehicle of social processes suggests partial solutions for the problems and fascinating opportunities for research. Within the study of contentious politics, the analysis of identities and repertoires as conversation provides an opportunity to tunnel under linguistic and culturalist reductionism by treating construction and deployment of relevant stories as objects of explanation.

With few pauses for plumed tapirs or jungle declarations, let me lay out that line of reasoning in simple chunks. So far, students of social construction have produced competing specifications of its locus and character—in autonomously evolving mentalities, in language, in mental processes, or elsewhere. They have divided less explicitly but just as deeply on the amenability of social construction to systematic, falsifiable description and explanation. At one end of the seesaw, we have a Jacques Rancière urging social historians to recognize their enterprise frankly as poetry, at the other, John Mohr and Roberto Franzosi devising precise methods for describing discourses, then attaching them to their social settings. Even those who consider social construction to be coherent and explicable have not offered systematic accounts of its operation that identify significant causal analogies from one situation to the next.

One way to open the way toward a systematic account is to consider the place of standard stories in social construction. For reasons that lie deep in childhood learning, cultural immersion, or perhaps even in the structure of human brains, people usually recount, analyze, judge, remember, and reorganize social experiences as *standard stories* in which a small number of self-motivated entities interact within a constricted, contiguous time and space. Although prior and externally imposed conditions enter standard stories as accidents, facilities, and constraints, all meaningful action occurs as consequences of the designated actors' deliberations and impulses.

Actors in such stories range from you and me as we work out how we missed our scheduled appointment yesterday to all downtrodden Mexicans and their oppressors through five centuries of history. Both Marcos's whimsical account of a parrot's illicit romance and the Zapatistas' identification of themselves with centuries of heroic resistance come to us in the form of standard stories. Indeed, one refers obliquely to the other, since the plumed serpent, a frequent motif in Aztec statuary, represents the Aztec demigod Quetzalcoatl.

People's construction, negotiation, and deployment of standard stories do a wide variety of important social work. That work certainly includes the formation of Mexican national history and the histories of particular dissident movements, but it also includes autobiography, self-justification, social movement mobilization, jury deliberation, moral condemnation, cementing of agreements, and documentation of nationalist claims. Literary critic Dan Hofstadter puts it well: "It is sometimes believed . . . that if one shapes events into a story, this shaping will somehow bind or heal them, make sense out of occurrences that are essentially wounded and without hope of meaning" (Hofstadter 1996, 296).

Stories emerge from active social interchange, modify as a result of social interchange, but in their turn constrain social interchange as well. They embody ideas concerning what forms of action and interaction are possible, feasible, desirable, and efficacious, hence at least by implication what forms of action and interaction would be impossible, impracticable, undesirable, or ineffectual. Even if the individuals involved harbor other ideas, the embedding of stories in social networks seriously constrains interactions, hence collective actions, of which people in those networks are capable.

Although people store standard stories in their brains person by person, anyone who listens carefully on the subway, in a bar, or on a city street will soon recognize their incessant creation, employment, and social reconstruction in conversation. People package arguments in stories, reply to queries by means of stories, challenge each other's stories, modify or amplify their stories as the flow of conversation dictates, and sometimes even construct collective stories for presentation to third parties. They recast events after the fact in standard story form.

We observe interim products of the collective version in social movements and other varieties of contentious politics: political organizers spend a significant part of their effort on the creation and broadcast of collective standard stories that will facilitate communication, coordination, and commitment on the part of participants, allies, bystanders, and even objects of collective claims. When antagonists settle conflicts, they typically create retrospective accounts of what was at issue and how it got resolved. "Stories, stories, stories!" exclaims E. Valentine Daniel early in a moving study of Sri Lanka's interethnic violence. "I have never known for sure if I am their prisoner or their jailer" (Daniel 1996, 4).

What is more, the presence of a certain story constrains social interaction, defines an array of possible interactions and their likely outcomes, and thereby limits what can happen next. Stories play a significant part in the path-dependency of conversation and of social interaction as a whole. Once the Zapatistas found a worldwide audience for their claims to speak for the Mexican dispossessed at large, they received support from a wide variety of dissidents outside of Mexico. But they also incited counterclaims from other Mexican activists who denied Zapatista priority—and sometimes even Zapatista authenticity—in these regards.

The prevalence of stories poses critical analytical and pedagogical problems for social science. Few social processes actually have causal structures that conform to the logical requirements of standard stories. Most social processes involve unanticipated consequences, cumulative effects, indirect effects, and effects mediated by their social and physical environment, none of which fit the causal structure of standard stories. Even those few that correspond roughly to the formats of standard stories—for example, chess matches and some kinds of bureaucratic decision making—typically rest on extensive if usually implicit institutional foundations and previous histories. The fact that stories change though negotiation and retrospective recasting means that even when the causal structure remains plausible post hoc collectors of stories must respect them as social constructions rather than as faithful chronologies or reliable explanations.

Analysts of social processes who wish to explain stories must therefore translate material that comes to them largely in the form of standard stories created in the course of social interaction—and consolidated after the fact—into other idioms that better represent their actual causal structure. Every skilled survey researcher implicitly recognizes this condition both by interrogating the stories that respondents tell and by breaking up interview schedules into nonstory interchanges. Collectors of biographies and autobiographies likewise pour much of their expertise into critique and reconstruction (Chamberlayne, Bornat, and Wengraf 2000). Following programs called by such names as interpretation, discourse, narrative, and cultural analysis, however, many historians and social scientists have committed themselves to the view that standard stories do provide viable explanations of social processes, that the principal responsibility of social interpreters is the construction of superior standard stories, or even that nothing accessible to analysis exists beyond the limits of the standard stories that participants in social processes tell.

Teachers and writers of history and social science who wish to communicate nonstory explanations of social processes thus face audiences whose members have extensive training and strong investments in packaging social processes as standard stories. Teachers and writers of nonstory history and social science therefore have a choice between working within the stringent limits set by standard stories and instructing their audiences in the analysis of causal mechanisms and sequences that do not correspond to standard stories.

However they resolve that dilemma, teachers and writers of history and social science also confront the challenge of describing, explaining, challenging, and altering both the stories that participants in social processes tell about what is happening to them or others and the stories that analysts, critics, observers, and even fellow professionals tell about particular social processes, situations, and outcomes. Thus, the hermeneutic circle becomes a spiral of description, explication, explanation, critique, and back to description.

These problems pervade the study of social life in general. We could pursue them into description and explanation of inequality, sexuality, population change, or work. Within the field of contentious politics where we began, they clearly reappear in the analysis of collective identities and repertoires. Standard stories locate identities within individual bodies as some combination of attribute, experience, and consciousness, then derive collective identities from the attributes, experiences, and consciousness shared by many individuals. In political life, however, collective identities always form as combinations of relations with others, representations of those relations, and shared understandings of those relations. The identity *Zapatista* combines relations to many others, including fellow Zapatistas and the Mexican state; representations of those relations by means of names, symbols, practices, and stories; shared understandings grounded in the relations and their representations.

The word *identity* itself conveys contrary meanings. The *American Heritage Dictionary* offers a delightfully contradictory set of definitions for *identity:*

1. The collective aspect of the set of characteristics by which a thing is definitively recognizable or known

2. The set of behavioral or personal characteristics by which an individual is recognizable as a member of a group
3. The quality or condition of being exactly the same as something else
4. The quality or condition of being or remaining the same
5. The personality of an individual regarded as a persisting entity
6. An equality satisfied by all values of the variables for which the expressions involved in the equality are defined

On one side, we find uniqueness; on the other, common properties. Analysts of social identities have never quite resolved the contradiction.

So long as they insist that *identity* include the irreducible, unique set of attributes distinguishing an individual from all other individuals—what makes you you—analysts never will resolve the contradiction between uniqueness and common properties. They can come close, however, by recognizing that social identities at all scales, from individual to international, combine three elements: relations, boundaries, and stories. Let us think of an individual as one kind of *social site*—a locus of coordinated social action. Other social sites include households, neighborhoods, and organizations. From the perspective of any particular social site, an identity is its experience of transactions with another social site: individual to individual, individual to neighborhood, household to organization, and so on. We can sum up all the transactions between two sites over some period as their social relation. Every social site has as many identities as it has social relations. The uniqueness of any social site, in this perspective, does not consist of its individual attributes but of its particular combination of social relations.

Every social relation includes a boundary between the sites involved. At the individual level, the boundary falls somewhere between you and me. At the collective level, it falls between us and them. Boundary construction is a fundamental social process. That process is crucial to the production of identities. It depends closely on the adoption and modification of shared stories about the boundary, stories of the kind we have seen the Zapatistas telling about the distinction between themselves and their oppressors. Boundary stories typically include names for the sites on either side of the line, accounts of where they came from, and imputations of shared attributes to the entities on each side of the line.

Seen from a distance, boundary stories have some peculiar characteristics. Just as an individual who comes to a certain relationship as the honorable, responsible partner sometimes enters other relationships as predatory or irresponsible, enforcement of identity stories occurs chiefly at the boundary: Confrontations between Arabs and Jews become sharp and uniform at the frontier between them. But away from the boundary, who is an Arab or who is a Jew (not to mention what accepting one identity or the other entails for everyday behavior) remains a matter of intense dispute. As a matter of fact, distinction of one side from the other does not require homogeneity on either side. It merely requires enactment of uniformity at the boundary. Yet, at the extreme, that very enactment promotes hatred and destruction across the boundary.

Boundary stories often form and operate in the zone of contentious politics, the zone where people make discontinuous, public, collective claims on each other (McAdam, Tarrow, and Tilly 2001, ch. 1). Claim making becomes political when governments—or, more generally, individuals or organizations that control concentrated means of coercion—become parties to the claims, as claimants, objects of claims, or stakeholders. When leaders of two ethnic factions compete for recognition as valid interlocutors for their ethnic category, for example, the governments to which the interlocutors would speak inevitably figure as stakeholders. Contention occurs everywhere, but contentious *politics* involves governments, at least as third parties.

Collective identities activated in contentious politics vary along a continuum whose poles we can call embedded and detached. At the *embedded* pole, we observe clumps of relations, representations, and understandings that pervade a wide range of routine social interaction as well as form the bases of collective claim making. Under most circumstances, the identities *woman, Nahuatl-speaker, neighbor,* and *peasant* fall toward the embedded end of the continuum. At the *detached* pole, we observe clumps of relations, representations, and understandings that constitute identities in contentious claim making but rarely appear explicitly in routine social interaction. Under most circumstances the identities *citizen, worker, American,* and *socialist* fall toward the detached end of the continuum.

Political organizers, to be sure, often work to detach previously embedded identities by creating connections among fragmented populations (as when residents of many urban neighborhoods come to identify themselves as victims of the same corrupt city administration) or to embed currently detached identities by installing them in a wide range of routine social relations (as when promoters of a certain ethnic identity create ethnic institutions, exclusionary practices, and privileges). Whether embedded or detached, a wide range of contentious politics includes crucial performances in which people not only demand, request, attack, petition, or otherwise make specific claims on powerholders, but also act out statements of the type We are Alpha, We speak for Beta, or We insist on being recognized as Gamma. In the public performances of twentieth-century social movements, indeed, far more collective effort goes into assertions of the WUNC type—We are Worthy, Unified, Numerous, and Committed Xs—than into the specific presentation of concrete demands.

Further pursuit of that observation would take us to a number of topics dear to my heart: the interdependence between prescribed and unruly forms of politics, the emergence of the social movement as a distinctive and now perhaps fading vehicle of claim making, and so on. Most of them show up later in the book. Here, however, I simply want to call attention to the analogy between identity deployment in contentious politics and conversation in general. (Chapter 9 pursues the analogy further.)

It is not just that identity processes involve conversations, although identity-oriented conversations often have the richness we have seen in the Zapatista self-portrayal. More important, the striking, jazzy combination of improvisation, innovation, and constraint that characterizes conversation also characterizes interactions among parties to collective identity work. The previous histories of relations among the parties, previous representations of those relations, and previous shared understandings all channel collective assertions of identity, but stereotyped repetition of old stories decreases credibility and viability of the identities thus invoked, just as strictly grammatical and formulaic speech (except when offered in jest) typically marks the speaker as a suspect outsider—perhaps even as a humanoid computer.

Similar reasoning applies to contentious repertoires. Whether in the ritual executions, processions, celebrations, and militia marches of the early French Revolution or the public meetings, petition drives, lobbying, demonstrations, and association-forming of contemporary Western social movements, we witness the conversational combination of incessant improvisation, innovation, and constraint. Claim-making repertoires center on relational transactions: relations with fellow participants, relations with objects of claims, relations with audiences, and often relations with authorities who intervene forcefully or otherwise. They involve strategic interaction. They modify in the long run as a result of changes in the parties, in relations among them, and in their settings, all of which proceed in partial independence of contentious politics. But they also modify in the short run as a consequence of contention itself, as when Cuban revolutionaries imprinted models for bearded, cigar-chomping *guerrilleros* or black Americans established the sit-in as a standard way of making claims. Here, too, analogies with conversation—serious, high-stakes conversation—strike the eye.

This book will disappoint many specialists in stories, identities, and/or political change. With regard to stories, it neglects formal linguistic structure, content analysis, narrative theory, and the construction of individual biographies. With respect to identities, it pays little attention to their learning, modification, and negotiation in routine social life. When it comes to political change, it gives far less attention to measurement and modeling than does the bulk of my own research on the subject. So far, few scholars have pursued systematic studies of interactions among stories, identities, and political change. I have crafted this book to stimulate new work at that promising intersection of social processes.

The following chapters fall into four overlapping segments. The chapters of part I, including this introduction, deal especially with stories, explanations, and their interplay. Part II emphasizes political identities, from the small scale to the large. Part III's chapters look more closely at collective voice, especially as it appears in different sorts of political interactions. In part IV we examine large-scale political processes with an eye to the places of stories, identity construction, and collective conversation in those processes.

Before everything becomes deadly serious, let us recognize that conversation, contentious politics, and social life in general often center not on strategic interaction for high stakes but on persiflage, seduction, concealment, and play: Parrots, macaws, and plumed tapirs matter to sociability, offer pleasure that reinforces social ties, and provide contexts for the interpretation of political contention. I hope only to have shown that social construction pervades contentious politics, critically involves stories, shapes political change, and presents a deep, engaging explanatory challenge to the next generation of social researchers here or elsewhere. Now you know what sort of beast I found one night, emerging from a handsome speckled egg and what I propose we do with it.

2

Softcore Solipsism

In 1963, E. P. Thompson roared onto the terrain of class analysis like an invading army. Descending from the heights of literary criticism and biography, he daringly attacked on two fronts, machine-gunning mechanistic Marxism at the same time as he cannonaded conservative condescension. At least for England from the 1780s to the 1830s, he swept the field, persuading a wide range of readers that something he called the "making" of a working class occurred through a sustained series of struggles and convincing the rest that they now had a new, seductive leftist thesis to combat.

With a literary historian's panache, Thompson mustered an extraordinary range of evidence for his thesis, drawing connections between political philosophy and popular culture, enormously broadening the conception of relevant texts, giving popular utterances and crowd actions a literary standing they had rarely achieved before. His victorious vision of class formation in England inspired numerous historians of other Western countries to search for parallel constructions in their own territories and periods, so much so that the phrase Making of the _____ Working Class attained the immortality of a cliché.

Like European appropriation of Asian and African territories, Thompson's conquest of British class analysis laid down a terrible burden for his successors. Just as anticolonial leaders once felt obliged to advertise their own democratic commitments while condemning the actual operation of French or British democracy, in order to demonstrate their own advance over previous understandings, today's leftist historians feel compelled to reject Thompson's account of class formation without ceding popular history's terrain to Whig self-congratulation or Tory disdain.

"Softcore Solipsism" originally appeared in _Labour/Le Travail_ 34 (fall 1994): 259–268, and appears with permission of the editor and the Canadian Committee of Labour History.

Declining confidence in the capacity of organized parties and militant workers to check the power of states and capital, much less to bring about just and prosperous regimes, encourages the same historians to turn inward for consolation, seeking hope in improved critical understanding rather than expanded capacity for collective action. As faith in revolution fell, faith in deconstruction rose.

Both Patrick Joyce and James Vernon, the objects of this chapter, have sought refuge from Marxist realism in linguistic analysis. Joyce has done so fretfully and Vernon with shrill bravado. Each proposes his own interpretation of English popular culture and its creeds as an alternative to the Thompsonian history of class formation. In the baker's dozen of essays that fill his *Visions of the People* (1991), Joyce explores a wide variety of materials recording political discourse, popular literature, slogans, demands, theater, dialect, and much more, asking to what extent their uses set workers off from other people and to what degree they conveyed direct awareness of class difference as a formative experience and source of grievances. Joyce concentrates on Lancashire and the North between 1848 and 1914, eventually concluding with great unease that something like widely shared class consciousness began to emerge not in Thompson's 1790s but around World War I.

Vernon's *Politics and the People* (1993), for its part, takes on all of England from 1815 to 1867, but uses as recurrent points of reference his doctoral dissertation studying the public politics in Boston, Lewes, South Devon, Tower Hamlets, and Oldham. Although his announced period overlaps the one examined by Thompson (whose "early savaging" of Vernon's work the preface mentions), Vernon does not aim his empirical investigation at Thompson's account of political action between 1815 and 1832. Instead, he looks chiefly at post-Reform politics to document his claim that for ordinary English people the public sphere, far from opening to democratic participation, actually narrowed dramatically between 1832 and 1867.

Despite avoiding direct confrontation with Thompson's treatment of 1780 to 1832, Joyce and Vernon both seek self-consciously to displace Thompsonian analysis of class formation. They do so by means of three maneuvers: denial that economic experience shapes class consciousness, insistence on the variety of economic and social experience, embedding of all meaningful experience in language. In so doing, each makes two further moves he does not quite recognize and therefore does not bother to defend. The first is to adopt radical individualism, an assumption that the only significant historical events or causes consist of mental states and their alterations. The second is to doubt the intersubjective verifiability of statements about social life. Together, the two moves take them into the territory of softcore solipsism.

Hardcore solipsism, a venerable philosophical doctrine, denies the possibility of any knowledge beyond that of the knower's own individual experience. According to hardcore solipsism, all efforts to communicate, persuade, explain, much less accumulate collective knowledge, face insuperable barriers. No consistent believer in hardcore solipsism could pretend to write authoritative historical analyses. Joyce and Vernon opt for softcore solipsism by recognizing (however uncertainly) collective actors, by claiming to know something about what nineteenth-century workers thought, by treating language as subject to systematic analysis, and by persisting in the effort—useless according to strict solipsistic doctrine—to teach others their interpretations of British history. Fixed on the task of refuting Thompson and his ilk, furthermore, they center their analyses on questions of consciousness, on knowing what different groups of ordinary people actually thought at various times in the nineteenth and twentieth centuries. In the process, they abandon agency, cause, and effect except insofar as conscious deliberation causes individual action.

The abandonment of agency extends to Joyce's and Vernon's prose, which abounds in weak verbs and passive voice. A characteristic series of evasions appears in Vernon's introduction to his analysis of print as a means of control:

> Of course the danger was that this language with its appeals to a new rational public could be, as indeed it was, appropriated by radicals to demand that all those possessing reason should be included as citizens of the official political nation. Central to this discourse was the post-Enlightenment perception of print as the universal tool of reason, an ideal form for rational political debate that was available to all. However, I hope to show in this chapter that print was far from universal, instead it was used to reconstitute the public political sphere in an ever-more restrictive fashion, excluding groups believed to be "irrational" like women and the illiterate poor from public political debate. (Vernon 1993, 105)

The passage immediately raises the question: whodunnit? *Who* used print to reconstitute the public political sphere, and why? Vernon supplies no answer. We begin to understand why his book's very first epigraph comes from Michel Foucault.

Vernon's and Joyce's occultation of agency separates them from conventional historical narrative, in which limited numbers of well-defined motivated actors, situated in specific places and times, express their ideas and impulses in visible actions which produce discernible consequences, those consequences typically being the objects of explanation. Conventional narrative entails not only claims to reasonably reliable knowledge of actors, motives, ideas, impulses, actions, and consequences but also (1) postulation of actors and action as more or less self-contained, and (2) imputation of cause and effect within the narrative sequence. Softcore solipsism makes most of these elements difficult, and a denial of agency makes them impossible.

Vernon and Joyce also rule out alternative modes of social-scientific analysis, which require less access to other people's consciousness as well as allowing actors, actions, and environment to interact continuously, but demand even stronger conceptions of causal connection. Either solipsism or the denial of agency suffices to command rejection of these forms of social analysis. In short, the Joyce–Vernon philosophical position obliterates any possibility of historical explanation. It also undermines any grounds they might propose for accepting the validity of their analyses in preference to Thompson's or anyone else's.

As a practical matter, Joyce and Vernon pour much of their effort into twinned enterprises: (1) identifying alternative discourses to those of class; (2) finding new sorts of evidence to illustrate those discourses. Neither enterprise, however, advances any rationale for believing its results. Hardcore or softcore, solipsism lays on its advocates the burden of proof that what they are saying deserves more attention than the chattering of birds.

Vernon and Joyce shrug off that burden almost without comment. About the closest either comes is in the admission on Vernon's penultimate page:

> This, of course, leaves me open to the accusation that, by turning the triumphant teleologies of the dominant narratives of English political history on their head, I have simply provided a different, if equally dogmatic, narrative which also closes down other interpretive possibilities—the closure of the public political sphere merely replacing the forward march of labour and the triumph of Liberal democracy. Clearly, I can not deny the possibility of such a reading, although I may want to add the obligatory academic qualifications and caveats, stressing the slow uneven and incomplete nature of the closure of politics. Or, more truthfully if less properly, I could claim that it was never my intention to close down other readings, but that in subjects as well studied as nineteenth-century English politics only the most novel and bold (some would say foolhardy) of narratives can break the interpretive log-jam, opening up the space for a multiplicity of other readings. (Vernon 1993, 338)

Behind the statement's brash opportunism glowers despair at the possibility of using evidence to adjudicate the relative validity of competing historical accounts. Without relative truth claims backed by systematic evidence, Vernon apparently senses, history slumps into literary criticism. If historical analysis consists of nothing but language games, of course, one game is as good as another. Thus, the objective of academic effort reduces to the provision of multiple perspectives on ultimately indeterminate events. In this view, Vernon and Joyce break sharply with the realist epistemology and ontology of E. P. Thompson. (In the face of this sort of negation, Thompson told me a few years before his death that he had long disapproved of my penchant for social science but now saw that despite my failings we both stood on the same [realist] side of a widening, dangerous divide.)

Joyce and Vernon nevertheless remain captives of Thompson to a far greater degree than they acknowledge. First, they focus on the explication of plebeian consciousness in a very Thompsonian manner. Second, they rely on the assembly of numerous texts—now defined with the great breadth to which Thompson accustomed us—to substantiate that explication of consciousness. They engage in Thompsonian hermeneutics. Thompson must take the credit or blame for the sheer power of his argument and practical example, as well as for his own tendency to center his rare methodological discussions on the relationship between experience and consciousness. Thompson thereby undermined one of his own most important teachings. For it was Thompson above all who argued that class was not an individual state of mind, not even the collective mentality of a single group, but a dynamic, contested relationship among sets of people.

Anyone who adopts language as the analytic base for the treatment of class should, in fact, immediately recognize the significance of Thompson's teaching. Language is a deeply social medium, heavily dependent on interpersonal negotiation and creation. In solitary confinement, humans never learn to speak. The minimum set for the study of language consists not of a single thinking individual, but of two persons in communication with each other. To the degree that the linguistic turn brought historians toward solipsism, it led entirely in the wrong direction.

Historians do not wander alone through the epistemological and ontological wilderness. Social scientists and historians alike have frequently made the same mistake: interpreting social relations as if they were individual attributes. The program many social scientists call methodological individualism makes a virtue of just such a procedure. In the analysis of work and labor markets, economists have commonly supposed that people's jobs and incomes resulted directly from their individual human capital through the impersonal operation of something mysterious called the market (sometimes attenuated, but only attenuated, by the preferences of workers and employers). But the organization of jobs, work, and compensation actually centers on constantly renegotiated relations between workers and employers. Ethnicity and nationality likewise consist not of individual characteristics but of labeled connections among people. The individualization of identity causes great confusion in social analysis.

Identities reside in interpersonal relations. That is why the possession of multiple identities—highly problematic in an individualistic perspective—poses so little practical difficulty to most human beings. (The only people I have ever met who had more or less unitary identities were either psychiatric patients or fanatics, or both.) To be a daughter is to live in a certain relationship to a parent; to be a slave is to endure a certain relation to a master; to be a citizen is to hold certain rights and obligations vis-à-vis a specific state; to belong to a working class is to share with other people a certain relation to capitalists. Precisely: When he insisted on class as a relation among groups, E. P. Thompson rejected its reduction to individual characteristics, including individual consciousness. Alas, historians did not hear him well, any more than social scientists in general have understood the centrality of transactions, not individuals, in social life. Language, culture, identity, and class all reside not in single minds but in dynamic, contingent, negotiated relations among human beings.

Patrick Joyce has not gotten the message. Although at one point he remarks, "The sense of class is defined in relation to, and usually over and against, other classes" (Joyce 1991, 11), he soon abandons his relational insight. Joyce tortures himself on a rack of his own manufacture: He stretches himself to the breaking point among believing that class matters, that class isn't everything, that class does not exist, that what other people have thought to be class was actually populism. At several points he even reaches for an idealist world in which doctrines contend more or less independently of human agents or minds; on three separate pages (14, 96, and 332), for example, he approvingly quotes Fredric Jameson, via James Epstein, as saying that "the dialogue of class struggle is (normally) one in which two opposed discourses fight it out within the general unity of a shared code."

Joyce's epistemological and ontological hesitation encumbers a crucial early passage:

> That is to say, if class "position" is not considered in the light of the very problematic nature of proletarianisation, then one is led to ask in what respect is the phenomenon to hand a matter of "working-class consciousness" (presumably an outlook based on the perception of workers' shared experience as manual proletarians), rather than cultural and political traditions *per se*, or extra-proletarian identifications such as "the people," or the primary producers. Of course, we can define class as we like, in terms as cultural as we wish, but we should be aware that we are doing this, and that this will change one of the major meanings of class, both within Marxism and beyond it. (Joyce 1991, 4)

Translation: A working class exists to the extent that manufacturing wage earners share angry awareness of their condition, an awareness stemming directly from participation in similar labor processes. To the degree that workers draw shared awareness from symbols, experiences, traditions, and influences other than their similar conditions of work, they do not form a class. (This view motivates Joyce's rejection of Eric Hobsbawm's evidence for working-class formation during the later nineteenth century: "Because manual workers chose to wear cloth caps and support football teams," Joyce remarks, "it does not follow that they saw the social order in terms of class" [Joyce 1991, 8].) But since labor processes actually changed so variously, no possible homogeneity could result from working conditions. Joyce quickly censors this last argument, recognizing its base-superstructure implication that if labor processes *were* uniform, so too would be class and class consciousness. He can't make up his mind.

At book's end, Joyce is still fretting over the correct terms to describe what he has found. "Perhaps," he remarks,

> in line with the emphasis on discourse evident in this book, it is better to talk of a "master narrative" rather than of a "master identity," though it does in fact seem the case that the labouring poor of the industrial England of the time interpreted this narrative in a remarkably uniform way, making out of it what is here called a dominant tradition. (Joyce 1991, 331)

That dominant tradition, he continues, concerns "an excluded and virtuous people doing battle in its pilgrim's progress against the forces of privilege, faction, darkness and ignorance. 'The people' itself, as has been seen, could variously be seen as 'the poor,' 'the labouring poor,' even 'the working classes'" (Joyce 1991, 332). Joyce then toys indecisively with the possibility that the tradition represents a class's shared consciousness, even if it does not embody class consciousness. By this time he has greatly enriched our knowledge of nineteenth-century popular culture, but by most standards he has also documented the salience of working-

class identities in relation to employers, landlords, merchants, and aristocrats. Relational rather than solipsistic views of class, politics, and identities would have
greatly clarified Joyce's visions of the people.

Fortunately for our enlightenment, Joyce confines most of his tortured indeci-
sion over these matters to the introduction and conclusion of his *Visions of the People*. Joyce serves his readers a doubt sandwich: a hearty slab of old-fashioned research between two layers of uncertainty. Between the dubious beginning and end,
he offers a knowledgeable tour of nineteenth-century working-class collective life
in Lancashire and adjacent regions. He undertakes a survey of the forms and appeals of working-class leadership, investigates the deliberate employment of class
terminology in political appeals, sketches the range of prevalent political analyses
from radicalism through classical populism to Liberalism, reviews ideas forwarded
or accepted by textile workers, turns to the distinguishing markers of working-class
culture, calls attention to public representations of past and present, examines popular language, art, ballads, dialect literature, and theater—in short, lays out an array
of material of which any social historian could be proud, and which the rest of us
can plunder to our profit.

Joyce shows how, far from appealing only to false consciousness, both Tories and
Liberals offered programs that resonated with genuine working-class preoccupations, indeed adapted and publicized their appeals in order to garner working-class
support. He provides a telling account, for example, of Gladstone's great themes,
moral entitlement, and masses against the classes, showing how they resonated with
everyday concerns. More generally, he displays the richness of ideas, locutions, and
practices identifying working people with nation, class, and region, not to mention
the ease with which ordinary people participated in these multiple identities.

James Vernon offers a similar sense of richness, but pursues a more consistent,
forceful, and surprising argument than Joyce. His sandwich differs from Joyce's; between an introduction and conclusion boldly stating very broad claims, Vernon
presents eight dense and valuable chapters describing his five parliamentary constituencies, intermittently pausing to remind readers of the general argument. He
documents the modest increase in the electorate occasioned by the 1832 Reform
Act; the slight redistribution of electors among social categories at that point; the
formal exclusion of women from local and parliamentary politics; the construction
of civic spaces and monuments for the display of mass involvement in public politics; authorities' attempts to fashion municipal ceremonies into manifestations of
allegiance to the regime; the expanded use of print media in politics; print's partial supersession of nonverbal iconography and of oratory; the increasing crystal-
lization of party boundaries and doctrines; struggles among radicals, reformers, and
manipulators for control of the local organizational apparatus of government and
party; the emergence and containment of temperance-seeking women as a political force; the displacement of torchlight processions and other rough out-of-doors
performances by orderly public gatherings; the salience and dramatization of political leaders, and much more.

Before closing, Vernon devotes a chapter to arguing that "popular constitutionalism"—the emphasis on rights of freeborn Englishmen and related ideas—remained the "master narrative" of English politics at least through 1867. He thus picks up the clue concerning narratives Joyce placed in his own conclusions. Vernon's analysis of popular constitutionalism, however, leads him to the conclusion that ordinary people assumed social and political identities that "are not done justice by Patrick Joyce's 'family of populisms'" (Vernon 1993, 297). Those identities included religious affiliation, attachment to the crown, and a shifting variety of other ties.

Implicitly, Vernon also breaks with Joyce's analysis in another important regard. While Joyce accepts the now-standard postmodernist argument that the embedding of social experience in language blocks any escape from linguistic analysis, Vernon invokes a number of nonlinguistic elements: buildings, monuments, public spaces, partisan colors, ribbons, and other nonverbal markers of political relations. He neither argues that their meanings reside entirely in discourse nor subordinates them to language. On the contrary, he declares, "Civic landscapes can be read as cultural texts in themselves, texts of equal significance to the ceremonies and other symbolic practices that were staged upon them" (49). What is more, he treats the size and location of civic buildings and ceremonies as themselves conveying information about local politics. Reaching out like Thompson and Joyce for a vast range of cultural material, he bursts through ostensibly unbreakable linguistic barriers to reliable knowledge that Joyce and many more thoroughgoing postmodernists have stressed.

Vernon eventually takes the histories of his five constituencies to show a radical narrowing of political participation, hence of democracy, between the two reform acts, between 1832 and 1867. By political participation, however, he means subjectivity, something like a sense of empowerment. Politics, for Vernon, takes a very subjective form:

> The point is not that the nineteenth-century political subject had confounded the postmodern critique of the autonomous, rational, centred individual, but that it pretended it had, addressing people as though their identities were stable and coherent. Of course that was, and still is, the business (even the purpose) of politics. It is not just that we need politics to make sense of the often very chaotic world around us, but that it is arguably impossible to create a politics capable of attracting popular support which does seek to transcend differences both within and between decentred individual and collective actors with some kind of unifying identity. (Vernon 1993, 335)

(Challenge: Find the agents in that passage!) Politics exists, according to this account, in order to provide individuals with a sense of identity.

Repeatedly, Vernon glosses his findings as demonstrating the constriction of political participation in this subjectivist sense. Speaking of a shift from oral to print culture, for example, he summarizes his argument in this way:

> Citizenship of the political nation was provisional upon the possession of reason, virtue, and independence, and therefore mass political participation had to occur

within the private realm of the home, a setting conducive to rational political debate and thought, unlike the often passionate and emotive public arena of the streets. Therefore, despite all the legislation which historians have traditionally seen as heralding a brave new world of mass democratic politics—the electoral reforms of 1832, 1867, and 1884, the reduction and eventual abolition of stamp duties, the "anti-corruption" legislation, the introduction of the secret ballot in 1872—this period witnessed a marked decline in people's ability to shape the political appeals available to them as the official political subject was redefined in the image of print. (Vernon 1993, 107)

Several important observations lurk in this dark passage. First, the version of liberalism promulgated by such thinkers as John Stuart Mill did presume a level of civic competence that justified exclusion of incompetent, immoral, and dependent persons from public power. Second, fashioning of durable organizational and ideological connections between local and national politics generally standardizes the identities, interests, programs, and forms of action that have currency; it therefore frustrates some identities, interests, programs, and forms of action. Third, the formation of national parties and their production of a self-promoting literature favor official lines and give party activists an augmented interest in suppressing idiosyncrasy, diversity, and dissent.

Finally, bargaining over rights usually suppresses some previously available forms of behavior as it ratifies others, as when workers gained the legal right to strike at the price of abandoning a wide range of threatening or retaliatory tactics and accepting the state's jurisdiction over the declaration, conduct, and settlement of strikes. Yet, Vernon's dismissal of "mass democratic politics" gains its main force from his concentration on subjectivities, on the opportunity for each individual to place her personal desires on the public agenda, or at least to find a match between her own preoccupations and portions of the public agenda. Democracy, in this view, inheres in self-expression. Since Vernon claims his analysis shows that "the invention of democracy in England was then a sham" (336), we had better remember what definition of democracy he has in mind.

By other quite defensible criteria, after all, Britain did democratize during the nineteenth century, indeed served as a pioneer and model of democratization. Let us leave aside formal standards such as the number of voters and substantive standards such as equalization of living standards, although both point in a mildly democratic direction over the century as a whole. Drawing on widely held notions of democracy, let us say that a state is democratic to the degree that (1) it installs broad, equal rights and obligations of citizenship; (2) citizens collectively exercise effective control over the policies and personnel of government; (3) citizens enjoy protection against arbitrary action by agents of the state.

By such standards, no completely democratic state has ever existed, and most of the contemporary world's states fall far short of democracy. Nevertheless, if the rights and obligations of citizenship broaden and/or equalize, if collective control over governmental policies and personnel increase, or if protections against arbitrary action extend, the state in question democratizes. According to these criteria, the very evidence of ordinary people's increasing, if contained, involvement in nationally connected politics that Vernon presents so well establishes a modest but real increase in democracy.

Does that dispose of the question? Of course not. For Vernon is raising profound questions about democratic regimes, perhaps profounder than he acknowledges. At what cost to autonomy, spontaneity, and diversity do ordinary people become involved in the politics of parties, elections, patriotism, interest groups, and public policy? Is the experience of meaningful democratic participation only possible at a small scale, in the absence of large state bureaucracies? Many anarchists, libertarians, socialists, and political philosophers have thought so. If Vernon had chosen to frame his analysis as a contribution to democratic theory rather than as a dispute with previous accounts of nineteenth-century British history, we could all have benefited from his frank engagement with the great philosophical issues. His adoption of softcore solipsism, however, blinded him to that opportunity.

A pity—with talented researchers like Patrick Joyce and James Vernon at work, labor history will survive, even prosper in spite of philosophical debilitation. But it will cumulate faster and more effectively if a renewed realism, however linguistic or historicist, prevails.

3

The Trouble with Stories

Born in England but soon transplanted to Ontario, Stephen Leacock left Canada to do a Ph.D. with Thorstein Veblen at the University of Chicago. After four years, Leacock returned definitively to Canada, but this time to Montreal; he eventually chaired McGill University's department of economics and political science. In that vein, his *Elements of Political Science* merited translation into seventeen languages. As Leacock matured, however, he turned increasingly from economics and political science to humor such as his droll classic *Literary Lapses*. He titled that book's final story "A, B, and C: The Human Element in Mathematics." "The student of arithmetic," wrote Leacock,

> who has mastered the first four rules of his art, and successfully striven with money sums and fractions, finds himself confronted by an unbroken expanse of questions known as problems. These are short stories of adventure and industry with the end omitted, and though betraying a strong family resemblance, are not without a certain element of romance.
>
> The characters in the plot of a problem are three people called A, B, and C. The form of the question is generally of this sort:
>
> "A, B, and C do a certain piece of work. A can do as much work in one hour as B in two, or C in four. Find how long they work at it." (Leacock 1957, 141)

A, B, and C rowed on rivers, pumped water from cisterns, dug ditches, and otherwise competed strenuously, always to the disadvantage of C. Leacock reveals what he learned from survivor D: C died of exhaustion after yet another grueling contest with A and B. A then lost interest in competition as B languished in his grief

An earlier version of this chapter appeared as "The Trouble with Stories," in Ronald Aminzade and Bernice Pescosolido, eds., *The Social Worlds of Higher Education: Handbook for Teaching in a New Century*, pp. 256–270, © 1999 by Pine Forge Press. Reprinted by permission of Sage Publications.

until he "abjured mathematics and devoted himself to writing the History of the Swiss Family Robinson in words of one syllable" (Leacock 1957, 146).

Under Stephen Leacock's pen, the abstract relations of algebra give way to human interest stories. His readers can chuckle because they instantly recognize the conceit. Alas, the same does not hold for social science's readers. The trouble with reading, writing, and learning social science is straightforward but formidable: People ordinarily cast their accounts of social life as stories—stories, as we shall see, with distinctive causal structures. Such stories do crucial work in patching social life together. But social science's strongest insights do not take the form of stories, and often undermine the stories people tell.

By stories, I do not mean rhetoric, the artful use of language to convince readers that the writer tells the truth. Nor do I mean the straightforward chronologies of events that appear in such sources as personnel records, marriage registers, and machine inspection logs. Although reading notes, court proceedings, political tracts, and advertisements sometimes incorporate stories in the narrow sense I am pursuing here, I am not including all of them under the heading "story." I mean the sequential, explanatory recounting of connected, self-propelled people and events that we sometimes call tales, fables, or narratives. Let us call these sequential, explanatory accounts of self-motivated human action *standard stories*.

STANDARD STORIES

To construct a standard story, start with a limited number of interacting characters, individual or collective. Your characters may be persons, but they may also be organizations such as churches and states or even abstract categories such as social classes and regions. Treat your characters as independent, conscious, and self-motivated. Make all their significant actions occur as consequences of their own deliberations or impulses. Limit the time and space within which your characters interact. With the possible exception of externally generated accidents—you can call them "chance" or "acts of God"—make sure everything that happens results directly from your characters' actions.

Now supply your characters with specific motives, capacities, and resources. Furnish the time and place within which they're interacting with objects you and they can construe as barriers, openings, threats, opportunities, and tools—as facilities and constraints bearing on their action. Set your characters in motion. From their starting point, make sure all their actions follow your rules of plausibility, and produce effects on others that likewise follow your rules of plausibility. Trace the accumulated effects of their actions to some interesting outcome. Better yet, work your way backward from some interesting outcome, following all the same rules. Congratulations: You've just constructed a standard story!

In writing your standard story, you've crafted a text that resembles a play, a TV sitcom episode, a fable, a news item, or a novel. But you've also produced something like the following:

- The account that a jury constructs from the testimony and evidence laid out during a trial
- A biography or autobiography of a single character
- Explanations that people piece together at the scene of a grisly accident
- Histories that nationalists recount as they say why they have prior rights to a given territory
- Speeches of social movement leaders who are linking today's actions or demands to the movement's past
- The selective (and perhaps fanciful) account of his past with which a taxi driver regales his captive passengers during a long ride to the airport
- How people apologize for, or justify, their violations of other people's expectations: "I'm sorry, but _____ "
- What victims of a crime or a disaster demand when authorities say they don't know how or why it happened
- Conversations people carry on as they judge other people's sins, good deeds, successes, and failures
- How bosses and workers reply to the question "Why don't you folks ever hire any Xs?"

Standard stories, in short, pop up everywhere. They lend themselves to vivid, compelling accounts of what has happened, what will happen, or what should happen. They do essential work in social life, cementing people's commitments to common projects, helping people make sense of what is going on, channeling collective decisions and judgments, spurring people to action they would otherwise be reluctant to pursue. Telling stories even helps people recognize difficulties in their own perceptions, explanations, or actions, as when I tell a friend about a recent adventure only to remark—or to have my friend point out—a previously unnoticed contradiction among the supposed facts I have laid out.

STORIES IN ACTION

The social scientific technique of interviewing (especially in the forms we call life histories or oral histories) benefits from the readiness of humans to package memory in standard stories. Although all of us have recollections we would rather not share with interviewers, in my own interviewing I have generally found people delighted to talk about past experiences and adept at placing those experiences in coherent sequences. Indeed, humans are so good at making sense of social processes after the fact by means of standard stories that skilled interviewers must spend much of their energy probing, checking, looking for discrepancies, and then reconstructing the accounts their respondents offer them.

In teaching social science to North American and European students, I have been impressed by the ingenuity and persistence with which they pack explanations into standard stories. For example, whatever else we have learned about inequality, social scientists have made clear that a great deal of social inequality results from indirect, unintended, collective, and environmentally mediated effects that fit very badly into standard stories. Yet students discussing inequality tend to offer two competing variants on the same standard story: that individuals or categories of individuals who differ significantly in ability and motivation arrive at various tests, judged by others, on which they perform with differential success, whereupon those others reward them unequally *or* that powerful gatekeepers follow their own preferences in sorting individuals or whole categories of individuals who arrive at certain choice points, thereby allocating them differential rewards.

Both variants respect the rules of standard stories: self-motivated actors in delimited time and space, conscious actions that cause most or all of the significant effects. Such a standard story shapes likely disagreements: over which variant is more accurate, over whether and why categories of people do differ significantly in ability and motivation, over whether existing performance tests measure capacities properly, over whether gatekeepers operate out of prejudice, and so on. Although many people in and out of social science explain inequality in these ways, either variant of the story omits or contradicts major inequality-generating causal sequences well established by social scientific research.

Such a story conflicts, for example, with explanations in which inequality at work forms as a by-product of hiring through existing, socially homogeneous personal networks of people already on the job—which happens to be the most common form of job recruitment through most of the contemporary capitalist world. That sort of confrontation between preferred standard stories and well-documented causal processes presents teachers and students of social science with serious difficulties, but also with great opportunities to rethink conventional explanations of social life. Later sections of this chapter examine the difficulties and opportunities in detail.

By no means does trouble with stories occur in pedagogy alone. It bedevils social scientific analysis wherever that analysis takes place: in field observation, in historical reconstruction, in polling, on the editorial page, in everyday conversation, or in classrooms. Even veteran analysts of incremental, interactive, indirect, unintended, collective, and environmentally mediated causal processes in social life—I include myself—easily slip into interpreting new social situations as if standard stories adequately represented their causal structures. Although when discussing what we can do about weaknesses of stories I will describe one sort of teaching that concentrates on the construction of more adequate stories, I see no yawning gulf between teaching and research: Sophistication and effectiveness in one promotes sophistication and effectiveness in the other. At a minimum, teachers and researchers must learn the pitfalls of assuming that standard stories adequately represent causes and effects as they unfold in social processes.

For specialized purposes, of course, people frequently offer other sorts of accounts than the ones I have called standard stories. Novelists and poets occasionally write descriptions of human beings who engage in inexplicable actions, respond to hidden forces, or experience all life as chaos. Patients reporting their medical histories commonly depart from standard stories to enumerate successions of mishaps. Religious and political doctrines often include great historical arcs that fulfill some powerful plan or immanent principle: progress, decline, destiny, just retribution. A book called *The Story of the Atom* may well include standard stories about Albert Einstein and Niels Bohr, but much of its account is likely to center on explications of physical principles. Standard stories stand out among all the accounts we sometimes call stories by their combination of unified time and place, limited sets of self-motivated actors, and cause-effect relations centered on those actors' deliberated actions. Such stories predominate in everyday descriptions, explanations, and evaluations of human social behavior.

Why do standard stories occupy such central places in social life? I see two main possibilities; they do not exclude each other. First, standard story structures may correspond closely to the ways that human brains store, retrieve, and manipulate information about social processes. Brains seem to array objects, including social objects, in virtual spatial and temporal relations to each other; to assign objects attributes that are available as explanations of their behavior; and to assemble complex situations as interactions of self-motivated objects within delimited spaces and times. If so, preference for standard story accounts and availability of storytelling as a wide-ranging social tool could spring from deep currents in the human organism.

Perhaps, however, brains and nervous systems do no more than accommodate storytelling as one among many possible ways of organizing social accounts. Perhaps people learn the structure of stories just as they learn the maps of cities and the melodies of favorite songs. In that case, we might reasonably expect different populations to vary in their emphasis on storytelling, and we might well discover that Westerners acquired a preference for standard story packaging of social life through a long, distinctive history. Through that long history, we might find that people extended storytelling from an initial narrow invention to a wide range of applications.

Here, as always, the exact interplay between nature and nurture, between wired-in capacity and cultural immersion, between genetic determination and historical transformation presents a great challenge to our long-term understanding and explanation of social life. But in the short run, we need only this conclusion: For whatever reasons, today's Westerners (and maybe all peoples) have a strong tendency to organize conversations about social processes in standard story form.

DISCIPLINARY STORIES

Each of the academic disciplines that concentrates on the explanation of some aspect of human behavior has made its own adjustment to the dominance of standard stories. Linguists, geographers, psychologists, historians, paleontologists, economists, anthropologists, political scientists, and sociologists all have characteristic ways of dealing with—or keeping their distance from—standard stories. Many historians, for example, insist that such stories accurately represent the causal structure of social life. They write their histories as tales of conscious, self-motivated actors. When they get to the large scales of wars, great transformations, and civilizations, however, historians split between those who refer to collective actors (e.g., classes and nations) in standard story form and those who resort to abstract causal forces such as mentalities, cultures, technologies, and forms of power.

Psychologists take other approaches to stories. They divide among a dwindling number of storytelling analysts who continue to treat whole individuals as conscious, acting entities and a variety of reductionists who trace observable human behavior to the operation of genes, neurons, hormones, and/or subconscious mental processes. Economists divide differently, with many analysts of individual economic behavior adopting a highly stylized version of the standard story that centers on deliberate decision making within well-defined constraints while analysts of macroeconomic processes introduce nonstory mediating mechanisms: impersonal markets, technologies, resource endowments, and flows of information, capital, goods, or labor. For all their differences in other regards, political scientists, anthropologists, and sociologists maintain similar relations to standard stories. Within each of the three disciplines, some specialists conduct almost all of their analyses in standard story form, while others reject stories in favor of explanations based on nonstory structures and processes such as markets, networks, self-sustaining cultures, physical environments, and evolutionary selection.

What place should stories occupy in social science? In ordinary circumstances, well-told standard stories convey what is going on far more forcefully than the mathematical equations, lists of concepts, statistical tables, or schematic diagrams social scientists commonly chalk up on their blackboards. Why, then, shouldn't social scientists turn to fiction and biography as models for their own efforts? After all, non–social scientists often reserve their highest praise for social scientific work that "reads like a novel." Wouldn't a course in story writing therefore provide the best introduction to social scientific analysis?

No, it wouldn't, at least not if the point of social science is to describe and explain social processes. The difficulty lies in the logical structure of storytelling. Remember its elements: (1) limited number of interacting characters, (2) limited time and space, (3) independent, conscious, self-motivated actions, (4) with the exception of externally generated accidents, all actions resulting from previous actions by the characters. Standard stories work that way, but on the whole social processes do not.

Consider some examples:

- Within a high-fertility population, as improved nutrition or prevention of children's diseases reduces infant mortality, the population grows more rapidly and experiences a rise in life expectancy.
- Job seekers who get their information about employment opportunities from other people who are already close to them do less well in the job market, on the average, than job seekers who get their information from more distant acquaintances.
- Despite the sometimes sensational salaries of athletes, entertainers, and CEOs, the higher we go up the ladder of annual income in the United States, the larger looms inherited wealth, and the smaller the share that wages of any kind constitute current revenues.
- In Figure 3.1a, locations B and C are obviously peripheral, while A and D hardly differ from their neighbors in centrality. In Figure 3.1b, however, the addition of a connection between B and C has made them much more central than any of their predecessors, while A and D have also gained in their access to others.
- In U.S. cities, children from low-income households often live in rundown, crowded housing where dust mites and cockroaches proliferate. Those pests trigger asthma attacks, which keep poorer children out of school or hamper their performance in school.

a

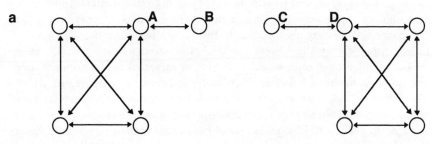

b

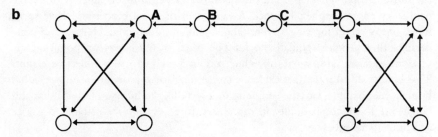

Figure 3.1   Changes in Centrality

Each of these cases calls for qualifications and explanations. The rise in life expectancy as a consequence of declining infant mortality registers the passage of larger surviving cohorts into higher age groups, and soon reaches a limit unless death rates start declining for those higher age groups as well. More distant acquaintances provide relatively effective news about available jobs not because individually they have better information but because collectively they connect job seekers with a wider range of opportunities than do close friends and kin. Inherited wealth actually places the bulk of rich Americans in their high positions and means that much of their income arrives as returns from capital rather than salaries. Connecting apparently peripheral locations that possess complementary resources describes the work of effective entrepreneurs, brokers, and matchmakers; it frequently changes whole organizational configurations rapidly. Missing school and being sick in school not only reduce children's exposure to education but also promote children's confusion, inattention, and discouragement, which further damage learning.

The point of these obvious examples is two-fold: In each case, strong, recurrent causal mechanisms are operating, but in none of them do the crucial causal mechanisms correspond to the structure of standard storytelling. Of course we can tell standard stories about some aspects in each of these situations: how microbe hunters track down baby-killing diseases, how individual job seekers actually find employment, why parents bequeath wealth to their children, under what circumstances entrepreneurs notice good fits between unconnected locations, or how poor children experience schools. But these cases differ from the conventional matter of storytelling because central cause-effect relations are indirect, incremental, interactive, unintended, collective, or mediated by the nonhuman environment rather than being direct, willed consequences of individual actions. The standard stories we construct for such processes miss their central causal connections. Most significant social processes fall into a nonstory mode. Most of them do so because at least some crucial causes within them are indirect, incremental, interactive, unintended, collective, and/or mediated by the nonhuman environment.

Personally, I have nothing against standard stories. I read them eagerly, make arguments with them, remember things by telling myself stories, and gladly overhear the stories people tell each other on the subway. I began this chapter with a standard story about Stephen Leacock. As a student of social processes, I have spent much of my career locating, transcribing, cataloging, analyzing, retelling, and pondering other people's standard stories. The pages of my books on popular contention overflow with stories in which ordinary people make collective claims. That massive effort to extract evidence concerning social processes from stories has brought me to appreciate the centrality of storytelling in human life, but it has also taught me the incompatibility in causal structure between most standard stories and most social processes.

THE SEARCH FOR CAUSES

Refusal to recognize the limits of standard storytelling creates major problems for social analysts. In one light, the problems stem from distortion produced by forcing social processes into stories about self-motivated actors. In the opposite light, they consist of failures to specify causal mechanisms that actually drive social processes. To clarify what is at issue in the confrontation between standard storytelling and social science explanation, we can use a rough distinction among the four dominant ontologies and explanatory strategies adopted by analysts of social life: methodological individualism, phenomenological individualism, holism, and relational realism. Let us review them and their connections with storytelling in turn.

Methodological individualism treats independent choice-making persons as the fundamental units and starting points of social scientific analysis. Its explanations pivot on mental events: choices or decisions. People make choices that forward their interests, preferences, or utilities within constraints set by personal resources and environmental settings. What causes those choices? Other mental events, in the form of calculations concerning the likely outcomes of different actions.

Methodological individualism has the great advantages of simplicity and generality—if and when it works. For the moment, it faces three large difficulties, two of them upstream and one of them downstream. Upstream (that is, before the point of decision that constitutes its central object of explanation), (1) few actual human behaviors seem to fit its requirement of optimizing choices among well-defined alternatives, and (2) supposedly fixed elements such as preferences and computations of outcomes actually wobble and interact in the course of social action. Downstream (that is, once a decision is supposedly made), we confront difficulty when, (3) methodological individualism so far lacks a plausible account of the causal chains by which decisions produce their effects on individual action, social interaction, and complex social processes.

Methodological individualists, however, can take standard storytelling in their stride. They are already talking about self-motivated actors—the fewer, the better—within delimited times and places whose deliberated decisions produce all the effects worth mentioning. Their problem does not result from intrinsic incompatibility of their causal accounts with storytelling but from the implausibility of the standard stories their causal accounts entail.

Phenomenological individualists likewise move easily on standard story terrain. They center descriptions and explanations of social processes on human consciousness. At the extreme of solipsism, indeed, the social world dissolves into individual consciousness, and systematic explanation of social processes faces an insuperable barrier: the impossibility of any observer's entering into her neighbor's awareness, much less explaining it. In less extreme forms, however, phenomenological individualists pursue a familiar variety of explanation. Through empathy, deduction, criticism, or some other means, they reconstruct the meanings, feelings, ideologies, and theories that presumably motivate social action. They can deal more easily than methodological individualists with collective actors such as churches, states, classes, or regions, to which they impute varieties and degrees of shared consciousness. At that point, nevertheless, phenomenological individualists confront the same explanatory obstacles as methodological individualists: upstream, accounting for change and interaction of the conscious states that presumably produce social action; downstream, showing how those conscious states create their effects.

Holists have commonly prided themselves on escaping precisely those obstacles by recognizing the interdependence of individual actions, their constraint by previously existing social structure, and their coalescence into self-regulating systems. Structures sketched by holists range in scale from friendships to civilizations, in content from fluid communications to evolutionary universals, in structure from gossamer webs to iron cages. What unifies holistic approaches is their imputation of self-generating properties to social aggregates and their explanation of particular social events by connections to the larger social systems within which they occur. The great failures of systems theories lie in two main areas: (1) the absence of sturdy, well-documented causal mechanisms that are actually observable in operation, and (2) the prevalence of poorly explicated functional explanations, in which events, relations, institutions, or social processes exist because they serve some requirement of the system as a whole. Although they certainly describe their major actors—social systems—as self-propelling, and sometimes describe social systems as having characteristic life histories, holists usually avoid standard storytelling.

Relational analysis focuses on the transaction, interaction, information flow, exchange, mutual influence, or social tie as its elementary unit. For relational realists, individuals, groups, and social systems are contingent, changing social products of interaction. Relational realists vary greatly in the prominence they ascribe to culture: to shared understandings and their representations. At one extreme, hard-nosed network theorists treat the geometry of connections as having a logic that operates quite independently of the network's symbolic content. At the other extreme, conversational analysts treat the back-and-forth of social speech as inescapably drenched with meaning. In between, students of organizational processes who reject the idea that organizations are self-maintaining systems often trace webs of culturally conditioned interdependency among persons and positions within the organization.

At both extremes and in between, relational analysis maintains a curious connection with storytelling. It simultaneously denies the self-propulsion of a story's characters and affirms the centrality of mutual influences among characters that give standard storytelling its continuity. Relational analyses enjoy the advantages of providing excellent descriptive templates for social processes and identifying robust regularities in social interaction. At least in principle, they offer the promise of treating standard stories not as descriptions or explanations of social processes but as changing, contingent *products* of social interaction. In fact, they could account for the production and use of nonstandard stories as well.

To be sure, in real life and in social science most attempts at explanation of social processes involve syntheses, amalgams, and compromises among some or all of our four basic approaches: methodological individualism, phenomenological individualism, holism, and relational analysis. It is not hard, for example, to conceive of individuals as making rational choices within strict limits set by encompassing and self-regulating social systems, as in the model of a buyer or seller who enters a competitive market.

Similarly, relational analysts often go on to argue that the structures created by interaction—hierarchies, paired categories, industries, and so on—have emergent properties, operate according to powerful laws, and shape social relations among their participants; to that extent, relational realists edge toward systems theories. Still, each of the four explanatory traditions generates some relatively pure and exclusive accounts of social life; even in compromised form each presents characteristically different difficulties, and at the limit all four cannot be valid. None of the four, furthermore, offers an explanatory structure that fits comfortably with the standard stories in which people ordinarily cast their social accounts.

In most circumstances, standard storytelling provides an execrable guide to social explanation. Its directly connected and self-motivated actors, deliberated actions, circumscribed fields of action, and limited inventory of causes badly represent the ontology and causal structure of most social processes. There are exceptions—some games, some battles, some markets, and some decision making within formal organizations approximate the ontology and causal structure of standard stories. But these are extreme cases, notable especially for the hidden institutional supports that make them possible. Most social processes involve cause-effect relations that are indirect, incremental, interactive, unintended, collective, and/or mediated by the nonhuman environment.

HOW TO CONFRONT STORYTELLING

Hence a three-faced problem: how to cut through the limits set by prevalent stories on the explanation of social processes; how to convey valid explanations of social processes when audiences customarily wrap their own explanations in storytelling; how to describe and explain the creation, transformation, and effects of existing standard stories.

The first is, surprisingly, the easiest. Well-versed practitioners of methodological individualism, phenomenological individualism, holism, and relational analysis have all at times learned to resist standard story interpretations of their subject matter and to adopt formalisms that assist them in imposing an alternative frame: mathematical models, diagrams, simulations, conceptual schemes, measurement devices, and more. It may be painful, and some skilled practitioners abandon their training, but such learned self-discipline comes with apprenticeship to the trade.

Communication with nonspecialists who customarily cast their social accounts in standard stories sets a greater challenge. Teachers of mathematics' or chemistry's emphatically nonstory structures to novices have several advantages over social scientists: Almost no one thinks mathematics or chemistry should or does follow the rules of storytelling; students have no previous training in mathematics or chemistry as a series of stories to shed before they can learn more adequate models; students grudgingly or eagerly accept that learning the formal structure of mathematics or chemistry will give them future benefits. None of these, regrettably, applies to social science.

On the contrary, most people, including some teachers of social science, think that social life actually does conform to the requirements of storytelling—self-motivated actors, deliberated actions, and the lot. In addition, people (or at least Western people) ordinarily carry on their moral reasoning in a standard story mode; they judge actual or possible actions by their conscious motives and their immediately foreseeable effects; this fact lies behind the frequent complaint that social scientific explanations deny the responsibility, autonomy, and/or moral worth of individuals.

More complexities follow. People ordinarily join (1) moral judgments, (2) conceptions of what is possible, (3) ideas of what is desirable within that realm of possibility, and (4) causal accounts of social life. A discussion of what people should do presumes that they can do it, and the justification for their doing so usually includes judgments about the likely consequences of their doing so. As a result, people do not readily accept analysts' attempts to pry those elements of moral thinking apart. (Perhaps for that very reason young people who are beginning to question the moral systems within which they grew up develop greater receptivity to social science than their fellows.)

That is not all. Before they encounter social scientific disciplines, students and nonspecialist readers have had years of practice in constructing social explanations by means of storytelling; they do not cast off that practice easily. Finally, the benefits of doing so are much harder to discern than in the case of mathematics or chemistry; indeed, what most students and some professionals hope to find in social science is the ability to construct more persuasive standard stories. Social scientists do not easily cut through the veil of resistance.

What can social scientists do about it? Here are some of the possibilities:

- Study the social processes that condition how and why similar stories strike one audience as quite authentic and another as utterly phony
- Teach competing ways of representing particular social processes: not only as storytelling and as alternative social scientific models but also as metaphor, machine, and political rhetoric; compare premises, procedures, and results of these competing representations, showing what is distinctive and valuable about the social scientific ones
- Dramatize the existence of social processes, configurations, or outcomes for which available standard stories offer implausible explanations, demonstrably

false explanations, contradictory explanations, or no explanations at all, and for
which coherent social scientific explanations exist

- More precisely and aggressively, create and use simulations of social processes
  (whether simple games or complex symbolic representations) that challenge
  available standard stories, embody social scientifically plausible causes and effects, produce empirically verifiable outcomes, and allow participants to investigate the consequences of altering inputs or causal structures

- Trace standard story shadows of nonstory processes, as by following a series of
  interdependent life histories, each itself in coherent standard story form, before examining the intersection and variation of those lives: how, for example,
  do variable relations to the same school system, firm, or labor market create
  contrasting trajectories and solidarities?

- Go even farther in the same direction and subvert storytelling: embed nonstory explanations in ostensibly storytelling form, for example by recounting
  the same social process—a military battle, flow of information through a hospital, or racial integration of a school system—from multiple perspectives, one
  standard story per participant, until the problem shifts to accounting for differences and connections among the experiences of participants

- Observe how the relationship and conversation between interviewer and re-
  spondent shape the responses that survey analysts later interpret as evidence of
  respondents' individual traits, preferences, intentions, and/or propensities

- Simulate and investigate what happens when participants in standard stories
  become aware of and respond deliberately to cause-effect relations that are indirect, incremental, interactive, unintended, collective, and/or mediated by the
  nonhuman environment, thus approximating what many theorists have advo-
  cated as "reflexive" social science

- Tunnel under standard stories themselves by creating compelling explanations
  for both (1) the stories that participants in social processes tell about what is
  happening to them or others, (2) the stories that analysts, critics, observers, and
  even other social scientists tell about particular social processes, situations, and
  outcomes; using systematic knowledge of the social processes involved, for example, explain how and why police, criminals, judges, prosecutors, priests, social workers, and criminologists come to tell different stories about crime

From the last alternative unfolds a huge, promising program of social scientific
work. Analysts of social construction have generally contented themselves with
demonstrating that entities earlier interpreters have taken to be irreducibly real—
identities, nations, states, genders, and more—consist of or depend on elaborate,
contingent, but compelling cultural webs. They have not offered verifiable descriptions or explanations of the processes by which the relevant social construction takes
place. They have taken social construction to be a blank wall, an opaque screen, or
an impenetrable thicket, impossible to tunnel under. Since standard stories constitute one of the major zones of social construction, however, any systematic account

of the processes by which people generate, transform, respond to, and deploy standard stories will serve as a model for tunneling under constructionist analyses in general—taking them seriously, but identifying the social constructions involved as objects of explanation.

Here is a challenge to social science worthy of a lifetime's effort. To explain how, why, and with what effects people fashion standard stories will require a commodious, sophisticated theory. It will entail mapping the various contents, forms, and contexts of stories, tracing how they change, pinpointing the social work people do with them, saying how some of them become fixed in laws, national traditions, or religious rituals, others form and flow like jazz, while still others circulate as jokes, insults, potted biographies, excuses, moral pronouncements, and ad hoc explanations. Surely hermeneutic and text-analytic methods will not suffice; attention will shift to the social processes that precipitate standard stories. We should enjoy the irony—that a major obstacle to social explanation should become the object of social explanation.

We have some models for that sort of analysis. In the study of language, of art forms, of well-articulated ideologies, of contentious repertoires, of kinship systems, of other phenomena where change in shared understandings clearly occurs and significantly affects participants' interactions, sociologists and other social scientists have already accumulated experience in tunneling under social construction. Not that they have reached high consensus or manufactured models that will easily export to the explanation of standard stories or other equally complex phenomena. However we evaluate the models currently available in these fields, their existence establishes the possibility in principle of taking the prevalence, variety, and power of standard stories as an explanatory challenge.

An even greater challenge lies farther along the same road. Social scientists must eventually reconcile three apparently contradictory features of social life:

1. Recurrence of a limited set of causal mechanisms in a wide variety of situations
2. The incessant improvisation that occurs in social interaction
3. The great weight of particular histories, congealed as particular cultural configurations, on social interaction

Each is so compelling that it has acquired its own advocates: advocates of general covering laws for human behavior, advocates of social life as nothing but piecemeal improvisation; advocates of deep historical and cultural determinism-cum-particularism. In fact, all three operate and interact. The three features combine in producing path-dependent social processes that never quite repeat themselves, ceaseless flux in relations among participants, and strong but partial causal analogies from one iteration of a social process to the next.

We see the trio in the field of inequality, where similar processes of exploitation, resistance, and control recur in disparate circumstances, yet actual participants in any one of those circumstances negotiate, innovate, cheat, resist, and adapt without cease, and all this improvisation occurs within strong limits, particular to the time and place, set by accumulated culture, so much so that within the same setting inequalities by gender, race, and citizenship operate as if they belonged to distinct idioms within a common language. We see the trio again in contentious politics, where an analyst of mobilization notices similar causal connections in a vast array of situations, where on the ground improvisation is not only prevalent but essential, and where the forms of interaction themselves occur within or at the perimeters of previously established forms.

Although the production of standard stories surely conforms to causal principles and permits variation in storytelling style, storytelling lodges especially in the third category, in the social arrangements by which the accumulated collective past weighs on the present and the future. Social interaction generates stories that justify and facilitate further social interaction, but it does so within limits set by the stories people already share as a consequence of previous interactions. It would be a triumph of social analysis to tell the true story of how storytelling arises and how it affects our conduct of social life.

ENLIGHTENMENT AND EXPLANATION

The prevalence of standard stories poses two significant problems for teachers and students of social science. *First*, both teachers and students make choices, implicit and explicit, between conceiving of social science as (a) enlightenment or (b) science, but for most people the paths to enlightenment pass through standard stories; substituting one standard story for another rather than complementing standard stories by means of science. *Second*, the actual causal structure of social processes—the indispensable core of any social scientific explanation—usually contradicts the logical and causal structure of standard stories. As a consequence, teachers of social science choose, however unconsciously, how to connect their presentation of the subject with standard stories.

Figure 3.2 schematizes the choice. At one extreme, teachers can emphasize social science as enlightenment by formulating and telling superior stories. In what way superior? From a social scientific viewpoint, superior stories have these qualities:

- They include all the major actors (including collective and nonhuman actors) a valid causal account of the events in question would identify and relate.
- Within the social interactions they describe, they accurately represent cause-effect relations among actions of participants in the story, even if they neglect indirect, incremental, and other effects that are not visible in the participants' interactions.
- They provide effective means of connecting the story with times, places, actors, and actions outside its purview.

- They offer means of relating causes explicitly invoked by the story with other causes that are indirect, incremental, interactive, unintended, collective, and/or mediated by the nonhuman environment.

Superior stories, that is, do not identify all the relevant cause-effect relations, but they remain consistent with fuller, more adequate causal accounts.

In the case of social movements, for example, an *inferior* but commonly credited story says that people who have failed in fair, normal competition vent their frustration in collective complaints, to which right-thinking people respond by pointing to established channels for the expression of political preferences. The story is inferior because solid evidence concerning social movement recruitment and participation regularly contradicts its empirical implications and because the causal connections it alleges—notably the chain from failure to frustration to collective action—do not hold up to close observation.

A *superior*, social scientifically validated story says that people join social movements as a consequence of their relations with other people who have already experienced injustice or otherwise become aware of fellow humans' experience with injustice. Neither story adequately represents the significance of network connections in recruitment to social movements, but within the social interactions it does represent the second story comes much closer to social processes actually governing social movement activism. Thus, the superior story makes a contribution to the teaching of social science as enlightenment.

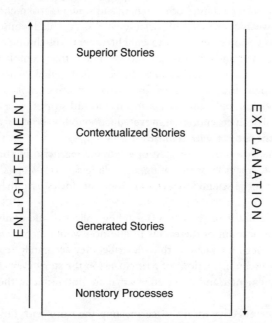

Figure 3.2   Ways to Present and Pursue Social Science

At the other extreme—nonstory processes—we can decide to teach, learn, and use social science as a deliberate integration of social interaction into causal chains, significant parts of which are indirect, incremental, interactive, unintended, collective, and/or mediated by the nonhuman environment. Thus, we can construct, verify, and communicate models of social movements in which intentions, awareness, and deliberated action take place in tight interdependence with social processes that are not immediately visible to social movement participants. This sort of teaching, learning, and using is essential to the discovery of new explanations and the full criticism of prevalent stories, hence crucial to the education of professional social scientists. It is essential because cause-effect relations within social processes do not, in fact, conform to standard stories.

In between the two extremes, we can also choose to pursue social science as an effort to contextualize existing stories or to generate them. *Contextualizing* stories involves identifying the social situations in which certain kinds of stories arise and tracing the consequences of adopting those stories rather than others that are, in principle, available. Thus, we might analyze the conditions under which a connected but previously unmobilized population forms a story about its distinctive national origins, makes claims for political recognition on the basis of that story, and then lives the consequences of having adopted that particular story rather than some other that might have been available.

The even more ambitious program of *generating* stories consists of analyzing the processes by which people actually create, adopt, negotiate, and alter the stories they employ in routine social life. Here, in principle, the analyst should be able to simulate and predict both form and content of stories as they enter the social interactions of juries, social movement activists, newscasters, co-workers, and people in general. Storytelling is such a fundamental, pervasive social process that it is hard to imagine effective generation of stories without deep understanding of nonstory processes. Thus, each rung in the ladder from explanation to enlightenment depends on those below it: Construction of superior stories rests on some ability to contextualize them, contextualization requires some awareness of processes that generate stories, and the analysis of generation requires partial knowledge of the nonstory causal processes at work in social life.

To teach superior stories and the capacity to detect and criticize inferior stories, however, amply serves enlightenment. Social science as enlightenment can profitably concentrate on critical examination and reconstruction of widely employed standard stories. Since most students of social science go off into other walks of life, and since almost all of them continue to conduct their lives by means of stories and responses to other people's stories, social science as enlightenment should enrich and clarify social experience. An enlightenment-oriented social scientific education can equip those nonspecialist citizens to identify, compare, classify, criticize, improve, or even deploy standard stories. On the presumption that knowing how powerful everyday processes actually work prepares the knowers for more effective encounters with social life, social scientific teaching can serve well by concentrating on standard stories. If that sort of education then sensitizes nonspecialists to indirect, incremental, interactive, unintended, collective, and/or environmentally mediated causal links to the stories people tell, so much the better.

Part II

POLITICAL IDENTITIES

4

Stein Rokkan
and Political Identities

My onetime collaborator Stein Rokkan curiously twinned a strongly relational sensitivity to social processes and a fundamentally individualistic conceptual apparatus. It goes without saying that his were two-egg twins, often at war with each other, an intellectual Cain and Abel. Relational sensibility probably came easily to Rokkan because of the jarring confrontation between his Norwegian origins and a vast international network in which he occupied as many different identities as connections (see Torsvik 1981). Nevertheless, he borrowed deep individualism from his frequent coworkers the survey researchers, who imagined a world peopled by independent individuals, each one supposedly having a distinct, coherent mentality that explained his or her individual behavior.

Rokkan never escaped from ambivalence between individuals and relations. Analyzing the effects of the secret ballot, for example, he remarked:

> A personal choice was placed before the worker that made him, at least temporarily, independent of his immediate environment: was he primarily a worker or primarily a citizen of the broader local or national community? Secret voting made it possible for the inarticulate rank and file to escape the pressures of their organizations, and at the same time it put the onus of political visibility on the activists within the working-class movement. (Rokkan 1970, 154)

In this scenario, political actors make individual choices among identities in the same way that hardware store customers choose among the can openers on the shelf.

Proceeding in this fashion, Rokkan adopted the dominant prejudice of the social sciences: He accepted the existence of reasoning, reasonable individuals, each

An earlier version of this chapter appeared as "Stein Rokkan et les Identités Politiques," *Revue Internationale de Politique Comparée* 2 (1995), 27–45; I have translated it from the French original.

of them possessing a more or less unified consciousness, each one's actions motivated by that consciousness. In individual experience, according to that doctrine, the presence of multiple identities threatens to undermine the coherence of thought and action. For Rokkan and others, that sort of individualism blocked understanding (or at least adequate representation) of social relations that constrain electoral choices.

Yet, the same Rokkan proved himself capable of formulating a deeply relational conception of a political center:

> Centres can be minimally defined as privileged locations within a territory where key military/administrative, economic and cultural resource-holders most frequently meet; with established arenas for deliberations, negotiations and decision-making; where people convene for ritual ceremonies of affirmation of identity; with monuments that symbolize this identity; with the largest proportion of the economically active population engaged in the processing and communication of information and instructions over long distances. Centres, then, are both locations providing services and nodes in a communications network. These two simple concepts of degree of centralization and centrality pull together the key concepts in any consideration of central structures— resource endowments, distances, communications—measured in terms of the three conventional dimensions of differentiation: political control, economic dominance, cultural standardization. Typically, a center controls the bulk of the transactions among resource-holders across a territory; it is closer than any alternative site (location) to the resource-rich areas within the territory; and it is able to dominate the communication flow through a standard language and a set of institutions for regular consultation and representation. (Rokkan and Urwin 1982, 5; for similar conceptions, see Dodgshon 1998; Hohenberg and Lees 1985; Meier 1962; Skinner 1964)

This time the essential social process does not take place in individual consciousness but in transactions among persons. Here, Rokkan is adopting relational ontology.

Unlike me, Rokkan never took a dogmatic position on one side or the other. At the start of a remarkable autobiographical report presented to the French Association for Political Science in 1976, Rokkan apologized for his big schemata:

> You will see immediately that it is a matter of sketches, efforts, and drafts. I have published a certain number of these models, but I have never been satisfied by what I have done. As soon as I have published one version of a model I have been struck by new logical or empirical difficulties and have taken up the effort again, rethinking the structure of concepts and variables. (Rokkan 1976, 1)

Later he traced the path that led from the individualism of his survey analyses to the relational sensibility of his European conceptual maps. That path passed through examination of the social contexts within which people make political choices, then back to historical origins of those contexts, especially their variation from one European country to another. Without recognizing the ontological boundary he had crossed, Rokkan complained of his first democratization models:

"I noticed that the first model was too atomizing; it treated each case separately without taking account of environmental effects stemming from the geopolitical location of the territory in question" (Rokkan 1976, 8–9). The desire to contextualize individual choices led Rokkan directly to analysis of relations among persons, among groups, and among territories.

At his death, Rokkan was working on his never-completed masterwork *Economy, Territory, and Identity*. That book analyzed political experiences of peripheral regions including Scandinavia. It sent roots even more deeply into relational soil than his earlier analyses had, in two different ways: first, by showing how much any particular country's domestic politics operated as a function of its variable relations to the world outside that country; second, by stressing language as principle and means of political identification. If language, then communication, conversation, and social relations.

Let me not claim that Stein Rokkan anticipated recent attempts to attach analyses of political identity to a relational base (e.g., Aminzade 2000; Auyero 2000; Brubaker 1993; Brubaker and Cooper 2000; Cerulo 1997; Hanagan 1994; Østergard 1991, 1992; Somers 1992, 1993; Wendt 1994). Given his search for deep historical origins of political cleavages in different parts of Europe, he would, I suppose, have been unsympathetic to current labeling of ethnic and linguistic identities in terms of strategy, contingency, and social construction (Anderson 1991; Brubaker and Cooper 2000; Burguière and Grew 2001; Comaroff 1991; Guardino 1994; Gal 1987; Hechter 2000; Laitin 1998; Segal 1988; Shell 1993; Tishkov 1997). Presuming that temporal priority signaled causality, Rokkan excavated cleavages as if he were an archaeologist looking for the subterranean foundations of visible structures.

Yet, it seems to me that before his premature death in 1979 Rokkan was already posing questions to which today's students of identity are still trying to form useful replies:

- Among the many identities political actors have at their disposal, why do only some of them become bases of public collective action?
- What processes lead people to slaughter each other according to religious, ethnic, and political identities?
- Why do identity-based demands occur in waves and incite each other instead of appearing in response to regular rhythms of economic and demographic change?
- When a heterogeneous empire—Ottoman, Soviet, or otherwise—organizes its administration around titular nationalities, what happens to those identities when the empire disintegrates?

These are the sorts of questions that impel this effort to extend, complete, and perhaps to correct the ideas of Stein Rokkan. The best proof of its utility will be the light cast on the formation and mobilization of ethnic and national identities. But to get there it helps to frame the inquiry in terms of collective identity at large.

Faced with the proliferation and mutation of public identities in Eastern Europe, I imagine Rokkan would have taken three apparently contradictory steps:

1. Localization of such identities as Russian, Abkhazian, Macedonian, Croatian, or Albanian in relations among populations rather than in the characters of the peoples thus designated
2. Search for cultural materials deployed in these identities in a long process of historical accumulation
3. Placement of these analyses within a series of extremely broad comparisons

In that perspective, a latter-day Rokkanian would undertake a relational and comparative investigation of the formation of political identities. That is the point of this chapter: to sketch early stages of that great enterprise. Those stages are, to be sure, rather conceptual and schematic, without solid evidence, but based (like Stein Rokkan's thought) on long reflection about concrete political processes in Europe over multiple centuries. The study of revolutions, popular contention, states, and the growth of capitalism inevitably raises questions concerning political identity.

Remember our strongly relational postulate: Rather than living inside human bodies, true identities invariably live in ties among persons. (More generally, they live in relations among social sites, but "persons" will do for present purposes.) Their ways of life vary according to the context. Identities deployed by a married couple differ in many regards from those that link a merchant to her customers, which in turn differ from the identities at work within a capitalist firm. We need some basic concepts. We can begin by following the ontological chain from social transactions to groups through ties, categories, and social networks. Even individuals emerge from *social transactions,* which means that a single human body ordinarily provides the material bases for a number of distinct personalities differentiated by type of transaction.

As trust and duration increase, some of these transactions acquire stories of their own. They acquire memories, expectations, understandings, rights, and obligations; we can call those bundles of transactions *social ties.* A social tie becomes stronger according to the multiple of its (1) frequency, (2) intensity, and (3) range of behavior. Similar ties among at least three persons constitute a *social network.* Obviously, networks vary with respect to extent, density, centralization, and many other dimensions (Emirbayer and Goodwin 1994; Knoke 1990; Wellman 1988).

Social categories include regional, racial, ethnic, or political identities to the extent that a single criterion, simple or complex, distinguishes a set of actors. By no means do all social networks constitute categories, or vice versa, a truth illustrated by chains of sexual or monetary connections in which the third participant knows nothing of the first, the fourth knows nothing of the second, and so on. A category exists when the actors involved in a certain kind of tie, real or potential, recognize its application to their transactions. That application may be symmetrical, as in relations among members of the same religion, who thus belong to the same category. It may also be asymmetrical, with the actors accepting a significant division between them; the distinction between masters and slaves, for example, defines two interdependent categories. A category becomes stronger to the extent that a simple verification of mutual membership imposes obligations on actors who have not previously met; if the simple fact of belonging to the same nationality or religion allows X, previously unknown to Y, to demand help from Y, that category is strong. Thus, a social network built on ties of cohabitation, sexual relations, and lineage following principles of common origin becomes an ethnic group.

This is then the essential identity chain: transaction, tie, network, category, and group. An identity is simply the social experience of one of these elements coupled with public representation of that experience. The experience of friendship, a type of social tie, constitutes the identity *friend*. The experience of belonging to a religious group constitutes a religious identity. Although carriers of identities internalize knowledge of its practices, the identity itself exists in relations to others, whether at the level of transactions, ties, networks, or groups. Far from being a source of difficulty, exercise of multiple identities is the normal, indispensable condition of human social life. It is a necessary complement to the proliferation of social relations. A truly unitary identity would ironically resemble *folie à deux:* just one relation to all the world. We begin to see the analogy with spoken language, rather than with an interior monologue. Every socially competent person knows how to vary her conversation according to the character of her interlocutor, thus according to the social relation defined by the interacting parties.

Following that analogy, notice that actors build and negotiate each of the different sorts of identity using the cultural means at their disposal and drawing on collective memory, adopting or adapting available models. The history of a certain relation (or type of relation) therefore limits subsequent constructions of that relation. Notice also that each actor deploys her own history when interpreting each transaction, tie, network, category, or group. That fact challenges any representation of identity as a straightforward reflection or expression of social position. Here is the essential point: Identities depend on social transactions, multiply as a function of the multiplicity of social relations, and result from socially organized negotiation and interpretation.

In the political world, however, not all identities are equal. Some of them lend themselves to mobilization and collective action, others do not. Activation of those that do serve collectively varies markedly in time and space, the same persons participate in collective action under different identities on different occasions, and the risks people are ready to take on behalf of one identity or another vary enormously. Since World War II, for example, over the world as a whole the proportion of large-scale lethal combats in which participants define their differences as ethnic or national has increased decade by decade. In the fields of revolutions, rebellions, and civil wars, conflicts in which participants define themselves in terms of social class have declined noticeably as ethnic and national definitions have risen (Gurr 1993a, 1993b, 2000; Gurr and Harff 1994; Holsti 1991, 1996; Kushner

2001). This does not mean that in everyday life ethnicity was becoming more central while class conflicts lost importance. It means that the political context of the later twentieth century increasingly favored the activation of ethnic categories, or at least ethnic representation of all sorts of conflict.

How and why? We enter hotly contested ground. Let me nevertheless attempt a preliminary mapping. First, we need a distinction between the *mechanisms* and the *forms* of identity mobilization. It is becoming increasingly clear that activation of previously existing solidarities sustained by ties and social networks plays a fundamental role as a mechanism of mobilization in political action and social movements (Deneckere 1990; Diani 1988, 1990; Fernandez and McAdam 1988; Giugni and Passy 2001; Hirsch 1990; McAdam and Paulsen 1993; Ohlemacher 1993; Opp and Gern 1993; Passy 1998). But if it brakes or blocks mobilization of categories and groups lacking some minimum density of ties and networks, this phenomenon does not alone determine which groups or categories actually mobilize. We must also consider relations between potential actors and their political contexts. At first glance, such a formulation seems to exclude nothing. But it follows a distinctive perspective that has emerged in the study of social movements over the last few decades, the analysis of political opportunity structures (see Cultures et Conflits 1993; Duyvendak 1994; Giugni and Kriesi 1990; Koopmans 1993; McAdam, McCarthy, and Zald 1988; Tarrow 1998; Zdravom'islova 1993).

In that perspective, within limits set by interpersonal understandings concerning what is possible, desirable, and effective, daily life creates capacities and propensities for claim making. But the organization and action of powerful actors—the level of repression, state centralization, availability of allies, and so forth—channel current claims. Compared to what we might conclude from a straightforward reading of the interests at risk in public politics, shared culture, capacity, and political context strongly limit mobilization and making of collective claims. If marginal groups rarely make their way into public politics, that is not because they are content with their lot but because the existing structure of political opportunities inhibits them.

Even in this cartoon form, the argument suggests ways of explaining the mobilization and demobilization of ostensibly national or ethnic movements. To bypass theoretical complications, let me offer a series of conjectures concerning conditions favoring mobilization of various identities, with no more than passing illustrations of each conjecture. These will be top-down conjectures, seen from the viewpoint of powerful actors. From the bottom up, we must explore the conditions under which ordinary people who lack political voice acquire the means of making claims. Bottom-up analysis can rely on a vast accumulation of previous research, while top-down analysis clearly needs renewal. Let us therefore emphasize the top-down view. Here are the conjectures:

1. As a result of previous history, each connected set of political actors at the local, national, or international level readily recognizes certain types of politi-

cal identities but rejects others as invalid, even if the latter exist in routine social life. At each level specialists in certification of identities often arise; for
example, the United Nations specializes in the certification of nations and
states.

2. Recognition of a class of identities and of certain actors as certified participants in that class offers its beneficiaries significant, concrete political advantages, including privileged access to public authorities and recognized voice
in public debate. Thus, the European Union is step by step defining the qualifications of individuals and groups across the continent for citizenship in Europe as a whole.

3. For each class of identities exists a set of performances that, properly executed
and approved, support the demand of an actor to be recognized as a valid interlocutor of a certain type, to possess the proper relations of that type, therefore to deserve the rights attached to that type of identity. The performances
in question always consist of public *inter*actions with other constituted actors.
They include proof of the actor's character and capacity to act. Following the
laws of each country, for example, clusters of workers who ask for recognition as parties to public decisions must establish their qualifications to speak
for their fellow workers in the public arena.

4. Acceptance of an actor as a participant in a certified identity imposes on that
actor and other members of the system a set of obligations, including abandonment of previously possible (or even acceptable) actions that violate the
rules of the game in the new arena. During the nineteenth century, legalization of trade unions and of strikes generally required labor leaders to disavow
machine breaking as a means of combat, while after World War II admission
to the United Nations required new states to abandon (at least in principle)
international terrorism.

5. Networks, categories, and groups falling under the control of a political system vary enormously in their capacity to carry out such qualifying performances, but actors can alter their organization and behavior in conformity with
expectations of authorities that control processes of admission and exclusion.
In our time, establishing that a category constitutes or represents a nation is
much more difficult than forming a special-interest association, but three
centuries ago the opposite was true.

6. Nevertheless, each admission or exclusion of an actor modifies somewhat the
structure of power and the rules of the game prevailing in a political system.
The arrival of just a few feminists in positions of power tends to foil the later
exclusion of other actors for the sole reason of their gender composition,
while the suppression of any association whatsoever threatens the rights of
other associations that remain in public life.

7. From these conditions flows a triple battle, first, around establishment or suppression of whole classes of identities, second, around recognition or exclusion of certain actors as valid participants within their class, and finally, around

the particular claims of the actors. During the French Revolution's early months, bourgeois militias often changed themselves into National Guard units and demanded public authorization as such (battle for recognition of a class of identities), more proletarian armed units had greater difficulty achieving recognition (battle around demands of particular actors for recognition), and once recognized National Guard units often demanded public action against their enemies (battle around concrete claims).

These conjectures apply to multiple political levels, from communal life to international relations. Let us take just three illustrations: transformations of popular contention in Great Britain, varieties of social movements in contemporary Western Europe, and recent ethnic or nationalist mobilizations. The first two cases will clarify how the conjectures apply to the third.

In Great Britain (England, Wales, and Scotland) between 1750 and 1850, the forms of popular political life underwent a deep transformation (Belchem 1990; Charlesworth 1983; Palmer 1988; Plotz 2000; Stevenson 1992; Thompson 1991; Tilly 1995d). From a world of Rough Music, machine breaking, and forcible ejection of popular enemies British people moved into another world of public meetings, demonstrations, and electoral campaigns. A full explanation of that transition requires detailed examination of changes in the state, the economy, and popular life. What matters here, however, is to observe how much public political identities changed over the transition.

During the eighteenth century, the British elite already followed the practices of forming specialized societies for the pursuit of political or charitable activity, as well as using ties of kinship and patronage as bases of political identity. But those practices generally excluded ordinary people. Ordinary people typically took public positions as members of authorized communities: local ratepayers, constituted trades, religious congregations, members of local markets. In those identities they attacked tax collectors, punished workers who accepted less than the prevailing wage, and seized for local resale grain that was on its way to other markets. Beginning around 1780, however, as capital concentration proceeded and the British state became more heavily involved in warfare, some segments of the populace began to create new forms of action and new political identities.

Let me simplify radically by saying that social movement logic began to prevail, with self-designated groups claiming to represent the grievances and demands of important population segments. These groups often took the form of specialized associations, as in antislavery societies (see Drescher 1994). But they likewise adopted the strategy of the public meeting, most often less open to true debate than to demonstrations of popular support for a political program. The demonstration, the petition campaign, and the pamphlet war likewise made their position-taking visible.

That deep transformation of the means of popular contention implied a shift in the dramatis personae of political life. Instead of authorized communities, public life began to feature political associations, workers' organizations, supporters of candidates, followers of causes. Local assemblies, it is true, continued to play critical parts in the preparation of addresses and petitions to Parliament, but even there we can see a shift toward the acting out of unity and respectability to back adherence to political programs. During the 1820s, under the leadership of Daniel O'Connell, successive versions of the Catholic Association in the United Kingdom (the somewhat misnamed amalgamation of Great Britain with Ireland in 1801) opened the way to other associations, notably those oriented to parliamentary reform. Despite dissolution of the Catholic Association, the legislation of 1829 that "emancipated" Catholics by increasing their access to public office responded directly to a huge popular campaign organized through the Catholic Association and opposed by Protestant popular associations. Overall, the passage of Catholic Emancipation ratified and encouraged mass mobilization by means of popular associations.

Almost immediately, reformist political entrepreneurs generalized the forms of association (for example, the Political Unions) they had invented during unsuccessful reform campaigns of 1815 to 1819. They mounted an unprecedented political mobilization. The Reform Act of 1832 resulted from that mobilization. It gave the vote to property holders while excluding from suffrage the mass of workers whose mobilization had frightened the ruling classes. Worker-based Chartism of 1838 to 1848 then responded directly to the failures of the 1832 legislation. The exclusion of most workers in 1832 after the mass mobilization of 1830–1832 explains the surprising weight of the Chartist program on voting rights and parliamentary representation rather than on economic advantages. Thenceforth, political associations and workers' societies occupied central places in Great Britain's public life. A new category of political identities, constituted by new relations between citizens and authorities, became available to people who shared an interest. This history, I believe, conforms closely to the political processes described in my earlier conjectures.

We can see remarkable parallels in contemporary social movements (Amenta, Halfmann, and Young 1999; Ayres 1998; Casquette 1998; Connell 1990; Duyvendak 1994; Giugni, McAdam, and Tilly 1998; Hanagan 1994, 1998; Ibarra and Tejerina 1998; Krieger 1999; McCammon et al. 2001; Ray and Korteweg 1999; Tarrow 1998; Taylor and Whittier 1998). Although interpreters of new social movements (e.g., Melucci 1992; Touraine 1985) have sometimes claimed otherwise, in this domain, movement activists have not been creating whole new categories of identity as political associations once did. They have instead made new entries into long-established categories. The idea and practice of simultaneously creating associations (Antislavery Society) and broader identities (abolitionist) for social movement ends generalized in Western Europe and North America during the nineteenth century. From there they spread to the rest of the world with the diffusion of contested elections and parliamentary politics.

Social movements center on sustained challenges to authorities in the names of populations otherwise lacking direct representation. The challenge takes the form of repeated public performances expressing the worthiness, unity, number, and commitment of adherents to the cause and (where possible) of the unrepresented population. Public meetings, demonstrations, petitions, pamphlets, symbols, slogans, and programs of direct action often belong to the social movement repertoire. Organizers of social movements do three kinds of work:

1. Identifying a group (for example an antinuclear association) with a threatened or wronged population (for example, all humanity, residents of a region, or mothers), thus demanding recognition of two linked identities
2. Organizing an array of public performances (demonstrations, meetings, etc.) that simultaneously dramatize demands for recognition, programs, and the movement's special character
3. Suppressing all signs of division, weakness, corruption, or triviality in the public image presented by the movement

As movement veterans know, all three usually require large, persistent efforts. Since every social movement actually builds on a contingent coalition, organizing is always hard, sometimes risky, and often thankless. Today, national and international social movements ordinarily connect social movement activists and provide a basis for popular mobilization as well as for wider dissemination of programs. Since World War II, careers in the partly contradictory specialty of social movement professional have opened up (Walker 1991; Zald and McCarthy 1987).

Recent studies of Western European social movements demonstrate how much the form and strategy of movement actors vary with regional and national structures of political opportunity. In Germany, for example, antinuclear organizations and environmental activists commonly adopt a federal structure, while French organizations in the same fields usually adopt more centralized national structures (Giugni and Kriesi 1990; Giugni and Passy 1993; Kitschelt 1986, 1993). In France, as Jan Willem Duyvendak observes, relatively close integration of movements and political parties occurs as well:

> In general, it is hard to close one's eyes to connections between left parties and the new social movements. Yet these close ties vary with the type of movement. *Instrumental* movements were especially practical for the big left parties: the solidarity movement for the Socialists and Communists and the peace movement (via the organization called Movement for Peace) for the Communists. The themes adopted by those movements could easily be formulated in terms already familiar in the old left. The ecological movement, in contrast, opposed old left ideas on the goals to be sought. That does not mean the ecological movement operated entirely out of politics. Given its lack of genuine integration into the big left parties, especially during the 1980s, that movement found itself obliged to create its own political representation. (Duyvendak 1994, 278)

Even the gay movement, according to Duyvendak's analysis, attached itself to the party system, depending heavily on the Socialist Party in times of crisis. Thus, the national structure of political opportunity both channels and facilitates social movement work. The very identities of movement actors depend on their connections with other political actors.

Mutatis mutandis, a similar analysis helps decode today's nationalist mobilizations. To schematize again, before the French Revolution, European mobilizations in the names of nations occurred mainly in two circumstances. Either an empire sought to incorporate directly a population that had hitherto enjoyed extensive autonomy, or a monarch tried to impose his religion on a population that followed a different religious tradition. In these two cases, imperial action often incited rebellions in defense of previous liberties and in the name of a distinct people. Defenders of a threatened people, however, did not invoke a general principle of national self-determination; they always appealed to particular previous privileges that incorporation would violate. Indeed, they often brandished specific charters and treaties guaranteeing their privileges.

With the Revolution and (especially) Napoleonic conquests, European states established the principle of national self-determination. France certainly applied that principle selectively, denying France's own linguistic minorities any claim to self-determination, and expanding France's frontiers substantially by means of military conquest. But the treaties that closed the Napoleonic Wars inscribed the principle of self-determination on Europe's map. With the nineteenth century, the age of state nationalism arrived. From that time, major European states strove from the top down to impose national administrations and cultures.

The top-down effort produced two critical and contradictory effects: (1) It increased the value of control over a state to those who could seize power, but (2) it also stimulated resistance on the part of those whom the top-down process excluded from power. Thus, top-down nationalism incited bottom-up nationalism. The principle of self-determination justified resistance, especially where rulers of neighboring states had something to gain from supporting the rights of minorities they considered oppressed. The Ottoman Empire's disintegration under European attacks provides the major example of that process. It exemplifies the interaction between political opportunity structure and performances on the parts of actors seeking ratification of an advantageous identity.

The process was very selective. Among the hundreds of European populations possessing distinctive combinations of language, religion, culture, and geographic origin, only twenty or thirty became serious candidates for the equation 1 Nation = 1 State. Lapps, Ruthenians, Auvergnats, Frisians, Gypsies, Vlachs, Uniates, Lutherans, even Andalucians have not demanded separate states for centuries. In conformity to the conjectures offered earlier, the establishment of such an identity requires rare circumstances: a population sufficiently numerous and concentrated to support a state; a plausible history of coherence and continuity; a set of nationalist leaders; indigenous or borrowed military capacity; support from neighboring states; acceptance by the major powers. During the nineteenth century, Greeks and Belgians fulfilled these conditions, but Bretons, Basques, and Finns did not. Today political entrepreneurs in fragments of the former Soviet Union—the Caucasus, Tatarstan, and elsewhere—are trying to meet the same tests, with uncertain results.

Obviously this analysis contradicts the self-descriptions of spokespersons for currently stateless nationalities, who (exactly like the organizers of Britain's parliamentary reform and leaders of contemporary social movements) almost always work with fragile coalitions but strive mightily to suppress evidence of internal dissension. In order to be credible, a claimant to nationhood must not only maintain a unified front but also construct a long, coherent history that will pass review by other parties to its certification. That is a difficult task in a world where migration, trade, information, and marriage incessantly cross population boundaries and where jobs, housing, commerce, and social life organize in ethnic networks that do not necessarily conform to those announced by nationalist chiefs. The very efforts of nationalist organizers reveal the contingency and the orientation to political opportunity of the collective performances that they promote.

These observations suggest modifications to Stein Rokkan's ideas even as they draw inspiration from Rokkan's own work. By searching backward in time for the origins of contemporary Europe's political cleavages, Rokkan assumed continuities in regional character that the cases reviewed here contradict. But his sketch of a relational approach to political processes allows us to get past that contradiction. Accumulated history always provides material for construction of identities, always sets limits to identity construction, and increases the likelihood that certain social relations will become the bases of identity construction. Yet, history also leaves space open for the creative talent of identity builders.

5

Political Identities in History

If William Cobbett acted the proper British patriot during his Canadian military service of 1784 to 1791 and played tory loyalist during his Philadelphia exile of 1792 to 1800, he soon thereafter turned toward a radical critique of Britain's ruling class. During the surge of working-class action and mobilization for political reform that followed the Napoleonic Wars' ending in 1815, his *Political Register* and other writings transmitted radical messages across Britain. In a vivid dramatization of his claimed political genealogy, Cobbett carried Thomas Paine's bones from America to England on his return from another American exile in 1819. He advised popular Princess Caroline in her futile bid for coronation with her estranged husband George IV in 1820–1821. He then continued to write eloquently for parliamentary reform and for justice in the countryside through the next decade. During the tumultuous British election campaign of May–June 1826, Cobbett plunged even more deeply into national politics: He stood for parliament in the borough of Preston, Lancashire.

After having been a hotbed of working-class mobilization between 1815 and 1820, in 1826 Lancashire entered its fifth straight year of intensifying strikes, accelerating attacks on industrial machinery, and swelling workers' demands for political reform. Handloom weavers were trying desperately to maintain their slipping position by means of attacks on power looms in cotton mills. In this time of mounting class conflict, Cobbett's radical temper appealed to industrial workers as well as to the agricultural laborers who formed the particular object of his sympathy and a substantial body of his supporters (Dyck 1992, 1993).

An earlier version of this chapter appeared as "Political Identities," in Michael P. Hanagan, Leslie Page Moch, and Wayne te Brake, eds., *Challenging Authority: The Historical Study of Contentious Politics*. Minneapolis: University of Minnesota Press, 1998.

Preston, a major cotton-textile town, maintained one of England's most generous suffrage provisions. In addition to the usual landlords, rentiers, professionals, merchants, and manufacturers, a number of workers actually voted there. As a center of Irish immigration, Preston also housed many Catholic electors—a significant fact when a massive new mobilization on behalf of Catholic political rights had begun in Ireland and British reformers were lining up in favor of those rights, which tories generally opposed. Cobbett arrived in Preston committed to both radical reform and Catholic Emancipation: not only manhood suffrage and frequent parliamentary sessions but also full eligibility of Catholics for nonreligious public office.

Far more than legal electors, however, thronged the hustings in Cobbett's support; he attracted a large following of disfranchised workers, both male and female. They sported Cobbett's colors: light green and white in this election, since green was the independent color, and his independent opponent had already preempted plain green. His supporters met him outside of town, paraded with a band in his honor, carried flags nobly depicting their hero as well as a series of political motifs, displayed hefty green-leaved branches, and cheered his long speeches. (Those green branches may merely have shown partisan colors, but they also recalled a tradition of liberty trees that ran back to the American and French Revolutions.) During the house-to-house canvass of early June, Cobbett and his four sons became the toast of working-class Preston.

Once the polling began on 10 June 1826, nevertheless, Cobbett's life grew more difficult. Cobbett had entered the Preston race against whig E. G. Stanley and independent John Wood. They had agreed not to require of Preston's Catholic voters the oath of supremacy, which involved a public repudiation of papal authority. Then Robert Barrie (navy captain and resident commissioner in Kingston, Ontario) entered for the tories, with the apparent intent of scaring off Cobbett's supporters by demanding the oath.

Preston's mayor Nicholas Grimshaw and his election officials collaborated with Barrie and against Cobbett not only by insisting on the Anglican oath but also by physically blocking Cobbett's electors from the polls (Spater 1982, II: 458–463). Preston's electors customarily voted in tallies, standard-sized groups of voters who proceeded to poll for their candidate, then give way to an equal-sized group of supporters for another candidate until the inability of one side to supply its next tally signaled the election's outcome. Tallies enormously slowed down an election's progress, but they reduced violent jostling for places in the electoral queue and provided opportunities for the demonstration of a candidate's mass support, complete with banners, ribbons, and colors. By means of challenges, of harassment, and of delays that discouraged faint-hearted voters, authorities could use the tally system against threatening candidates.

That happened at Preston in 1826. Mayor Grimshaw's forces not only instituted the tally system and deliberately slowed it down—the entire poll finally consumed fifteen days—but also built segregated channels to the hustings for each of the candidate's electors. "One of the worst examples of slow voting," reports Frank O'Gorman,

> came at Preston in 1826, when William Cobbett was a candidate. Day after day he justifiably complained that the slow progress of the poll threatened to disfranchise half of the Preston electorate and to damage his own prospects. . . . Only when mob violence threatened to get out of hand did the mayor agree to speed up the poll, in this case by abandoning the use of tallies. (O'Gorman 1989, 135–136)

Mob violence? In response to complaints from mayor Grimshaw about intimidation of electors, troops from the King's Dragoon Guards and Foot Guards occupied the city on 16 June. Cobbett accused the mayor of calling in troops for the express purpose of "terrifying my voters, and preventing them from exercising their rights" (Spater 1982, II: 462). Obliquely, the military concurred: On orders from regional commanding general Sir John Byng, who "disapproves very much of the Troops being allowed to remain, without the existence of an actual riot," Captain Charles Hall soon moved his forces out of town (HO 40/20 [Public Record Office, Kew, Home Office Papers, series 40, box 20]).

They did not, however, go far or long. After billeting a short distance away, they came back a few days later. Major Eckersley, Manchester commander of dragoons, wrote Undersecretary Henry Hobhouse at the Home Office on 22 June about the return of troops to Preston:

> The Mayor of Preston reports, under date of last evening, that in consequence of the most serious outrages which had been committed by a Mob, armed with Bludgeons, at one of the Entrances of the Poll Booth for the Election now holding in that Borough, preventing the access of Voters to the Hustings, Captain Barrie, one of the Candidates had protested against the admission of any more Voters, until free access was allowed to every Voter; and that being in vain tried to force a free access by means of the Civil Power, except to such persons as the Mob chose to admit, he had been under the necessity of calling upon the Troop of Cavalry, stationed at Kirkham, to place itself at Broughton, four miles from Preston, on the road to Garstang, this morning by eight o'clock, to remain there until the close of the Election on Monday next, unless circumstances should arise which might justify him or the Magistrates in bringing it into Preston. (HO 40/20)

Cobbett's people had fought to reach the polls despite the mayor's interposition, and the many special constables Grimshaw had recruited (the "Civil Power" of Eckersley's dispatch) could not contain them. The "Bludgeons" Eckersley mentioned consisted of Cobbett's supporters' electoral staves cut into fours; until dragoons drove them away, Cobbett's forces used their cudgels to keep supporters of Barrie and Stanley out of the channel that Grimshaw had assigned to Cobbett's electors. Eventually, Cobbett himself, despairing of election as the authorities turned back his voters by the dozen, opened his channel to Wood's electors (Cobbett [1829] 1977, Letter I). Both sides used force to influence the outcome. Cobbett's side lost.

Despite his electoral defeat, Cobbett later exulted in recollections of the Preston campaign. In his *Political Register,* he boasted:

> I went to the North a total stranger as to person. I had no friends. Yet, on my first entrance into Preston, I was met and accompanied by, at least, ten thousand people, and was received with marks of attention and respect surpassing those ever shown to any other man . . . calumniators of mine began to comfort themselves with the thought that I was a "Poor Old Man"; and that I could not possibly last long. It was an "old man," recollected, who could travel five hundred miles, make speeches of half an hour long twice a day for a month; put down the saucy, the rich, the tyrannical; that could be jostled out of his majority at an election; and that could return towards his home through forty miles of huzzas from the lips of a hundred and fifty thousand people. (Cobbett 1933, 202)

At age sixty-three, Cobbett found such a reception a vigorous vindication of his long radical career.

Government spies among the region's workers, to be sure, reported the situation differently. The worker-spy who signed his frequent reports George Bradbury, George Bradley, and G__ B__ portrayed northern radicalism as a conspiracy abetted at a distance by Cobbett. In a letter from Walsall dated 19 June he reported:

> I was invited to Preston to assist in the return of W. Cobbet to Parliament and to Consider of any Measures along with others of the Party alluded to in my Communication of the 27th of May to further the ultimate ends of these Men whose work is to get a Voice in Parliament for the purpose of spreading principles subversive of the national faith, There principle object was it not for the Six Acts [repressive legislation passed in 1819] to call Meetings at all places at one time where they can spread their principles under the specious pretex of Equal Representation in the House of Commons . . . the secret idea is to carry by force of arms those [wild?] measures which have devastated every Country where they have gaind the Ascendency—and in 1819 secret instructions were given to prepare every Man his own Picke head and to stick it in the ground below the Reach of the Plough—and Nearly all were in Lancashire and Yorkshire of that party prepared for any Chance which might offer. I began a Reformer and soon became a principle leader when I found on being admitted to Confidence their object was Republican Government to be effected by force or otherwise as Circumstances offer. (HO 40/20)

As summer wore on, Bradbury/Bradley warned increasingly of the possibility of armed insurrection—a threat that no doubt justified his government pay, but that also represented the current talk of some determined radicals and recalled a series of regional working-class rebellions between 1816 and 1820.

British politics of the 1820s deserves attention not only for the exploits of such heroic radicals as William Cobbett but also for the great transformations of popular political life that were occurring. In the course of struggles over parliamentary reform, workers' rights, and Catholic Emancipation, British people were fashioning forms of political participation that marked public life for another century.

They were installing public meetings, demonstrations, mass associations, petition campaigns, firm-by-firm strikes, and related forms of claim making as the standard repertoire in Great Britain. That momentous transition strongly affected Britain's popular politics, including the identities people assumed as they made collective claims. It therefore permits some general observations concerning political identities wherever and whenever they appear. Let me sum up conclusions from previous chapters. For all their enormous variation in form and content:

- Political identities are always, everywhere relational and collective.
- They therefore alter as political networks, opportunities, and strategies shift.
- They always include the adoption of shared stories concerning we-they boundaries—stories about how the boundaries arose and what they separate.
- The validation of political identities depends on contingent performances to which other parties' acceptance or rejection of the asserted relation is crucial.
- That validation both constrains and facilitates collective action by those who share the identity.
- Deep differences separate political identities embedded in routine social life from those that appear chiefly in public life.

These propositions break with two very different but common ways of understanding political identities: (1) as straightforward activation of durable personal traits, whether individual or collective; (2) as malleable features of individual consciousness.

The first view appears incessantly in interest-based accounts of political participation, which generally depend on some version of methodological individualism. The second view recurs in analyses of political commitment as a process of self-realization and correlates closely with an assumption of phenomenological individualism, the doctrine that personal consciousness is the primary—or, at a sollipsistic extreme, the only—social reality. Obviously, my view denies neither personal traits nor individual psyches, but places relations among actors at the center of social processes. It sees identities as relational and collective.

But what does "relational and collective" mean? A *political identity* is an actor's experience of a shared social relation in which at least one of the parties—including third parties—is an individual or organization controlling concentrated means of coercion. (If the coercion-controlling organization in question enjoys some routine jurisdiction over all persons within a delimited territory, we call it a *government*; to the extent that it lacks rivals and superiors within its territory, we call it a *state*.) Political identities usually double with shared public *representations* of both relation and experience. Thus, in Preston of May–June 1826 Cobbett's supporters as such shared relations not only to their hero but also to competing candidates, Mayor Grimshaw, the borough of Preston, the British state, and its ever-ready dragoons. They represented that shared identity by wearing colors, bearing staves, marching, attending meetings, drinking toasts, and jeering Cobbett's opponents.

Well before 1826, British elections provided occasions for the assertion of political identities by electors and nonelectors alike. In parallel with civic festivals and
public executions, elections permitted ordinary people to fill the streets, voice their
preferences, criticize authorities, and identify themselves collectively by means of
symbols, shouts, songs, or dress (Epstein 1990; Laqueur 1989; Linebaugh 1992;
O'Gorman 1992).That candidates often spent lavishly on food, drink, cockades, and
other gifts for nonelectors (including families of electors) does not gainsay the political interest of ordinary people in British parliamentary elections. Ordinary people and local leaders had complementary interests: In addition to treats, plebeian
participants in elections gained affirmations of solidarity, claims to patronage, and
protected opportunities to voice their preferences. On the other side, as often happens in public rituals, the capacity of a candidate to bring out orderly, committed
crowds in his support confirmed or denied his standing within the community and
thereby affected his subsequent credibility as patron or broker even when it had little influence over an election's outcome (cf. Benford and Hunt 1992; Marston 1989;
Paige and Paige 1981; Schneider 1995; Trexler 1981).

British election activities, then, asserted, displayed, or confirmed political identities: candidate, official, elector, partisan, keeper of the peace. Most of these identities,
furthermore, correlated weakly or nully with the identities of routine social life:
wife, son, neighbor, debtor, parishioner, butcher, baker, candlestickmaker. Such routine identities did often figure in local conflicts: Parents and children fought; neighbors massed to tear down houses of ill repute; debtors attacked creditors; parishioners demanded changes in church government; silk weavers collectively resisted
wage cuts imposed by their masters, and so on.

As a generation of feminists has insisted, Britain's available public political identities
rested on strong implicit assumptions about gender differences in political capacity.
But only contingently did these routine identities play significant, direct, acknowl-
edged parts in electoral proceedings, as when Catholics lined up against Anglicans in
disputes over suffrage, or weavers who saw their legal standing threatened gathered en
masse to assert their rights. Instead, elections then confined relevant identities to officials, constables, troops, candidates, supporters, electors, spectators, and few others.
Such identities were relational and collective: Individuals possessed them only as a
function of their relations to others and in company with others.

We must therefore distinguish carefully between identities that appear chiefly or
exclusively in public life and those that are embedded in routine social existence.
The first category typically includes candidate, supporter, party member, and election official, while the second covers the range of kinship, friendship, work, and
neighborhood. Of course, the distinction is relative in two senses. First, some identities pivot explicitly and importantly between the spheres; Mayor Grimshaw of
Preston remained mayor before, during, and after the 1826 election, just as Captain Hall's dragoons had chosen careers that moved them incessantly into and out
of the public political sphere. Second, ties of kinship, friendship, gender, work, and
neighborhood clearly underlie public political identities; Cobbett chose to stand

for parliament from Preston rather than some town with highly restricted suffrage precisely in the hope of inducing bloc voting from the city's less wealthy electors. Nevertheless, relations between public and routinely embedded identities were becoming increasingly distant and contingent. Electoral positions as special constable, political supporter, election official, or even candidate spilled over little or not at all into the relations of workers, masters, kinfolk, neighbors, or fellow members of the local market.

As the Preston election illustrates, relevant political identities were undergoing a momentous transition during the 1820s. Although organizers of political associations (both clandestine and public) had been working for a decade to weave national coalitions of reformers and radicals, neither candidates nor local supporters presented themselves in their guise as associational activists. If some continued to insist on local connections in good eighteenth-century style, by then candidates increasingly aligned themselves with nationally available categories: whig, tory, reformer, other. Despite recurrent displays of colors and symbols, however, their supporters (electors or not) still did not declare themselves publicly as party members but as local candidates' supporters. In two-seat elections, the standard distinctions among plumpers (those who cast just one vote, for their favorite), splitters (those who divided between two candidates of different tendencies), and straights (those who followed a party line) reveal the weak state of partisanship as a political identity (O'Gorman 1982, 1984, 1989; Phillips 1982, 1990, 1992).

Yet, in Preston and over the country as a whole available political identities were changing emphatically. National parties were consolidating; political unions and similar reform (or, for that matter, antireform) organizations had been proliferating since 1817; workers' associations had enjoyed a precarious legal existence since 1824 after decades of underground ebb and flow; a Catholic Association was beginning to mobilize masses in Ireland and to gain a substantial following in Great Britain; public meetings to promote political causes (often organized, secretly or otherwise, by special-purpose associations) were multiplying; drives to prepare mass petitions for parliament were becoming more common; and the combination of meetings, marches, pamphleteering, symbol mongering, and lobbying we now recognize as the apparatus of social movements was acquiring uneasy legality.

For more than a century, British authorities had generally repressed ordinary people who undertook such activities on the ground that they were usurping parliamentary privileges, that they were establishing subversive organizations, or that they were directly disturbing public order. But now, through just such struggles as we have seen unfolding in Preston, authorities were reluctantly conceding the rights of ordinary people who refrained from overt violence, openly seditious talk, or explicitly illegal programs (for example, the republicanism of which Bradbury/Bradley accused Cobbett and his cohorts) to assemble, to associate, to identify themselves collectively, to exhort each other, to state their views autonomously and publicly. Thus, parliament and the courts simultaneously validated new political identities and claimed their own prior right to do such validating.

Much was at stake in the validation of political identities, for once accepted they both constrained and facilitated collective action. Identities as candidates, electors, supporters, or officials imposed significant constraints on their holders, who found themselves bound by the laws and customs of electoral campaigns. Thus, candidates had no choice but to endure celebratory entries into town, give repeated speeches on the same theme, flatter local constituencies, treat supporters lavishly, and, in the event of victory, submit to being *chaired:* paraded in a brilliantly decorated chair, a sort of throne. But the same identities facilitated collective action by justifying assemblies, marches, cheers, epithets, and other expressions of opinion that outside of elections would have run the risk of severe repression. Indeed, postelectoral speeches generally signaled the end of license by explicitly calling for members of the community to forget their recently expressed differences and work together.

The increasing differentiation of a public political sphere with its distinctive identities correlated with significant changes in the forms of collective claim making. For intermittent years spread from 1758 to 1834, my research group has prepared a large catalog of British "contentious gatherings": occasions on which people outside the government gathered in publicly accessible places and made collective claims on others, claims which if realized would affect the others' interests (Tilly 1995d). During the eighteenth century, we may group the bulk of such British events as follows:

Claim making within authorized public assemblies (e.g., Lord Mayor's Day): Taking of positions by means of cheers, jeers, attacks, and displays of symbols; attacks on supporters of electoral candidates; parading and chairing of candidates; taking sides at public executions; attacks or professions of support for pilloried prisoners; salutation or deprecation of public figures (e.g., royalty) at theater; collective response to lines and characters in plays or other entertainments; breaking up of theaters at unsatisfactory performances

Celebrations and other popularly initiated gatherings: Collective cheering, jeering, or stoning of public figures or their conveyances; popularly initiated public celebrations of major events (e.g., John Wilkes's elections of the 1760s), with cheering, drinking, display of partisan symbols, fireworks, and so forth, sometimes with forced participation of reluctant persons; forced illuminations, including attacks on windows of householders who fail to illuminate; faction fights (e.g., Irish versus English, rival groups of military)

Attacks on popularly designated offenses and offenders: Rough Music; ridicule and/or destruction of symbols, effigies, and/or property of public figures and moral offenders; verbal and physical attacks on malefactors seen in public places; pulling down and/or sacking of dangerous or offensive houses, including workhouses and brothels; smashing of shops and bars whose proprietors are accused of unfair dealing or of violating public morality; collective seizures of food, often coupled with sacking the merchant's premises and/or public sale of the food below current market price; blockage or diversion of food shipments; destruction of tollgates; collective invasions of enclosed land, often including destruction of fences or hedges

Workers' sanctions over members of their trades: Turnouts by workers in multiple shops of a local trade; workers' marches to public authorities in trade disputes; donkeying, or otherwise humiliating, workers who violated collective agreements; destroying goods (e.g., silk in looms and/or the looms themselves) of workers or masters who violate collective agreements

Attacks on coercive authorities: Liberation of prisoners; resistance to police intervention in gatherings and entertainments; resistance to press gangs; fights between hunters and gamekeepers; battles between smugglers and royal officers; forcible opposition to evictions; military mutinies

In summary, we might call such claim-making events parochial, particular, and bifurcated: *parochial* because the events were chiefly limited in scope to a single locality; *particular* because the precise routines, participants, and symbols varied significantly from group to group, place to place, and issue to issue; *bifurcated* because they divided between events in which local people (1) took direct action on local objects as the occasion required and (2) appealed to patrons or intermediaries for intercession with powerful outsiders. Parochial, particular, bifurcated claim-making events generally emerged from routine local gatherings for work, marketing, recreation, or authorized rituals rather than from deliberately convened and preplanned assemblies of interested parties.

Such events contrasted with the emerging nineteenth-century forms of claim making, which we can characterize as cosmopolitan, modular, and autonomous: *cosmopolitan* because their scope so regularly exceeded a single locality, indeed, often extended to a national or even international scale; *modular* because standard forms served for a wide variety of claims, claimants, and localities; *autonomous* because the claimants took major initiatives in determining the time and place of their action. Public meetings, petition drives, firm-by-firm strikes, demonstrations, street marches, and other still-familiar forms of collective action constituted this emerging repertoire.

These newer forms of action not only frequently made claims on extralocal authorities and entailed coordination with claim-making groups in other localities but also offered strong assertions about the actors and the constituencies they represented—claims that they were worthy, unified, numerous, and committed, therefore deserving of serious political attention. By the 1820s, these cosmopolitan, modular, and autonomous means of claim making were rapidly displacing authorized celebrations, attacks on stigmatized offenders, and mass destruction of barriers. Here is one sign of the shift that was going on: During the 1750s and 1760s, 3 percent of the events in our catalog consist of preplanned public meetings outside of government auspices; by the 1830s, the figure rises to 24 percent.

The numbers matter less here than a salient contrast: The predominant eighteenth-century forms of claim making flowed directly from routine local activities such as markets or work and drew on the everyday identities embedded in those activities. The predominant nineteenth-century forms broke with routine activities and identities, calling people away to meetings, demonstrations, and other concerted actions in which they appeared not as spinners, neighbors, or tenants of particular landlords but as citizens, partisans, association members, or workers in general. They frequently shared those identities with many people outside their own localities. Even their geographies differed, on balance, from that of everyday life: Seats of authority, meeting halls, and major thoroughfares drew disproportionate shares of the action.

No need to exaggerate the novelty or the extent of the change from eighteenth to nineteenth century. During Britain's seventeenth-century revolutions and no doubt before, local people had reached out in coordinated claim making across the country. During the 1830s, agricultural laborers still smashed threshing machines, while workers who caught an informer in their local pub often drubbed him and drove him out of town. Nevertheless, between the 1750s and the 1830s the net shift in forms of claim making went much farther and changed local politics much more definitively than any previous transition of the sort. Britain's ordinary people entered and re-created the national political sphere as never before.

As familiar and inevitable as the transformation seems in retrospect, it has a puzzling side. People abandoned forms of direct action that had long brought results within their own fields for other forms that depended on extensive organization, that only worked cumulatively and indirectly, that hardly ever achieved their stated ends in a single outing. Social movement tactics of meeting, marching, demonstrating, and self-identifying seem ineffectual as compared with the destruction of threshing machines and the forceful expulsion of pariahs. Why should anyone exchange direct for indirect action?

The change occurred in part because authorities acquired increasingly effective means of repression such as organized police forces, in part because the organizational bases of the older performances disintegrated, in part because national affairs (where the older forms of direct action had rarely made much difference) became increasingly crucial to ordinary people's interests. But something else was happening as well: Indirect, cumulative, cosmopolitan, modular, and autonomous forms of action not only made specific claims on extralocal authorities but also asserted political identities on a larger than local scale. They asserted the existence of valid, weighty political claimants to participation in the national polity. They declared: We exist and have a right to exist. We have strength, coherence, and determination. National politics must take us into account.

Britain's creation of mass national politics had distinct historical properties that set off nineteenth-century Britain as a peculiar combination of aristocratic power and popular democracy. Yet, the transformation of political identities that occurred in Britain deserves close attention for its general implications. For not only in Great Britain but in general, to repeat: (1) Political identities are relational and collective; (2) they therefore alter as political networks, opportunities, and strategies shift; (3) the validation of political identities depends on contingent performances to which other parties' acceptance or rejection of the asserted relation is crucial; (4) their validation both constrains and facilitates collective action by those who share the identity; and (5) deep differences separate political identities embedded in routine social life from those that appear chiefly in public life.

These principles have enormously wide application. Because authorities and analysts alike have drawn stark lines between institutionalized and exceptional politics—between collective action and collective behavior, between elections and social movements, between moments of calm and moments of madness, between routine and revolutionary action—neither has seen the incessant interplay among standard political means, challenges, and innovations. Let us retrieve the old metaphor of *the polity* for a set of political identities that afford their holders routine access to some government. Then we can think of identity validation as an entry into such a polity, the constitution of a valid member. Each polity has a history; its existing membership and the processes by which they gained entry strongly constrain succeeding challenges and entries.

Each new challenge and entry entails innovation in two senses. First, promoters of a new identity constitute themselves and call attention to their worthiness, unity, numbers, and commitment by performances that are recognizable to existing members of the polity, but sufficiently novel to dramatize the new candidate's distinctive qualities to potential adherents and allies. Second, the success of an actor in gaining recognition, hence entry into the polity, alters the rules for the next round of challenges. Thus, the radicals and Catholics who were challenging in Britain during the 1820s established the mass-membership association as a legitimate basis for political claim making after centuries during which only churches had enjoyed a semblance of such rights, and those only within much more stringent limits than came to prevail in the 1830s.

Students of what they called New Social Movements of the 1960s and thereafter—especially movements for peace, women's rights, gay rights, and environmental protection—have often stressed the identity-affirming activities of those movements, in supposed contrast to the narrower interest orientations of preceding movements for suffrage or workers' rights. Their analysis combines a proper critique of narrow interest-group interpretations with a misunderstanding of earlier social movements (Calhoun 1993b). Identity affirmation has *always* played a crucial part in social movements, indeed provided one of their major rationales. Once we understand that the identities in question were relational and collective, constituted claims for recognition by public authorities, the contradiction between "interest" and "identity" interpretations disappears.

The establishment of identities results from political mobilization and struggle as well as action by authorities, but it also affects subsequent political processes. Anthony Marx (1998) offers the important comparison of racial categories in South Africa, the United States, and Brazil. After the Boer War, the white South African regime established a set of racial categories that corresponded only grossly to the much more differentiated populations in the country but became facts of life strongly affecting the fates of putative members of different categories. During Reconstruction and its Jim Crow aftermath, both individual states and the federal government of the United States built legal systems that redefined racial categories and attached differential advantage to them.

Brazil, arguably sustaining as much social and economic inequality by race as the United States, avoided legalizing racial distinctions to anything like the degree of South Africa and the United States. In the short and medium runs, the difference surely worked to the advantage of Brazil's black populations. But over the long run stringent racial categories provided bases for political mobilization and legal claims for redress in South Africa and the United States, while in Brazil the very absence of legalized racial categories, statistics, and agencies inhibited black collective action. Clearly, the legal validation of political identities works as both facility and constraint.

National processes of identity assertion have direct counterparts at an international scale. Nationalism provides the most obvious case in point (see Brubaker 1993; Hechter 2000). Nationalism in general asserts two main ideas: (1) The world's population divides, and ought to divide, into historically formed, connected, coherent, and relatively homogeneous nations; (2) nations should correspond to states, and vice versa. As it has prevailed over the last two centuries, nationalism therefore takes two related forms: top-down and bottom-up. Top-down nationalism involves the attempt by those who control a given state to homogenize its population culturally, to enforce a preferred understanding of its population's history, and to give obligations to the state priority over all other obligations. Bottom-up nationalism consists of efforts by ostensible representatives of populations that currently lack states of their own to establish the historical distinctness, coherence, connectedness, and determination of their followers, thereby claiming the right to political autonomy. The parallels with identity-affirming activities of social movements are dramatic.

Other fascinating parallels suggest themselves. We could follow the analogy into industrial relations, where the legalization of strikes simultaneously facilitated some workers' claim making vis-à-vis their employers, confirmed "strikers" and "union members" as political identities, and separated the strike from a whole series of sometimes-effective tactics—for example window breaking, community-wide marches, and attacks on nonstriking workers—that workers had previously employed. We could examine how relevant identities change in the course of what Sidney Tarrow calls protest cycles (Tarrow 1998). We could ask how international institutions form and acquire recognition (Wendt 1994). We could explore further the widespread nineteenth-century creation of political identities at a national scale, which played a crucial part in the development of strong citizenship and extensive democracy both in Britain and elsewhere. The point would remain the same: For all their apparent hardness and durability, political identities undergo incessant challenge and alteration as a consequence and constituent element of political struggle.

6

Micro, Macro, or Megrim?

Suppose you interview your neighborhood skinhead, asking how he sees himself and the world. Next, you witness a motorcycle rally of skinheads, including your neighbor, and hear them shout, "Freedom for skinheads." You then sit through a session of your national parliament, where you see a deputy denounce skinheads as a menace to democracy. Thereafter, you read a grave social historian who traces skinheads back to disruption of coherent communities by globalization, by television, by capitalism, or perhaps by all of them. Finally, you try to trace causal connections among your four different exposures to skinheads. Result: a vicious, vibrating megrim, a massive headache occupying fully half your brain. My job here is to explain what causes your megrim and how to cure it.

Jacques Rancière is one of those inconsiderate folks who bangs pots and doors while the person down the hall is suffering from an aching head. In *Les mots de l'histoire* he declares that historians of the *Annales* persuasion such as Lucien Febvre and Fernand Braudel cunningly avoided the reduction to mere timekeepers that full integration of history into social science would have entailed. Instead, says Rancière, they drew on the romantic inspiration of Jules Michelet and built on the great French tradition of human geography by inventing a history of mentalities. Their seductive new history summarized the cumulative experience of living in vast social spaces. Dealing with large, geographically based chunks of human experience, they could synthesize in terms of unities, common properties, grand themes.

An earlier version of this chapter appeared as "Micro, Macro, or Megrim?" in Jürgen Schlumbohm, ed., *Mikrogeschichte—Makrogeschichte: komplementär oder inkommensurabel?* vol. 7 (Göttingen: Wallstein Verlag; Göttinger Gespräche zur Geschichtswissenschaft, 1998).

In so doing, however, they imposed an impossible burden on historians of the democratic age, whose subject necessarily centered on division rather than unity. Hence a cruel choice:

> The social history of a democratic workers' era quickly faces a dilemma. Either it re-
> duces to a chronicle of proper names which lack discursive legitimacy and historical
> direction—description of a struggle, of an activist, of a party, of a union, or of a news-
> paper—or it is the science that reduces these particularities and surface agitations to
> their foundations by identifying the subterranean realities whose local and intermit-
> tent expression they form. (Rancière 1992, 193–194)

The stopgap effort to attach distinctive "sociabilities," "cultures," or even "men-talities" to particular working-class localities or trades stumbled from the start, ac-cording to Rancière, simply because the social units in question lacked the kinds of linguistic and geographic coherence that loaned plausibility to the grand histo-ries of Lucien Febvre, Fernand Braudel, and their disciples. Alas, the objection ap-plies equally well to any effort to treat Skinhead as a collective actor, to write a so-cial history of skinheads that connects the individual, the rally, the parliamentary epithet, and the historical synthesis.

Or equally badly, Rancière recommends escape from the historiographical dilemma through frank recognition of history's poetic genius, of its calling to make peace with its inescapable captor, human language, and to invent ways of convey-ing the complexity of experience by means of linguistic play. In fact, Rancière and his colleagues have invented both a false dilemma and an exit into a blind alley. They have done so by adopting an ontology that inserts a large, unnecessary dis-tance between microscopic and macroscopic social life.

Before reviewing that false dilemma, let me clear the way by insisting that some micro-macro problems do exist. A host of *methodological* difficulties face any histo-rian who seeks to derive descriptions of large-scale changes and collective events from records concerning individuals. *Literary* problems beset any analyst of demo-graphic transformations or international wars who wants to show how the people involved experienced them. *Technically*, sequences, distributions, and configurations consist of relations among elements rather than mere sums of those elements. Like all students of human social life, historians have created their own devices for con-necting microscopic and macroscopic observations in these regards: family recon-stitution, vignettes of representative persons, maps of geographic variation, and more. Anyone who treats both large-scale and small-scale phenomena in the same historical analysis adopts some set of these methodological, literary, and technical devices.

Genuinely serious micro-macro problems, however, lie elsewhere. They stem from logical and ontological incompatibility between elements that analysts of so-cial life invoke when dealing with small-scale and large-scale processes. As Rancière intuits but does not quite say, to the extent that social experience consists exclusively of individual mental events, collective processes amount at best to changing distributions of consciousness within collections of individuals. To the extent that relevant mental events consist of interior monologues in privately held languages, collective processes are illusory and the hope of discovering connections or common properties across large populations even more illusory. At best we might identify ways of speaking publicly that bear plausible relations to interior states and recur in a variety of situations. Within such a worldview, the micro-micro incompatibility makes any history beyond the experiences of exemplary individuals seem either impossible or trivial.

To see what is at issue more clearly, let us inventory the four main ontologies twentieth-century historians and social scientists have applied to social life: phenomenological individualism, methodological individualism, holism, and relational realism. Rancière and his fellows come closest to *phenomenological individualism*, the doctrine that individual consciousness is the primary or exclusive site of social life. Phenomenological individualism veers into solipsism when its adherents argue that adjacent minds have no access to each other's contents; therefore, no observer can escape the prison of her own awareness. Even short of that analytically self-destructive position, phenomenological individualists tend to regard states of body and mind—impulses, reflexes, desires, ideas, or programs—as the chief motors of social action. In principle, they have two ways to account for large-scale social structures and processes: (1) as summed individual responses to similar situations; (2) as distributions and/or connections among individual actions.

In the first case, historians sometimes constitute collective actors consisting of all the individuals within a category such as peasant or woman—precisely the practice about which Rancière complains. In the second case, they take a leaf from those political scientists who see national political life as a meeting place, synthesis, and outcome of that shifting distribution of attitudes we call public opinion or from the social psychologists who see individual X's action as providing a stimulus for individual Y's action. None of these strategies provides a workable account of large organizations or complex institutions. Macro-micro translations therefore bedevil phenomenological individualism.

Methodological individualism has less of a following in history than its phenomenological cousin, although it does engage many economic historians as well as a large share of historical analysts in economics and political science. Methodological individualism resembles its cousin in insisting on human individuals as the basic or unique social reality. It differs, however, in modeling individuals with thin consciousness or none at all. In more economistic versions of methodological individualism, the person in question contains a utility schedule and a set of assets, which interact to generate choices within well-defined constraints.

In every such analysis, to be sure, figures a market-like allocative structure that is external to the choice-making individual—but it is astonishing how rarely methodological individualists examine by what means those allocative structures actually do their work. As a consequence, large disjunctions emerge between microeconomics and macroeconomics, or more generally among choice-making practices of individuals, aggregate causes or consequences of individual choices, and organized institutions such as banks, firms, industries, and governments. Methodological individualists face severe micro-macro problems.

Historians and social scientists who sensed the weaknesses of phenomenological and methodological individualism have frequently turned to *holism*, the doctrine that social structures have their own self-sustaining logics. In its extreme form—once quite common in history but now unfashionable—a whole civilization, society, or culture undergoes a life of its own. Less extreme versions attribute self-reproducing powers to major institutions; treat certain segments of society as subordinating the rest to their interests; represent dominant mentalities, traditions, values, or cultural forms as regulators of social life; or assign inherent self-reproducing logics to industrialism, capitalism, feudalism, and other distinguishable varieties of social organization. For holists, the micro-macro problem runs in the other direction, for they must determine to what extent, how, and why small-scale social life, including individual experience, articulates with these overarching patterns. Holists ordinarily resolve the problem, if they do so at all, with some combination of socialization and sanctions, both positive and negative.

Relational realism, the doctrine that transactions, interactions, social ties, and conversations constitute the central stuff of social life, once predominated in social science, if not in history. Classical economists Karl Marx, Max Weber, and Georg Simmel all emphasized social relations, regarding both individuals and complex social structures as products of regularities in social relations. During the twentieth century, however, relational realism lost much of its ground to individualism and holism. Only in American pragmatism, various versions of network analysis, and some corners of organizational or labor economics did it prevail.

Since I saved it for last, you will not be surprised to learn that I think relational realism deserves revivification. In relational analysis, logical and ontological micro-macro problems dwindle to insignificance as compared with their almost intractable nature in phenomenological individualism, methodological individualism, and holism. They dwindle because relational realism concentrates on connections that concatenate aggregate and disaggregate readily, form organizational structures at the same time as they shape individual behavior. Relational analysts follow flows of communication, patron–client chains, employment networks, conversational connections, and power relations from the small scale to the large and back.

Intellectual genetic engineers can, of course, create hybrids of the four basic ontologies. A standard combination of phenomenological individualism and holism portrays a person in confrontation with society, each of the elements and their very confrontation having its own laws. Methodological individualists, I have already said, often assume the presence of a self-regulating market or other allocative institution. Individualists vary in how much they allow for emergents, structures that result from individual actions but once in existence exert independent effects on individual actions, much as music lovers enter a concert hall one by one, only to see the audience's distribution through the hall affect both the orchestra's performance and their own reactions to it (Barth 1981, 1–118; Bunge 1996, 248–253). Relational analysts commonly allow for partly autonomous individual processes as well as strong effects on interaction by such collectively created structures as social categories and centralized organizations. The existence of such combinations, however, neither denies nor solves the characteristically different micro-macro problems that result from the adoption of one ontology or another.

As one might guess from Jacques Rancière's frequent play with multiple meanings of the word *histoire*—as lived experience, written history, and stories people tell—the two individualisms and holisms have a crucial advantage over relational realism. They correspond to the mode in which people, or at least contemporary Western people, commonly organize their own accounts of social life. They incorporate, or at least accommodate, *stories* in which connected, self-propelled actors, individual or collective, cause events, outcomes, and each other's actions. Although relational analysts do not deny the existence of sentient individuals or collective actors, they typically make two moves that render their accounts incompatible with such stories. First, they portray both individuals and collectivities as continuously changing products of interaction. Second, they incessantly invoke indirect effects, cumulative effects, unintended effects, and effects mediated by the nonhuman environment.

I began my career as a historian in dismay over the way that chroniclers of the Vendée insisted on constructing the counterrevolution of 1793 in the form of individual and collective actors—Cathelineau, la Rochejacquelein, Carrière, The Peasantry, The Clergy, and so on—each having unitary mentalities that explained their actions. Really fierce disputes among historians of the counterrevolution, after all, concerned proper attribution of intentions and efficacy to different actors (Tilly 1964, 6–9). As a slow learner, however, it took me forty years to realize that historians of the French West were following practices that pervade social life, and that pervaded the *histoire événémentielle* against which the *Annales* historians originally rebelled (Tilly 1978a, 1996). To put my own account in story form: As Rancière intuits, some of the attraction to cultural anthropology that eventually drew Lucien Febvre's heirs away from their earlier infatuation with other social sciences surely sprang from the greater receptivity of interpretive anthropology to storytelling.

But stories as usually told inhibit explanation of social processes and erect almost insuperable barriers to the discovery of connections between micro and macro processes. Let me summarize my argument about stories all too quickly, without essential qualifications:

1. For reasons that lie deep in childhood learning, cultural immersion, or perhaps even in the structure of human brains, people usually recount, analyze, judge, remember, and reorganize social experiences as *standard stories* in which a small number of self-motivated entities interact within constricted, contiguous time and space. Although prior and externally imposed conditions enter standard stories as accidents, facilities, and constraints, all meaningful action occurs as consequences of the designated actors' deliberations and impulses.

2. People's construction, negotiation, and deployment of standard stories do a wide variety of important social work. That work certainly includes accounting for skinheads and counterrevolutions, but it also includes autobiography, self-justification, social movement mobilization, jury deliberation, moral condemnation, cementing of agreements, and documentation of nationalist claims.

3. Few social processes actually have causal structures that conform to the logical requirements of standard stories. Even those few—for example, chess matches and some kinds of bureaucratic decision making—typically rest on extensive if usually implicit institutional foundations and previous histories.

4. Analysts of social processes who wish to explain them must therefore translate material that comes to them largely in the form of standard stories created in the course of social interaction—and consolidated after the fact—into other idioms that better represent their actual causal structure.

5. Following programs called by such names as interpretation, discourse, narrative, and cultural analysis, many historians and social scientists have committed themselves to the view that standard stories do provide viable explanations of social processes, that the principal responsibility of historical analysts is the construction of superior standard stories, or even that nothing accessible to analysis exists beyond the limits of the standard stories participants in social processes tell.

Let me be clear about this: I enjoy well-told standard stories, often communicate in standard stories, frequently use standard stories to discipline my memory, and regard standard stories as doing crucial work in routine social life. Over forty years or so, my professional work has consisted largely of collecting, coding, criticizing, recasting, analyzing, and explaining standard stories in the form of administrative correspondence, newspaper reports, life-history interviews, historians' published accounts, and similar materials. Reflection on what I have been doing has finally led me to the conclusions I have just summarized.

What sorts of social processes contradict standard stories? All those in which indirect effects, incremental effects, unintended effects, collective effects, and/or effects mediated by the nonhuman environment play a significant part. Those conditions apply generally in the generation of inequality, organizational change, contentious politics, network-mediated communication, state transformation, revolutionary struggle, labor market operation, nationalism, and migration, to stick with topics about which I know something. My claim is that they apply just about everywhere else in social life.

Even if it turns out to be wrong in some regards, the claim has two beneficial features: First, it focuses attention on empirically verifiable causal mechanisms, which have been much neglected in recent social science and history. Second, it implies an empirical program identifying, examining, and explaining the stories people tell, then comparing and connecting those stories' logical structures with

our best causal accounts of relevant social processes. Whether or not my preliminary formulation holds up, we can hardly lose.

Let us reconsider the concocted skinhead story with which I began. It actually
concerns a common micro-macro problem, entails a choice among ontologies, and
embroils us with standard stories. Who or what are these skinheads? How shall we
describe and explain their identities? In particular, how do they constitute publicly
recognizable political identities?

The central difficulty is the one that so exercises Jacques Rancière: If, in the style
of standard stories, we assume that identities exist inside social units, we must characterize those units. We must choose among phenomenological individualism,
methodological individualism, holism, and some combination among them. If we
choose either individualism, the collective identity Skinhead becomes mysterious.
If we choose holism, we must construct an account of how individuals attach
themselves to the collective identity. If we choose a combination, we still lack the
means of transition from one version of the identity to another. How shall we reconcile your neighborhood skinhead's account of himself, the gathering of self-
identified skinheads, the deputy's reference to skinheads as a menacing political category, and the historian's imputation of collective continuity to skinheads?

Answer: Turn away from individualism and holism to relational realism. Recognize that a substantial part of social reality consists of transactions among social
units, that those transactions crystallize into ties, that they shape the social units involved, that they concatenate into variable structures. Identity will then become
not an essential feature of an individual or a group but a characteristic and consequence of social interaction. An identity is an actor's experience of a category, tie,
role, network, or group, coupled with a public representation of that experience;
the public representation often takes the form of a shared story.

The ubiquitous concept "identity" has remained blurred in political analysis for
three reasons: First, identity is in fact not private and individual but public and relational. Second, it spans the whole range of relational structures from category to
group. Third, any actor deploys multiple identities, at least one per tie, role, network, and group to which the actor is attached. That others often typify and respond to an actor by singling out one of those multiple identities—race, gender,
class, job, religious affiliation, national origin, or something else—by no means establishes the unity, or even the tight connectedness, of those identities. That sick-
ness or zealotry occasionally elevates one identity to overwhelming dominance of
an actor's consciousness and behavior, furthermore, does not gainsay the prevalence
of multiple identities among people who are neither sick nor zealots. It actually
takes sustained effort to endow actors with unitary identities. That effort, furthermore, more often impoverishes social life than enriches it. We often call it brain-
washing.

The widespread adoption of phenomenological individualism, however, makes
these homely truths hard to grasp. Phenomenological individualists have often
confused themselves with respect to identities by assuming that language entraps

individuals, that preexisting presumptions and categories of language provide filters through which all social experience passes, hence that reliable knowledge of social relations is impossible. Such a view disregards the deeply interactive character of language itself, its location in constantly negotiated conversations rather than individual minds. Indeed, language provides a medium for establishment and renegotiation of identities, seen as an actor's experience of a category, tie, network, or group, coupled with a public representation of that experience. The narrative offered in such a public representation ordinarily stresses interplays of social relations and individual traits: We are Xs by virtue of experiences we share with other Xs in relation to all those (very different) Ys.

Political identities share those linguistic properties. Political identities embed in social ties that accumulate their own shared understandings. Thus, to assert identity as a Chechnian or a Croat is not to summon up primeval consciousness but to draw a boundary separating oneself from specific others (in the instance, most often Russian, Serb, or Muslim), to claim solidarity with others on the same side of the boundary, and to invoke a certain sort of relationship to those on the opposite side. Skinheads become skinheads in relation to and distinction from other people—skinheads, nonskinheads, and antiskinheads. Similar relational constructions of identity occur repeatedly in social movements, racial conflicts, and interactions of trade diasporas with local communities. Such a view denies neither personal traits nor individual psyches, but places relations among actors at the core of social processes.

Have I fallen into Rancière's trap by proposing to absorb history wholly into social science, thus obliterating its individuality? Yes and no. Yes, the program I have outlined calls for rapprochement of social scientific and historical analyses. But it does not reduce history to mere timekeeper or to the teamster who simply brings wagonloads of facts for grinding in the great social scientific mill.

On the contrary, to the extent that social processes are path-dependent—that sequences and outcomes of causal mechanisms vary by space–time setting, that the order in which events happen affects how they happen, that small-scale or large-scale collective experience accumulates and congeals as culture—historians who understand the effects of context on social process will teach their fellows in something like the way that geologists, seismologists, ecologists, paleontologists, and other historically oriented physical scientists keep their universalizing brethren in touch with reality. They will perhaps recognize their affinity with Oliver Sacks, the superb clinician and historical analyst of neurological conditions, whose book on migraine—or megrim—inspired this chapter's title.

7

Social Movements and Other Political Interactions

In May 1828 the United Kingdom's House of Commons voted by a narrow margin to consider dissolution of 140-year-old legal barriers against Catholics' participation in national politics. On 10 June, however, the House of Lords blocked any such move by a majority of forty-eight. Four days later, the British Catholic Association therefore met in London's Freemasons Tavern to discuss strategy. Debate turned to whether Catholics, like the Protestant Dissenters who had in April seen their own interdiction from national politics removed, should offer collective securities for good behavior. Mr. Therry rose to oppose any such proposal:

> It has been asked what securities should we offer to Government? My answer is—our attachment to that Constitution—our love of country—a contribution of a portion of the fruits of our industry to the State—the employment of whatever wisdom and talents we may possess, and even the shedding of our blood, as before it has been shed, for the service of the State. [Applause.] (*Morning Chronicle* 16 June 1828, p. 2)

In the view vigorously applauded by Therry's auditors, British Catholics were already fulfilling the obligations of good citizens, including military service under the British flag, yet were being denied the privileges good citizens deserved. The long war with France, now thirteen years past, had proven Catholics to be reliable supporters of the nation's causes. Yet, arbitrary religious distinctions continued to deny them their rights. Their call for Catholic Emancipation (as they called it) insisted not on their special character as Roman Catholics but on their general character as citizens.

An earlier version of this chapter appeared as "Social Movements and (All Sorts of) Other Political Interactions—Local, National, and International—Including Identities. Several Divagations from a Common Path, Beginning with British Struggles over Catholic Emancipation, 1780–1829, and Ending with Contemporary Nationalism," *Theory and Society* 27 (1998), 453–480, reprinted with permission of Kluwer Academic Publishers. The title was, of course, a joke.

Members of the Catholic Association and their allies were demanding rights of citizenship by means of strategies that later generations came to recognize as social movement politics. In 1828, however, the forms of action we know as social movements were still contested political novelties. This chapter draws on current ideas concerning social movements first to examine what happened in the struggle for Catholic Emancipation, then to think out loud about analogies between social movements and other political processes at an international scale, especially assertions of nationalism.

The study of social movements has passed through three main phases since the 1960s (Jean Cohen 1985; Giugni and Kriesi 1990; Jenkins 1983; Mayer 1991; McAdam, McCarthy, and Zald 1988; McPhail 1991; Morris and Herring 1987; Rule 1988). As social movement activity rose in Western Europe and North America during that decade, analysts drew at first on two venerable theoretical traditions: (1) treatments of collective behavior as uninstitutionalized action driven by mass psychology, which had acquired a psychoanalytic edge in analyses of fascism, (2) natural-history conceptions of social movements modeled especially on the history of organized labor, but extended to other emancipatory movements such as suffrage and feminism.

Neither one proved adequate, logically or ideologically, for dealing with civil rights activism, student protests, and other new forms of contention—the more so because so many specialists came to the subject as sympathizers, advocates, or direct participants in the struggles they were interpreting, with a consequent investment in defending the new challengers against widespread accusations of impulsiveness, self-indulgence, and incoherence. Out of that ferment emerged overlapping perspectives known variously as political-process, rational-action, and resource-mobilization models of collective action and/or social movements. Differing considerably from one another, they nevertheless converged on the imputation of coherent understandings and intentions to social movement actors as well as on the grounding of their action in durable social organization and interests.

In addition to their mutual criticism, these new orthodoxies eventually generated dissent from several quarters, notably from interpreters of so-called New Social Movements, recent mobilizations oriented to environment, peace, sexual preference, communitarianism, and related issues. Critics complained variously that the stress on social organization, interests, resources, and strategic action

- exaggerated the instrumental character of these social movements (or perhaps of all social movements) while underestimating the importance of self-expression and collective experience;
- underestimated the contingency, plasticity, and willful self-transformation of the identities deployed in social movements (or at least in new social movements);
- assumed that all movements sought power within existing polities rather than alterations in social and political life as a whole; and
- missed the significance of shared beliefs in social movement activity.

The collapse of socialist regimes in Eastern Europe heightened the controversy, as many critics of state socialism and advocates of democracy came to argue that social movements in the newer style could help constitute civil society and thereby forward democratic transformation.

The burgeoning of nationalisms, ethnicities, and religiously defined political differences in the ruins of Yugoslavia and the Soviet Union reinforced analysts' concern about identity and belief in social movements and related phenomena. The spread of postmodern skepticism likewise led many students of collective struggle to treat it as a social construction, a set of expressive acts with dubious grounding in interests and social structure. Even short of postmodern epistemological despair, followers of the linguistic turn stepped up their interest in the discursive side of collective action: frames, narratives, and storytelling reconstructions of events.

Responding to these challenges, realists among students of social movements took the beliefs, identities, and symbolic work involved much more seriously than they or their predecessors had in the heyday of rational-choice, resource-mobilization, and political-process models. At the same time, realists invested a great deal of energy in examining how the characteristics and trajectories of social movements vary as a function of the political opportunity structures in which they operate—establishing, for example, differences between the forms taken by movement organizations in relatively centralized polities such as the Netherlands or France and relatively segmented polities such as Switzerland (Giugni and Passy 1993; Kriesi 1993).

Although no single view has emerged unquestioned from all this exploration, on the whole social movement analysts have ended up thinking that movements depend intimately on the social networks in which their participants are already embedded, that the identities deployed in collective contention are contingent but crucial, that movements operate within frames set by a historical accumulation of shared understandings, that political opportunity structure significantly constrains the histories of individual social movements, but that movement struggles and outcomes also transform political opportunity structures (Boggs 1986; della Porta 1995; della Porta and Diani 1999; Duyvendak 1994; Eyerman and Jamison 1991; Giugni 1995; Kitschelt 1993; Melucci 1992; Oberschall 1993; Ohlemacher 1993; Tarrow 1998).

Imperceptibly but powerfully, the same reorientations have moved many social movement analysts from an individualistic toward an interactional view of their subject. Three brands of individualism long prevailed in social movement studies: *methodological individualism*, with its imputations of interests and resources to one unitary actor (collective or individual) at a time; *phenomenological individualism*, with its effort to penetrate the consciousness of each actor (again collective or individual, but presumed unitary); *holism*, the presumption that social movements as such are unitary actors possessing standard orientations, behaviors, and life histories. All three of these assume self-directed units. In place of any individualism or holism, social movement analysts have made a net shift toward an interactional way of thinking we might summarize in the following concepts:

Actor: Any set of living bodies (including a single individual) to which human observers attribute coherent consciousness and intention

Category: A set of actors distinguished by a single criterion, simple or complex

Transaction: A bounded communication between one actor and another

Tie: A continuing series of transactions to which participants attach shared understandings, memories, forecasts, rights, and obligations

Role: A bundle of ties attached to a single actor

Network: A more or less homogeneous set of ties among three or more actors

Group: Coincidence of a category and a network

Organization: Group in which at least one actor has the right to speak authoritatively for the whole

Identity: An actor's experience of a category, tie, role, network, group, or organization, coupled with a public representation of that experience; the public representation often takes the form of a shared story, a narrative

The shift in orientation leads to an understanding of social movements as strongly patterned transactions within interlocking networks. The networks always include actors, ties, and identities, often include roles, groups, and organizations, but never sum up to a single solidary group. Analysts adopting this view, to the consternation of individualists and holists, identify social movements by looking for claim-making interactions between challengers and powerholders. Such a view is yielding important returns for the study of all sorts of social movements.

Only timidly, however, have the same analysts sought analogies and connections between social movements *stricto sensu* and other political processes likewise involving contingent identities, historically constructed frames of shared understanding, and variable political opportunity structure—phenomena such as nationalism, revolution, ethnic conflict, and creation of transnational institutions. Because it straddles national and international contexts, study of struggles over religious inclusion and exclusion with respect to citizenship opens a bridge to preliminary analysis of important analogies and connections.

In Great Britain (England, Wales, Scotland), in Ireland, and elsewhere, the histories of religious exclusions from political rights and of their general dissolution during the nineteenth century illustrate four points of great importance for political analysis in general.

First, those histories reveal powerful analogies between the processes driving social movements within national polities and a range of other processes, both "national" and "international," to which analysts of social movements have paid little attention; they therefore rectify common conceptions of social movements as sui generis.

Second, the identities people deploy in political claim making (including identities of religious affiliation, nationality, and citizenship) consist of contingent relationships with other people rather than inbuilt personal traits; they therefore alter as political networks, opportunities, and strategies shift.

Third, the histories show us incessant interaction between political processes that observers commonly distinguish as "domestic" and "international," processes that analysts frequently conceive of as quite independent one from the other.

Fourth, once we shift from conventional individualistic conceptions to transactional analyses of political processes, these three points become almost self-evident.

The history of Catholic exclusion and inclusion in the eighteenth- and nineteenth-century British polity provides dramatic evidence for all four points. The final success of Catholic Emancipation in 1829 resulted largely from the dynamics of a social movement, indeed from one of the first social movements ever to form anywhere at a national scale. The political processes observable in that movement for Catholic Emancipation we can also see operating today in the play of identities, mobilizations, political opportunities, and collective contention at local, national, and international levels; although social movements occupy distinctive niches within national polities, they also share properties with revolutions, nationalisms, ethnoreligious struggles, and a variety of other processes involving collective claim making. Like many other divisions within national polities, the ostensibly domestic issue of Catholic Emancipation intersected over and over with Britain's international relations, including questions of war and peace. Recognition of the identities, claims, and settlements involved in the struggle over Emancipation as transactions rather than expressions of individual proclivities greatly clarifies how they worked.

Catholic Emancipation alone cannot, of course, establish four enormous principles. But a clearly focused case in point will clarify what is at issue, as well as how the issues connect. Let us wander for a while among relevant British experience, reflections on social movements as distinctive political phenomena, and general discussions of interactions and analogies between national-level social movements and political processes at other scales.

RELIGION AND CITIZENSHIP IN GREAT BRITAIN

Ties between religious identity and political privilege have fluctuated enormously over the long run of European history. During the last millennium, Europe has seen everything from the Ottoman Empire's ready (if unequal) absorption of Christians and Jews to the Nazis' programmed annihilation of those Jews they could track down. Broadly speaking, political exclusion on the basis of religious identity increased with widespread persecution of Muslims, Jews, and Christian heretics during the fifteenth century, reached the state of war through much of Central and Western Europe during the sixteenth century, stabilized in the same regions from 1648 to 1789 with the Westphalian doctrine of *cujus regio ejus religio*, and then receded irregularly from the French Revolution onward through much of the continent.

Although religious prejudice and unofficial discrimination have persisted, sometimes even flourished as in nineteenth-century pogroms and the Dreyfus Case, categorical exclusions from political rights such as those practiced by fascists became rare by the twentieth century. Until recently, at least—whether the sharpening of state-identified religious divisions in the former Soviet Union, in disintegrated Yugoslavia, and potentially in France constitutes a reversal or a momentary aberration remains to be seen.

In Great Britain, the political program that eventually won the name Catholic Emancipation originated in wars, both civil and international. The struggles of 1688–1689 toppled Roman Catholic James II from the British throne, established Protestant William of Orange as king, and restored a Protestant ruling class in colonized Ireland. The Glorious Revolution of 1689 barred Catholics from public office, capping their exclusion with an officeholder's oath that denied tenets of the Catholic religion and (in the case of members of parliament, MPs) explicitly rejected the pope's authority:

> Members of Parliament were required to subscribe to (1) an oath of allegiance; (2) an oath abjuring any Stuart title to the throne; (3) an oath of supremacy ("I, A. B., do swear that I do . . . abjure as impious and heretical that damnable doctrine and position that princes excommunicated or deprived by the Pope . . . may be deposed or murdered by their subjects. . . . And I do declare that no foreign Prince, Person, Prelate, State or Potentate hath, or ought to have, any jurisdiction . . . or authority, ecclesiastical or spiritual within this realm"); (4) a declaration against the doctrine of transubstantiation, the invocation of the saints and the sacrifice of the Mass. (Hinde 1992, 161n)

As the political undertones of these requirements suggest, Britain's and Ireland's Catholics fell under the double suspicion of subservience to a foreign authority, the pope, and collaboration with Britain's historic enemy, France. (By the eighteenth century, the pope had not, in fact, intervened effectively in British affairs for centuries. But the French, from Mary Queen of Scots' time defenders of Stuart claims to the British crown, gave direct military support to a serious Irish rebellion as late as 1798, well within the memories of many participants in 1828's debate.) Although non-Anglican Protestants also suffered political disabilities under the settlement of 1689, in practice subsequent regimes shut Catholics out of parliament and public life much more effectively.

Oaths of abjuration individualized membership in the category "Catholic" and made it seem centrally a matter of belief. Certainly, Catholicism had implications for individual characteristics and behavior in the United Kingdom as it did elsewhere. But to be Catholic in the sense that was relevant for citizenship between 1689 and 1829 consisted of involvement in crucial social relations: relations to priests and the church hierarchy, relations to a publicly identified community of Catholic believers, relations to an Anglican establishment. Just as the category "worker" conveniently signals a bundle of personal characteristics but finally depends on distinction from and relation to the category "employer," the category "Catholic" finally designates a distinctive set of social relations. The distinction between Catholic and non-Catholic obviously existed before 1689 and after 1829; between the two dates, however, it coincided with a relation between fuller and lesser citizens. That coincidence came to be increasingly challenged as time went on.

Catholic exclusion had serious political consequences. When the British won Québec from France in the Seven Years War (1756–1763), the British Empire not only gained jurisdiction over an almost unanimously Catholic population but also pacified resistance to British control by large concessions to Québecois, hence to Catholic, self-rule. That settlement inserted a twin to Ireland into the British realm, but granted its Catholics more favorable conditions than their Irish coreligionists enjoyed. To the extent that the British incorporated Catholic Ireland into their economy and polity, furthermore, the Irish Protestant establishment became a less effective instrument of indirect rule, and the demands of Catholic Irish on both sides of the Irish Sea for either autonomy or representation swelled. The enlargement of armed forces during the American war, finally, rendered military recruiters increasingly eager to enroll Irish warriors, already reputed as mercenaries elsewhere in Europe, but barred from British military service by the required anti-Catholic oath.

Militarily inspired exemptions of Catholic soldiers from oath-taking during the later 1770s raised strident objections among defenders of Anglican supremacy. The exemptions directly incited formation of a nationwide Protestant Association to petition, agitate, and resist. Scottish Member of Parliament Lord George Gordon, whose vociferous opposition to Catholic claims made him head of the association in 1780, led an anti-Catholic campaign that concentrated on meetings and parliamentary petitions, but during June 1780 ramified into attacks on Catholic persons and (especially) property in London. A full 275 people died during those bloody struggles, chiefly at the hands of troops who were retaking control over London's streets. Among Britain's ruling classes, those so-called Gordon Riots gave popular anti-Catholicism an aura of violent unreason. By negation, advocacy of Catholics' political rights acquired the cachet of enlightenment.

From that time onward, an important fusion occurred. Catholic Emancipation became a standard (although by no means universal) demand of reformers and radicals who campaigned for parliamentary reform. By "reform" its advocates generally meant something like elimination of parliamentary seats controlled by patrons, more uniform qualifications for voting across the country, enlargement of the electorate, and frequent parliamentary elections. (Demands for universal suffrage, for manhood suffrage, or even for equal individual-by-individual representation among the propertied rarely gained much of a following before well into the nineteenth century.) Catholic Emancipation dovetailed neatly with such proposals, since it likewise called for granting a more equal and effective voice in public affairs to currently excluded people.

Both parliamentary reform and Catholic Emancipation surged, then collapsed as national political issues in Great Britain several times between the 1780s and the 1820s. But emancipation became more urgent during the Revolutionary and Napoleonic Wars, when William Pitt the Younger sought to still the Irish revolutionary movement that was undermining the British state's titanic war effort against France. Pitt helped create a (dubiously) United Kingdom of Great Britain and Ireland in 1801, which meant dissolving the separate Irish parliament and incorporating one hundred Irish Protestant members into what had been Britain's parliament. In the process, Pitt half-promised major political concessions to Catholics. King George III's hostility to compromising the Anglican establishment (and thereby a crown that was already suffering from the war-driven rise of parliamentary power) made that commitment impossible to keep. Pitt's consequent resignation by no means stifled Catholic demands. On the contrary, from 1801 to 1829 Catholic Emancipation remained one of the United Kingdom's thorniest political issues. The 1807 wartime resignation of the coalition "Ministry of All the Talents," for example, pivoted on the king's refusal to endorse admission of Catholics to high military ranks.

Much more than a king's attachment to Anglican privilege, however, made the issue contentious. Anti-Catholicism continued to enjoy wide popular appeal in Great Britain, the more so as Irish immigration (responding to industrial expansion in Britain and consequent industrial contraction in Ireland) accelerated. On the other side, Irish Catholic elites resisted the even greater separation from great decisions affecting their island's fate that had resulted from the transfer of the old Dublin parliament's powers—however Protestant it had been—to an English-dominated parliament in distant Westminster. Repeatedly during the 1820s, two movements coincided: an increasingly popular campaign for Catholic political rights led by lawyers, priests, and other elites in Ireland, and a coalition of radicals, reformers, and organized Catholics in support of Emancipation within Great Britain. Eventually, a countermovement of Protestant resistance to Catholic claims mobilized as well.

CATHOLIC EMANCIPATION AS A SOCIAL MOVEMENT

The interweaving movements reached their dénouement in 1829. During the previous six years, Irish Catholic barrister Daniel O'Connell and his allies had organized successive versions of a mass-membership Catholic Association in Ireland, with some following in Great Britain. They perfected a form of organization (drawn initially and ironically from Methodist models) with which radicals and reformers had experimented during the great mobilizations of 1816 to 1819. The association collected a monthly penny—the "Catholic rent"—from thousands of peasants and workers. With the proceeds it conducted an incessant, effective campaign of propaganda, coalition formation, lobbying, and public claim making. Each time the British government outlawed their association, O'Connell and friends fashioned a slightly reorganized (and renamed) successor to replace it.

Efforts by Protestant supporters of emancipation to get a bill through parliament failed in 1812, repeatedly from 1816 to 1822, and again in 1825. But in 1828 a related campaign to expand political rights of Protestant Dissenters (e.g., Baptists, Methodists, and Presbyterians) by repealing the seventeenth-century Test and Corporation Acts gained parliamentary and royal assent. Although it had the effect of removing important allies from the same side of the barrier, on balance such an opening made the moment auspicious for Catholic Emancipation. The regime that had defended Anglican supremacy by excluding non-Anglicans from office in principle (despite frequent exceptions in practice for Dissenters) lost some of its rationale for excluding Catholics.

The House of Lords and the king presented larger obstacles than the Commons, which by the 1820s had on the whole reconciled itself to some expansion of Catholic rights. The Lords included, of course, not only peers of the realm but also bishops of the Anglican Church, most of whom would not lightly sacrifice their organization's privileged political position. At their coronations, furthermore, British monarchs swore to defend Anglican primacy; in 1828, King George IV still feared that to approve Catholic Emancipation would violate his coronation oath.

When the House of Lords again forestalled emancipation in 1828, both Irish organizers and their British allies redoubled the emancipation campaign, not only expanding the Catholic Association but also staging massive meetings, marches, and petition drives. The technically illegal election of Catholic O'Connell to parliament from a seat in County Clare during the fall of 1828 directly challenged national authorities, especially when O'Connell proposed to take his place in Westminster at the new parliament's opening early in 1829.

This formidable mobilization, in turn, stimulated a large countermobilization by defenders of the Protestant Constitution, as they called it. In Great Britain and to a lesser extent in Ireland itself they organized Brunswick Clubs to produce meetings, marches, petitions, propaganda, and solidarity on behalf of the royal house of Brunswick. That the Commons, the Lords, and the king finally conceded major political rights—although far from perfect equality—to Catholics during the spring of 1829 resulted from an otherwise unresolvable crisis in both Ireland and Great Britain. It by no means represented a general conversion of Britons to religious toleration. Jews, for example, did not receive similar concessions until 1858. Nor did unofficial discrimination against Jews or Irish Catholics ever disappear from British life. We are speaking here of legal exclusion from political rights on the basis of religious identity.

British authorities played a double game, dealing with a predominantly anti-Catholic political mobilization in Great Britain and a massive, near-insurrectionary pro-Catholic mobilization in Ireland. A catalog of "contentious gatherings" (CGs: occasions on which ten or more people assembled publicly and somehow made collective claims) reported in one or more of seven British periodicals during

March 1829 provides evidence on the British side although, alas, it does not tell us the comparable story for Ireland (Tilly 1995d). During that turbulent month, the Commons finally passed its Emancipation bills and sent them on to the Lords. Altogether the month's catalog yields 153 CGs explicitly centering on support for or opposition to Catholic rights, plus another half dozen in which public responses to officials clearly resulted from the positions they had taken on Catholic Emancipation. (Because many reports come from parliamentary debates in which MPs reporting petition meetings took pains to mention places but neglected dates, some events in the March catalog surely happened in February, but they just as certainly belonged to the same wave of mobilization.)

A selection of about a tenth of all events from the month's catalog imparts its contentious flavor:

London: The minister and congregation of Crown Street Chapel assembled to sign a petition declaring, among other things, that

the engine of Romanism, with all its machinery, is still preserved entire, and ready to be brought into action as soon as opportunity and policy shall concur to set it in motion, and should the barriers of our happy Constitution, which now restrain its operation, be once removed, its influence would gradually increase, and from the nature of the very principle it imbibes and inculcates, its overbearing progress must terminate in the complete subjugation of Protestant liberties." (*Votes and Proceedings of Parliament,* 2 March 1829, pp. 336–337)

Arbroath, Dundee: The burgh's dean, guild, councillors, and brethren resolved that "all political disabilities, on account of religious opinions, are impolitic, unjust, and contrary to the spirit of Christianity" (*Mirror of Parliament,* 3 March 1829, p. 349).

Coventry: A public meeting issued an anti-Catholic petition signed by 3,915 persons, which generated a pro-Catholic counterpetition signed by 905 others (*Hansards,* 3 March 1829, p. 699).

Glasgow: After one group sent a large anti-Catholic petition to parliament, another set out a pro-Catholic petition for signing. A man stood at the premises' door "calling out to the people not to sign in favour of the Roman Catholics," a crowd gathered to hoot at all signers and knocked down one of them, police dispersed the crowd but arrested the victim rather than the perpetrator. For two more days crowds assembled and attacked people who came to sign the petition (*Mirror of Parliament,* 6 March 1829, p. 445).

Rothsay: After speeches emphasizing the Catholic threat, a meeting in Mr. M'Bryde's chapel dispersed, "some of the most unruly of them, thinking they would best show their admiration of the opinions of their pastor by a persecution of Catholics, proceeded to the house of the only Irishman in the place (a poor itinerant dealer in earthenware) and demolished every article on his premises" (*Times,* 10 March 1829, p. 4).

London: "A gang of pickpockets assembled yesterday evening in front of the entrance to the House of Lords, and shouted 'No Popery' as the Peers were retiring. Several gentlemen felt the effects of accidental contact with these light-fingered gentry as they passed through the avenues, which were occupied for nearly an hour by these miscreants" (*Times*, 10 March 1829, p. 3).

Cranbrook: In reaction to an anti-Catholic petition signed by "the lowest descriptions of persons, and of boys," "the Dissenters and other friends of civil and religious liberty" held a public meeting to support Catholic rights (*Mirror of Parliament*, 12 March 1829, p. 535).

Rye: Through his brother (the mayor) the borough's patron (an Anglican clergyman) called a meeting to launch an anti-Catholic petition, but "although the whole body of the select (members of the corporation) ranged themselves under the orders of their chief, and, although several paupers were also pressed into the service, the motion for a petition was lost by a majority against it of four to one" (*Times*, 12 March 1829, p. 3).

Inverness: A number of "boys and disorderly lads" burned an effigy representing Popery, paraded through town hoisting another effigy, then broke doors and windows at both the Catholic chapel and the police office (*Times*, 17 March 1829, p. 3).

Edinburgh: At a public meeting called in reaction to a pro-Catholic assembly, the provost and inhabitants started an anti-Catholic petition that eventually acquired 13,000 signatures (*Times*, 19 March 1829, p. 1).

Bothwell: The local minister ran a meeting in which he threatened hellfire for those who refused to sign a petition against concessions to Catholics (*Times*, 19 March 1829, p. 1314).

London: After the Commons' second-reading debate on emancipation, supporters unhitched the horses from the hackney coach into which Daniel O'Connell had retreated and attempted to draw him in triumph, but he forced his way out, and walked to his lodgings in the midst of thousands "shouting all the way 'Huzza for O'Connell, the man of the people, the champion of religious liberty;' 'George the Fourth for ever;' 'The Duke of Wellington, and long life to him;' 'Mr. Peel and the Parliament'" (*Times*, 19 March 1829, p. 4).

London: Two days later, several hundred people surrounded the duke of Wellington as he left the House of Lords "and assailed him with the most opprobrious epithets, and every sort of discordant yelling" (*Times*, 21 March 1829, p. 2).

East Looe: Free burgesses and inhabitants held a meeting to oppose any further concessions to Roman Catholics, initiating a petition eventually signed "by every person in the place" (*Mirror of Parliament*, 24 March 1829, p. 790).

Chesterfield: An anti-Catholic public meeting resulted in a petition signed by 4,000 people, which stimulated a counterpetition signed by 500 supporters of Catholic claims, "amongst whom were the whole of the magistrates resident in the district" (*Hansards*, 25 March 1829, pp. 1444–1445).

Pembroke: A county meeting concerning emancipation divided sharply, with the earl of Cawdor defending the measure and an Anglican clergyman exhorting the crowd against Catholics; after the county sheriff broke up the meeting, participants "broke the windows of those who were known to be favourable to the Catholics, and threw fire into the house of one person" (*Morning Chronicle,* 31 March 1829, p. 1).

Although such actions as effigy burning and unhitching a hero's carriage to draw it through the streets conformed to well-established eighteenth-century antecedents, on the whole these events followed the newly emerging logic of social movements. Meanwhile, priests and patriots connected by the Catholic Association were organizing similar social movement actions—but overwhelmingly on behalf of emancipation—through much of Ireland.

WHAT IS A SOCIAL MOVEMENT?

A social movement is a kind of campaign, parallel in many respects to an electoral campaign. This sort of campaign, however, demands righting of a wrong, most often a wrong suffered by a well-specified population. The population in question can range from a single individual to all humans, or even all living creatures. Whereas an electoral campaign pays off chiefly in the votes that finally result from it, a social movement pays off in the effective transmission of the message that its program's supporters are WUNC—(1) worthy, (2) unified, (3) numerous, and (4) committed. The elements compensate one another to some degree, for example, with a high value on worthiness ("respectability" in the language of 1829) making up for small numbers. Yet, a visibly low value on any one of them (a public demonstration of unworthiness, division, small numbers, and/or defection) discredits the whole movement.

Seen as means-end action, such a campaign has a peculiar diffuseness; as compared with striking, voting, smashing the loom of a nonstriking weaver, or running a miscreant out of town, its actions remain essentially symbolic, cumulative, and indirect, with almost no hope that any single event will achieve its stated objective of ending an injustice or persuading authorities to enact a needed law. Social movement mobilization gains its strength from an implicit threat to act in adjacent arenas: to withdraw support from public authorities, to provide sustenance to a regime's enemies, to move toward direct action or even rebellion. Skilled social movement organizers draw tacitly on such threats to bargain with the objects of their demands.

Social movements take place as conversations: not as solo performances but as interactions among parties. The most elementary set of parties consists of a claim-making actor, an object of the actor's claims, and an audience having a stake in the fate of at least one of them. But allies, competitors, enemies, authorities, and multiple audiences also frequently play parts in movement interactions. Therein lies the complexity of social movement organizing, not to mention the complexity of responses by authorities and objects of claims—third parties always complicate the interaction.

Examined from the viewpoint of challengers, social movement success depends in part on two varieties of mystification. First, beyond some minimum, worthiness, unity, numbers, and commitment almost necessarily contradict each other; to gain numbers, for example, generally requires compromise on worthiness, unity, and/or commitment. The actual work of organizers consists recurrently of patching together provisional coalitions, negotiating which of the multiple agendas participants bring with them will find public voice in their collective action, suppressing risky tactics, and above all hiding backstage struggle from public view.

Second, movement activists seek to present themselves and (if different) the objects of their solicitude as a solidary group, preferably as a group with a long history and with coherent existence outside the world of public claim making. Thus, feminists identify themselves with women's age-old struggles for rights in the streets and in everyday existence, while environmentalists present most of humankind as their eternal community. Organizers of the Catholic Emancipation campaign, including Daniel O'Connell, spent much of their energy striving to create a united public front and portraying their constituents as a long-suffering solidary population that had waited far too long for justice.

The two varieties of mystification address several different audiences. They encourage activists and supporters to make high estimates of the probability that fellow adherents will take risks and incur costs for the cause, hence that their own contributions will bear fruit. They warn authorities, objects of claims, opponents, rivals, and bystanders to take the movement seriously as a force that can affect their fates. Movements differ significantly in the relative attention they give to these various audiences, from the self-absorbed tests of daring organized by small clusters of terrorists to the signature of petitions by transient participants who wish some authority to know their opinion. These orientations frequently vary in the course of a given social movement, for example in transitions from (x) internal building to (y) ostentatious action to (z) fighting off competitors and enemies.

Neither in the case of Catholic Emancipation nor in general does mystification mean utter falsehood. Activists and constituents of social movements vary considerably in the extent to which they actually embody worthiness, unity, numbers, and commitment, and in the degree to which they spring from a single solidary group with collective life outside the world of public politics. To the extent that the two varieties of mystification contain elements of truth, furthermore, social movements generally mobilize more effectively; a segregated ethnic community threatened by outside attack, on the average, mobilizes more readily than do all those who suffer from attacks on civil liberties.

But the process whereby social movement activists achieve recognition as valid interlocutors for unjustly deprived populations does not resemble the fact-finding inquiries of novelists, social scientists, or investigative reporters. It resembles a court proceeding, in which those who make such claims, however self-evident to them, must establish themselves in the eyes of others—authorities, competitors, enemies, and relevant audiences—as voices that require attention and must commonly establish themselves in the face of vigorous opposition. They must prove that they qualify. Almost all such proofs entail suppression of some evidence and exaggeration of other evidence concerning the claimants' worthiness, unity, numbers, commitment, and grounding in a durable, coherent, solidary, deprived population.

Analysts of collective action, especially those who entertain sympathy for the actions they are studying, often insist on these mystified elements as intrinsic to social movements: the presence of solidarity, the construction of shared identities, the sense of grievance, the creation of sustaining organizations, and more. Without such features, analysts say, we have nothing but ordinary politics. Sometimes the myths fulfill themselves, building up the lineaments of durable connection among core participants. But most social movements remain far more contingent and volatile than their mystifications allow; these other elements do not define the social movement as a distinctive political phenomenon.

What does? Social movements involve collective claims on authorities. As earlier chapters have declared repeatedly, a social movement consists of a sustained challenge to powerholders in the name of a population living under the jurisdiction of those powerholders by means of repeated public displays of that population's numbers, commitment, unity, and worthiness (Diani 1992; Tarrow 1998; Tilly 1993–1994). As they developed in Great Britain and other West European countries during the early nineteenth century, the characteristic displays included creation of special-purpose associations, lobbying of officials, public meetings, demonstrations, marches, petitions, pamphlets, statements in mass media, posting or wearing of identifying signs, and deliberate adoption of distinctive slogans; while their relative weight varied considerably from movement to movement, these elements have coexisted since the early nineteenth century. Although the advocates and opponents of Catholic Emancipation had by no means mastered this full array of techniques in 1828 and 1829, they tried them all. They were, indeed, inventing the social movement as they went along.

Let me stress the fact of invention. For all its contentiousness, most of human history has proceeded without social movements, without sustained challenges to powerholders in the names of populations living under the jurisdiction of those powerholders by means of repeated public displays of those populations' numbers, commitment, unity, and worthiness. Rebellions, revolutions, avenging actions, rough justice, and many other forms of popular collective action have abounded, but not the associating, meeting, marching, petitioning, propagandizing, sloganeering, and brandishing of symbols that mark social movements.

With some eighteenth-century precedents, this second complex of interactions emerges as a way of doing political business in Western Europe during the nineteenth century; however we finally sort out the priorities, Britain shares credit for the invention. In Great Britain, the actual inventors were political entrepreneurs such as John Wilkes, Lord George Gordon, William Cobbett, and Francis Place. They, their collaborators, and their followers bargained out space for new forms of political action, bargained it out with local and national authorities, with rivals, with enemies, with the objects of their claims. The tales of contention over Catholic Emancipation in March 1829 provide glimpses of that bargaining.

MOVEMENT AND COUNTERMOVEMENT

From the beginning, movements often bred countermovements on the part of others whose advantages success for the movement's claims would threaten. British aristocrats had formed Brunswick Clubs, for example, explicitly to counter the Catholic Association's enormous success. They had then sought to build a popular anti-Catholic base. Notice the report from Edinburgh. Sir R. H. Inglis, who presented Edinburgh's anti-Catholic petition to parliament, reported that the local authorities' original plan had been to hold a sort of referendum, a public meeting at which people could vote for or against Catholic relief and "if no public meeting of those favourable to concession was held, none would be convened of those opposed to it" (*Times*, 19 March 1829, p. 1). But since pro-Catholic forces (no doubt aware that by sheer numbers Edinburgh's anti-Catholic legions would carry any general public assembly) had broken the agreement, held a meeting, and sent parliament a petition, the anti-Catholic organizers insisted on having their own say.

Supporters of emancipation put it differently: At a meeting of the Friends of Religious Liberty, "Brunswickers" had attempted to break up the proceedings. If the anti-Catholics had collected 13,000 signatures on their Edinburgh petition, Sir J. Macintosh reported on presenting the pro-Catholic petition to parliament that its 8,000 signatures began with:

> an unprecedentedly large meeting involving four-fifths or even nine-tenths of what, until such a leveling spirit seized the Honourable Gentlemen on the Bench below me, used without objection or exception to be called the respectable classes of the community in the ancient capital of the most Protestant part of this Protestant Empire, which, in my opinion, will perform one of the noblest duties of its high office of guardian to the Protestant interest of Europe by passing this Bill into a law. (*Morning Chronicle*, 27 March 1829, p. 2)

Macintosh echoed the ingenious arguments of several speakers at the Edinburgh meeting. They claimed that political disabilities segregated Catholics, drove them to defend their identities, and therefore made them less susceptible to cool reason. Full membership in the polity and full engagement in public discussion would, if permitted, eventually make them more skeptical of Catholic doctrine and papal authority. Macintosh went on to impugn Edinburgh Brunswickers for having padded their petition with nonresidents, for having circulated libelous tracts, and by implication for having appealed to the city's plebeians. Thus, he challenged their numbers, unity, and worthiness, if not their commitment to the anti-Catholic cause.

Both advocates and opponents of the Catholic cause in 1829 used a wide variety of techniques to forward their programs, but the central mechanism connected local political action directly to parliament. By the thousands, organizers drafted petitions, held local public meetings to publicize them, collected signatures, validated those signatures as best they could, and arranged for MPs to present them during parliamentary sessions. As the intensity of parliamentary debate increased, meetings and petitions multiplied. Each side tried to discredit the other's tactics and support, not only decrying false signatures (e.g., of women, boys, nonresidents, and other persons outside the political arena) but also complaining about "inflammatory placards" and incendiary speeches.

If Britons had enjoyed a limited right to petition for centuries, if Britain's seventeenth-century revolutions set a precedent of widespread popular mobilization, and if such eighteenth-century political entrepreneurs as John Wilkes and George Gordon had used public meetings, marches, and petitions quite effectively, never before had the full panoply of social movement organization, complete with mass-membership associations, come into play at a national scale (Tilly 1982). While recognizing eighteenth-century revolutions as possible challengers for the title and understanding that in Great Britain itself the distinctive elements of social movement practice came together in fits and starts from the time of Lord George Gordon's Protestant Association onward, we might even be able to call the Catholic Emancipation campaign the world's first national social movement. In Great Britain, only antislavery (whose national organization of 1787 marks it as an early riser) competes for the title.

By my counts of CGs and of parliamentary petitions, the scorecards over 1828 and 1829 as a whole ran like this:

	CGs 1828	Petitions 1828	CGs 1829	Petitions 1829
For Emancipation	16	732	99	1001
Against Emancipation	21	333	141	2169
Divided	4	0	2	0

The figures refer to Great Britain (England, Scotland, and Wales) alone. If these had been binding votes and Great Britain the only relevant arena of political action, Catholic Emancipation would clearly have failed as a political program. Comparable information from Ireland, on the other hand, would show overwhelming support for the Catholic cause (O'Ferrall 1985, 188–257). Only the virtual ungovernability of Ireland itself under the impact of Catholic Association mobilization moved the duke of Wellington and Robert Peel, reluctant parliamentary midwives of emancipation, to persuade an even more reluctant king that he had to keep the peace by making concessions.

Concessions, not capitulations. The very settlement reveals the sort of mixed bargain emancipation entailed. While removing most barriers to Catholic office holding in the United Kingdom, it included the following restrictions:

1. No Catholic could serve as Regent, Lord Lieutenant of Ireland, Lord Chancellor of England or Ireland, or hold any position in Anglican Church establishments, ecclesiastical courts, universities, or public schools.
2. Office-holding Catholics had to swear a new oath of loyalty to the king and the Hanoverian succession, denying the right of foreign princes including the Pope to exercise civil jurisdiction within the United Kingdom, denying any intention to subvert the Anglican establishment or the Protestant religion.
3. Forty-shilling freeholders (owners of property whose annual rent would be worth at least two pounds per year, who had previously voted in Ireland, and who had provided strong support for O'Connell) lost their franchise in favor of a ten-pound minimum with stronger guarantees against inflation of estimated property values.
4. The government dissolved the Catholic Association and barred successors from forming.

Cautious concession describes the bargain better than Catholic conquest or liberal largesse.

CONSEQUENCES

In conjunction with the earlier and less turbulent campaign over repeal of the Test and Corporation Acts, the partially successful social movement for Catholic Emancipation left a large dent in national politics. Those two rounds of legislation broke the hold of Anglicans over public office and parliament (Clark 1985). The Catholic Association made ordinary Irish people a formidable presence in British politics. Despite all the restrictions on Irish mobilization laid down by Wellington and Peel, their settlement ratified the legitimacy of mass-membership political associations and social movement tactics.

Almost immediately, advocates of parliamentary reform self-consciously took up the model and precedent to organize political unions and to initiate a campaign of meetings and petitions. This time, after more than half a century of striving, reformers gained a substantial victory; if the Reform Act of 1832 still excluded the majority of adult males (to say nothing of females) from suffrage, it enfranchised the commercial bourgeoisie, gave MPs to fast-growing industrial towns, eliminated parliamentary seats that had lain within the gift of a single patron, and forwarded the principle of representation according to (propertied) numbers rather than chartered privilege (Brock 1974; Cannon 1973; Phillips 1992; Phillips and Wetherell 1991). Catholic Emancipation did not cause the Reform Act, but it facilitated and channeled the political mobilization that led to reform.

Emancipation thus forwarded citizenship and democracy in Great Britain, directly through its dissolution of barriers to political participation, indirectly through its impact on parliamentary reform. Citizenship refers to a certain kind of tie: a continuing series of transactions between persons and agents of a given state in which each has enforceable rights and obligations uniquely by virtue of the persons' membership in an exclusive category, the native-born plus the naturalized. To the extent that the British state dissolved particular ties to its subject population based on local history and/or membership in locally implanted social categories while installing generalized classifications on the basis of political performance, it gave increasing weight to citizenship. Reducing barriers to the political participation of Dissenters and Catholics clearly moved in that direction.

Not all advances of citizenship promote democracy; in our own time, authoritarian regimes have often stressed a variety of citizenship in which most people qualify as citizens, but citizens' obligations are very extensive, greatly outweighing their rights. Democracy combines broad, relatively equal citizenship with (1) binding consultation of citizens with respect to governmental personnel and policies, (2) protection of citizens, including members of minorities, from arbitrary state action. This definition stands in a middle ground between formal criteria such as elections, legislatures, and constitutions, on the one hand, and substantive criteria such as solidarity, justice, and welfare, on the other. (Chapter 14 offers a more extended discussion of definitions and applications.)

By such a definition, emancipation democratized primarily by broadening and equalizing political rights, without significantly increasing the consultation of those who qualified as citizens or the protection of citizens against arbitrary action; simultaneous restrictions on voting and associational life in Ireland, indeed, attenuated the net movement toward democracy. Through direct and indirect effects, nevertheless, Britain's reduction of religious restrictions on citizenship in 1828 and 1829 marked an important moment for democratization.

In addition to its significance for British history, the emancipation campaign takes us back to the more general points that motivate this chapter: analogies between social movement dynamics and politics at other scales, negotiated contingency of political identities in movements and elsewhere, interactions between ostensibly "domestic" and "international" political processes, value of transactional rather than individualistic conceptions of political processes. In order to avoid endless elaboration, let us confine discussion to analogies between social movements and the politics of nationalism.

THE ANALOGY OF NATIONALISM

As a doctrine, nationalism asserts a series of propositions that had little currency two centuries ago, but came to seem like political common sense during the nineteenth century:

1. The whole world's population divides into nations, each of which shares a common origin, culture, and sense of destiny.
2. Each nation deserves its own state.
3. Each state has the right to create its own nation.
4. Given a nation's existence, its members have strong obligations to serve it and the state that embodies it. Those obligations override the claims of religion, family, and self-interest.

As propositions about how the world works, of course, each of these encounters enormous empirical and normative objections (Anderson 1991; Armstrong 1982; Bjørn, Grant, and Stringer 1994a, 1994b; Brubaker 1993; Comaroff 1991; Fullbrook 1993; Graubard 1993; Greenfeld 1992; Haas 1986; Hobsbawm 1990, 1994; Lerner 1991; Motyl 1992a; Noiriel 1991, 1993; Østergard 1991, 1992; Shell 1993; Smith 1990; Topalov 1991). But as justifications for social action, they all gained considerable currency in the Western world after 1789, then acquired worldwide scope with the dismantling of empires.

To be more precise and to focus on Europe, nationalist doctrines and practices took a zigzag course from 1492 to our own time. From 1492 to 1648, schematically, we witness a period in which Western and Central European powers struggled over the alignment between religion and state power, with outcomes varying among the establishment of state-dominated Protestant churches in Scandinavia, England, and parts of Germany, uneasy and unequal coexistence of multiple religions in Switzerland and the Dutch republic, expulsion and forced conversion of Jews and Muslims in Iberia, and decreasing toleration of a chartered Protestant minority in a France that kept its distance from the pope.

From 1648 to the 1790s, the European state system maintained a rough alignment of official religion with state identity, but the papacy continued to lose secular power, even within nominally Catholic states. The French Revolution and Napoleonic Wars started the severing of religion from national identity, with nonreligious or even antireligious definitions of citizenship coming to predominate. It is as if rulers discovered that religion usually encouraged international ties, which in turn subverted their programs of national hegemony. Religion bedded uncomfortably with nationalism.

As political process, nationalism consists of claim making in the name of these doctrines. It takes two forms: *top-down* and *bottom-up*. Top-down nationalism involves claims by agents of an existing state and their political allies, claims on presumed members of the nation identified with that state. Top-down nationalism includes the creation and imposition of a dominant language, origin myth, symbols, rituals, memberships, educational routines, and obligations by means of histories, literatures, curricula, museums, monuments, public assemblies, electoral procedures, state ceremonies, festivals, military service, and intervention in mass media. It entails the subordination or elimination of competing institutions and practices, at the extreme the exercise of control over wide ranges of resources and social life by state agents in the name of the nation's interest. Top-down nationalism has been rare in human history; over the roughly 10,000 years that states have existed somewhere in the world, most rulers have settled for assigning priority within their domains to their own cultural definitions and readings of their own interests, but coexisting more or less comfortably with composite subject populations having distinctive charters, cultures, and social routines. Although China stands as an important partial exception, top-down nationalism only became widely available, or even technically feasible, in most of the world's states during the nineteenth and twentieth centuries (Schram 1985, 1987; Shue 1988; Skinner 1964, 1985; Whitney 1970; Will 1994).

A fortiori for bottom-up nationalism, the mounting of demands for political autonomy and recognition by self-identified representatives of a coherent nation that lacks its own state. Historically, bottom-up nationalism has arisen chiefly in three circumstances: (1) when agents of an empire have sought to impose military, fiscal, or (especially) religious obligations on a previously protected minority, (2) when adjacent powers have attempted to undermine an empire by supporting the rebellion of peripheral populations within the empire, (3) when rulers of expanding states have undertaken thoroughgoing top-down nationalism in the presence of well-connected populations possessing distinctive cultural, political, and economic institutions. The first two have rarely stimulated strong assertions of national identity, especially with claims to separate statehood. The third—the encounter of top-down nationalism with well-connected minorities—has frequently done so. As a result, bottom-up nationalism surged during the nineteenth and twentieth centuries.

International relations played a significant part in both varieties of nationalism. Whether initiated by a state's agents or by an antistate minority, the claim to represent a nation could only succeed in relation to other powerholders, especially the rulers of major outside states. At least from the treaty of Cateau-Cambrésis (1559), settlements of large-scale European wars featured representation of multiple powers, a muster of those who had valid claims to rule, hence an implicit enumeration of those who *lacked* such claims. By the treaty of Westphalia (1648), the ruler's validated claim to represent a nation, at least as connected by a common religious tradition, came to figure among the criteria for recognition by the community of nations; one reason France and Sweden were able to keep Holy Roman Emperor Ferdinand III from representing all his domains as a single power at Westphalia was precisely the religious diversity of those scattered territories. Nevertheless, by the settlement of the Napoleonic Wars, shared religion had lost much of its force as a national political credential, while the concert of nations presumed more than ever before to decide collectively which states enjoyed sovereignty and who was qualified to rule them.

After World War I the League of Nations (boycotted by the United States) inherited some of the victorious powers' authority to certify nations. In the aftermath of World War II, the great powers delegated even more certifying power to the United Nations, practically ceding the work of credentialing to that body once massive decolonization began during the 1960s. The disintegration of the

Soviet Union and Yugoslavia both provoked and then fed upon disruption of the credentialing apparatus, as quick but disputed recognitions of some fragments (e.g., Slovenia, Croatia, and Ukraine) but not others incited military action on the parts of those who stood to lose political power, livelihood, or even lives as a function of outsiders' confirmation of others as their rightful rulers. Increasingly, then, the recognition of who constituted a valid nation (1) entered the process of state formation, (2) became the collective business of some concert of already-recognized nation-states, however heterogeneous their actual social composition, (3) generated international agencies specializing in recognition and its denial, (4) had enormous consequences for the relative power of different factions within constituted states.

As this account suggests, both top-down and bottom-up nationalisms share interesting properties with social movements. Like the claims social movement activists make on behalf of themselves and their ostensible constituencies, claims to nationhood always include a measure of mystification with respect to the relevant population's tenure, coherence, and solidarity with its self-identified spokespersons. They almost always incite counterclaims by rivals, enemies, and threatened power-holders. The identities they assert consist crucially of differences from and relations to others rather than actual internal solidarity. Their success rests at least as much on outside recognition as on internal consensus. And disciplined, stereotyped public demonstrations of "nationness," which typically require great internal coordination and repression, play a large part in that recognition. In this case, to be sure, the sheer ability to wield armed force effectively looms much larger than it does in most social movements.

WHERE NOW?

Nationalist performances are not simply social movements writ large, but they involve parallel political processes. To repeat:

First, the histories in question reveal powerful analogies between the processes driving social movements within national polities and a range of other processes, both "national" and "international," to which analysts of social movements have paid little attention; they therefore rectify common conceptions of social movements as sui generis.

Second, the identities people deploy in political claim making (including identities of religious affiliation, nationality, and citizenship) consist of contingent relationships with other people rather than inbuilt personal traits; they therefore alter as political networks, opportunities, and strategies shift.

Third, the histories show us incessant interaction between political processes observers commonly distinguish as "domestic" and "international," processes analysts frequently conceive of as quite independent one from the other.

Fourth, once we shift from conventional individualistic conceptions to transactional analyses of political processes, these three points become almost self-evident.

We could undertake similar reviews of other ostensibly local or international political processes, such as ethnic conflict, the creation of citizenship, militarization, democratization, dependent state formation, revolution, and war. Perhaps by now, however, the main point is obvious, tedious, even otiose: The endemic individualism of history and social science have long kept analysts from recognizing parallels and connections among political processes, parallels and connections that transcend geographic boundaries and scales. Perhaps Catholic Emancipation can direct us along the path of intellectual emancipation.

Part III

CONTENTIOUS VOICES

8

Voice in Contentious Politics

The year 1989 provided plenty of work for Europe's social movement watchers. Those who had until then settled for noting parallels between social movements in different countries found themselves obliged to explain not only connections among scattered movements but relations among the movements' political contexts. While the previous major wave of claim making experienced by Europe—in 1968—concentrated in the continent's western half, this time the initiative came from the east. That included the Soviet Union, long considered a special case. In the Baltic countries, in Czechoslovakia, in Romania, even in Albania, citizens poured into the streets to shout viva voce complaints they had previously only muttered in cafés or circulated in samizdat.

After his arrival as head of the Soviet Communist Party in 1985, Mikhail Gorbachev clearly announced his intention to reduce military expenditures, improve relations of the Soviet Union with the United States and the North Atlantic Treaty Organization (NATO), and to slow Soviet military intervention abroad. The costly, traumatic stalemate in Afghanistan (the Soviet Union's most serious standoff with the United States in years) had dimmed the Soviet army's prestige and raised doubts about the longstanding policy of military parity with the United States. Gorbachev's program of nonintervention and demilitarization even extended to the satellite countries of Eastern Europe.

When the Soviet Union began reducing military expenditures and announced its withdrawal from foreign intervention, citizens of other Eastern European countries started thinking that the probability of Soviet backing for their governments in the case of internal challenges had declined. Within the Soviet Union,

An earlier version of this chapter appeared as "Réclamer Viva Voce," *Cultures et Conflits* 5 (1992), 330–352; I have translated it from the French original.

inhabitants of non-Russian regions drew similar conclusions. Relaxation of the regime's repressive apparatus encouraged emergence of long-suppressed demands.

At that point, challenges multiplied in Poland, Hungary, Czechoslovakia, and East Germany. Everywhere except in Germany opposition forces had been forming for at least a decade. The Soviet warming of 1985 encouraged them. In June 1989, Poles chose 99 anticommunist deputies out of the 100 elected to the legislature's upper house in relatively free elections. In the lower house, the electoral law limited Solidarity to 35 percent of the seats. But the Peasant Party had broken its permanent alliance with the Communists in 1989. Its alignment with Solidarity produced a majority and gave Poland its first noncommunist prime minister since the arrival of socialism: Tadeusz Mazowiecki. The Soviets remained silent. Communists also lost power in Hungary, where the Socialist Workers' Party disbanded itself as a national referendum approved dismantling of communist factory cells, dissolution of communist militias, and publication of the party's accounts. On their side, Czechoslovak rulers managed to forbid demonstrations until November 1989. But a flood of East German refugees across the country, retrospective condemnation of Czechoslovakia's 1968 invasion by Hungarian and Polish armed forces on behalf of socialist unity, and rapid transformation of Czechoslovakia's ex-communist neighbors increased pressure on the regime. In mid-November, mass demonstrations in Prague and elsewhere shut down the governmental machinery, accelerating the formation of public opposition coordinated by Civic Forum. A series of improvisations brought Alexander Dubcek and Vaclav Havel to power.

Unlike their neighbors, East Germans had offered only weak public resistance to their communist regime before the collapse of 1989. But during the fall of 1989, Czechoslovak, Polish, and Hungarian authorities allowed thousands of East Germans to cross their frontiers on the way west. Nonintervention by Soviet forces and the incapacity of the East German government to stop the flow provided revealing signs of the big changes that were underway. East Germans then began to demonstrate for democratic reforms and against poor living conditions. When opposition leaders throughout Eastern Europe learned that the Soviet embassy in Prague had received a delegation from Civic Forum calmly instead of sending it packing, they drew their own conclusions. Soon, highly diverse popular rebellions swept away the communist heads of Romania, Bulgaria, and Albania. In addition, demands for independence or autonomy multiplied within Yugoslavia, Czechoslovakia, and the Soviet Union. The Soviet Union began the process of disaggregation that led to its disappearance in 1991.

Although each national movement had peculiarities resulting from its country's individual political history, the demonstrations, marches, and meetings that occurred throughout Eastern Europe in 1989 drew on a common stock of symbols and knowledge. They did not, however, spring from central coordination of parallel actions or even repetition of identical causes from one country to another. Instead events in one place stimulated events in another. We therefore face a theoretical problem. How should we conceive of connections among simultaneous but geographically dispersed movements, in order to understand how regime transformations spread so rapidly and widely? In this brief chapter, I will not document the day-to-day conflicts of 1989 or lay out a full explanatory model, but sketch ways of thinking about processes of this kind.

AVAILABLE IDEAS

As happened in the 1960s, the turmoil of 1989 and thereafter incited rethinking of available ideas about collective action. Users of existing models had considerable difficulty accounting for the rapid expansion of independence movements throughout Eastern Europe. Various models of political mobilization and collective action, including my own, arose in response to movements of the 1960s in Europe and America. They challenged the previously dominant idea of irrational "collective behavior," which had prevailed in academic discourse and in governmental pronouncements on riots, revolutions, and social movements. That line of argument found its most eloquent exponents in Neil Smelser, Ralph Turner, and Chalmers Johnson. Replying to the collective behavior tradition, models of collective action by such analysts as Francesco Alberoni, William Gamson, and George Rudé accented the rationality, solidity, organization, intentionality, and effectiveness of movement that earlier theorists had treated as spontaneous or irrational.

A second sort of critique bore on the Marxist idea of a broad historical trend in which groups—especially social classes—gained consciousness of themselves, formed social movements, and finally joined the master Social Movement that gave history meaning. While many models of collective behavior and of collective action assumed a more or less direct expression of material interests in collective action, Mancur Olson pointed out that the path from interests to action, far from being wide open, was strewn with roadblocks. Free riders were simply the most obvious of the obstacles—why should anyone take risks on behalf of uncertain, costly enterprises when others who would share the putative benefits were not obliged to participate? Olson's school assimilated collective action to the production of collective goods, thus giving an economistic flavor to the study of social movements.

From the two challenges to received opinion emerged an incomplete, often contradictory, and sometimes incoherent line of thought. It began with the idea that collective action is uncertain, costly, and deliberate. It made that action an outcome of the interplay among interest, organization, and consciousness. Later work on new social movements (e.g., that of Alain Touraine and his student Alberto Melucci) insisted on the importance of shared identities and rejected the assumption that governments channeled movements. But even that work accepted the general statement of what was to be explained.

The new line of thought had considerable advantages over its predecessors. Yet it assumed more or less independent actors whose particular situations and characters explained their action. Such a view led to the explanation of collective action group by group, one actor at a time, accepting unthinkingly the assumption that the object of explanation was the behavior of those who mounted protests. Analysts of the 1960s shared that assumption with the collective behavior theorists they had rejected. But such a setting of the problem obscures both actions of powerholders and interactions among parties to social movements. One can see why the available theoretical apparatus handicapped analysts of Eastern European events in 1989.

In summary, explanatory models of collective action have greatly evolved since the 1960s. The earliest models (including my own) now seem naïve with their simple rationalism, their ignoring of social context, their concentration on already existing political actors whose position remains more or less constant. Post-1960s improvements included the development of a more historical understanding of transformations in the means of collective action, deepened study of connections between the organization of routine social life and participation in conflict, and representation of political actors as changing, contingent, and constructed networks of persons that are themselves subject to political and ideological influence.

CONTRIBUTIONS AND LIMITS OF CURRENT MODELS

In the recent past a partial bifurcation has occurred in studies of collective action at large. One path includes complex analyses of rational action in which actors and interests are given a priori. The other takes a more historicist line, connecting collective action with political, economic, and ideological changes. Nevertheless, on the rational action side we find formal analysts such as Michael Hechter making serious efforts to specify effects of historical context, and on the historicist side we discover intense competition among competing general arguments (see Lichbach and Zuckerman 1997; McAdam, Tarrow, and Tilly 2001). Most analysts have come to accept the necessity of linking collective action to historical, economic, political, and ideological processes.

Studies of revolutions and of states have followed a parallel trajectory, although they have not converged with studies of social movements. Models of natural history in the style of Crane Brinton have given way to comparative histories in the style of Theda Skocpol. Studies of revolutions and of states have actually joined, to their mutual advantage (see, for example, Goodwin 2001). On the state's side, we see the gradual disappearance of typological and evolutionary approaches in favor of relating states historically to their social environments. Michael Mann, for example, treats states as complex structures within which many sinews of social power intertwine, but which collectively exert significant influence over social life.

Models of social movements have undergone a similar transformation. As earlier chapters have shown, the social movement in this narrower sense of the word emerged as a distinctive form of politics in Europe and North America during the nineteenth century. By the twentieth century it had become a standard way of doing political business throughout the more democratic parts of the world. During the 1960s, observers still often thought of the social movement as a sort of whale that rose from the sea only to plunge beneath the surface again, remaining essentially the same. From that conception followed the idea that one could follow a single movement—feminist, temperance, and so on—for decades, tracing its life history and course through the sea. But the topic became more historicist and skeptical on that score as interview studies, participation observation, and historical reconstruction confirmed a more discontinuous and contingent view of social movement operation.

Analysts introduced the distinction between social movement actions and social movement organizations, which previous studies had tended to conflate by thinking of the actions as work by continuously existing organizations. They noticed shifting participation in almost every long-lasting movement; of conflicts and changing coalitions within almost every movement; and unceasing strategic interaction among organizations, activists' social networks, competitors, and various authorities. These changes of awareness helped eliminate the view of social movements as coherent and continuous, hence to challenge movement leaders' own characteristic portrayal of their movements in those very terms. That challenge in turn raised questions about leaders' claims to speak directly for unified constituencies. Although studies of social movements continued to come disproportionately from movement sympathizers—hence a shortage of documentation concerning right-wing and high-risk movements—these changes of perspective introduced a measure of skepticism concerning the stories movement activists told about themselves.

Although the battle of definitions continues, researchers seem to be reaching agreement on social movements as forms of concerted political interaction depending on multiple organizations and networks, among which the specialized association has for 150 years occupied a special place. They generally agree, furthermore, that since 1945 social movement organizations have multiplied and professionalized in Western countries, often entering the well-trodden ground of interest-group representation. Students of the subject divide more sharply on whether the social movement we know formed as a particular form of politics in the era of the French Revolution or simply represents one variant on a much more general phenomenon. No one, however, doubts that social movements greatly increased in frequency and geographic range after 1789.

MOVEMENT CYCLES

Beginning with his studies of Italian conflicts between 1965 and 1975, Sidney Tarrow renewed the discussion of social movements with his model of protest cycles. According to Tarrow, successful claim making tends to stimulate new demands on the part of other actors. That happens because some actors recognize previously invisible opportunities, others emulate newly devised means of action, and still others find themselves threatened by the newcomers. Expansion of claim making occurs, according to this model, up to the point where rivals either establish themselves, rigidify their positions, exhaust their energies, destroy each other, or succumb to state repression called forth by those whose interests the claim making threatens.

Over such a cycle, early phases multiply innovations in collective action, create relatively open spaces for new collective experiments, and thus give the impression of a total break with the past. During later phases, more moderate claimants withdraw from the public arena, leaving more radical and marginal activists increasingly isolated and vulnerable. Each large cycle of this kind leaves its traces in the political system: formation of new groups, alterations of relations between citizens and public authorities, renewal of public discourse, and creation of new forms of collective action. But such results always fall short of hopes and fears at the peak of struggle. As a consequence, many movement participants reach later phases of a protest cycle disappointed and angry at leaders who have sold out, consoled only by the sense that they alone have remained pure. At the end of the 1965–1975 cycle, such experiences on the part of radical activists reinforced the idea of a break with the past, which in turn made the idea of new social movements more credible.

Tarrow's scheme rests on the idea of political opportunity structure. That structure, according to Tarrow's conception, limits all actors (although not equally), but varies from country to country and time to time. Collective action can swing rapidly without quick shifts in the character, internal organization, or immediate settings of political actors because political opportunities themselves change. The outbreak of war, the end of a war, and the death of a ruler provide cases in point. Yet, the principle is chiefly analytical. In practice, such changes in opportunity always generate simultaneous alterations in the mobilization and organization of potential collective actors. Still, the idea helps identify otherwise obscure parallels among such phenomena as revolutionary situations, ends of wars, and the disintegration of empires.

A revolutionary situation, for example, forms when at least two blocs within the same state claim control over the same state apparatus, and each receives support from some substantial segment of the citizenry. A revolutionary situation does not necessarily produce a revolutionary outcome, since old rulers can retake control or a state may split permanently. A full revolution—a transfer of state power through open struggle among blocs—never occurs, however, without a revolutionary situation. A revolutionary situation may begin with the declaration of independence by a subordinate segment of an existing state; for example, Soviet Estonia in 1990. It can occur through mobilization of a coalition among excluded actors; for example, the coalitions of intellectuals, bourgeois, and skilled workers that formed in many European countries during the revolutions of 1848. It can also occur through the segmentation of a previously dominant coalition, as in the cleavage between Roundheads and Cavaliers in England after 1640.

Revolutionary situations drive to the extreme a political situation that also occurs outside of revolutions: slippage of power over the state that threatens the interests of all actors having stakes in the present distribution of power, but that simultaneously opens opportunities to all other actors (including those in the ruling classes) enjoying the capacity to pursue their interests through rapid, decisive action.

Even when it does not produce large internal cleavages, the end of a war often has similar consequences. In major military mobilizations, almost all states promise participants in the war effort—civilian or military—more than they will actually be able to deliver at the peace. Expensive promises include services and payments for workers, officials, veterans, families of the dead and wounded, capitalists, and minorities that delay their claims for redress during the war. Moreover, states commonly erect exceptional controls over economic, political, and social life in wartime only to dismantle them at war's end, at the very time when they are demobilizing workers from war production and returning military personnel to civilian life. That relaxation of central controls promotes an explosion of deferred claims. The explosion often exceeds the state's capacity either to gratify or to repress. The more credibility the state loses during the war (defeat and foreign occupation being the extreme cases), the greater the chances of overflow.

Such processes threaten established rights and open the state to new demands. Consider the situation at the end of World War I. Every state involved in the Great War (including the presumably neutral Netherlands and the late-entering United States) faced challenges from political actors that had collaborated in the war effort. The greater a country's war losses, the more widespread the challenge. Russia, Austria, the Ottoman Empire, and Germany all experienced revolutionary situations, and Bulgaria came very close. With its huge strikes, factory occupations, and Fascist mobilization, Italy likewise came to the edge of a revolutionary situation between 1918 and 1921. Russia and Germany went through genuine revolutionary transfers of power, although Germany soon receded from its revolutionary regime of 1918.

France, Great Britain, and the United States did not come close to revolutionary situations, but revolution actually occurred in Ireland. All these countries faced great waves of claim making at war's end. Two major social movements—for prohibition of alcohol and for women's suffrage—actually saw their programs enacted into U.S. federal law in the war's aftermath. Thus, even the victors of World War I experienced their own versions of the war-end cycle.

Disintegration of empires, federations, and ruling coalitions likewise shares properties with revolutionary situations. Secession of a visible member transmits important signals to other members: diminution of the central authority's capacity to meet its own obligations and to enforce other parties' meeting of their obligations, increase in the likely costs of loyalty to the central authority, the sheer possibility of secession. Each secession, furthermore, opens up possible coalitions of remaining members with those who have departed. Mikhail Gorbachev tasted that bitter logic with the secession of Estonia, Latvia, and Lithuania from the Soviet Union.

All these political processes unfold following principles similar to those of Tar-row's social movement cycles. A successful round of claims promotes the emergence of new claims, competition among actors for political power sharpens, claims mul-tiply, claimants proliferate, and demands become broader before they begin to dis-sipate. As the process continues, militants invent and try new forms of organization, action, goal setting, claim making, combat with their rivals, discipline over their fol-lowers, protection of advantages they have acquired. At cycle's end, some actors have gained pieces of power, others have seen their political resources ravaged, public dis-course on the stakes of struggle has changed, and the array of acceptable ways of acting together—the repertoire of contention—has likewise undergone significant alterations.

In the course of such cycles, initial claims have two interesting characteristics. They require authorities to take seriously (if only to reject them vigorously) pro-grams they would otherwise have ignored. That serious consideration encourages mobilization and intervention on the part of other actors having interests, negative or positive, in the outcomes of the programs under contestation. The initial claims inevitably threaten the interests of others (nonclaimants) either because redistribu-tion of resources would undermine programs dear to other actors or because the programs in question would attack their interests directly. Revolutionary and non-revolutionary situations resemble each other in that regard.

The multiplication of revolutionary and nearly revolutionary situations in Eu-rope between 1847 and 1849 shared many features with less extreme protest cy-cles. The vulnerability of visible states to revolutionary programs encourages the emergence of revolutionary programs in other states, favors access of political ac-tors to revolutionary doctrine and expertise, and reduces the propensity of states that are themselves undergoing revolutionary changes to intervene on behalf of neighboring regimes threatened by revolution. The outbreak of revolutions in Bel-gium and the Kingdom of Naples early in 1848 heightened the significance of France's revolutionary moves later the same year.

Communication and shared belief play significant parts in such revolutionary processes. Three elements change as they advance: (1) common readings of state ca-pacity, (2) shared beliefs concerning the likely consequences of different claims and collective actions, and (3) relative capabilities of different actors to mobilize and act collectively. Those capabilities depend in their turn on the formation of new ac-tors by creation, mobilization, or coalition, the disintegration of existing actors, the diffusion of ideas and techniques, and the movement of experienced militants from setting to setting.

Except for natural disasters and military invasions, state capacity generally changes slowly. The rapidity of movement between nonrevolutionary and revolu-tionary situations, between inaction and action, between low and high levels of movement activity generally does not result from quick changes in state capacity but from the rapid diffusion of new information, beliefs, and evaluations of action's probable consequences.

BACK TO 1989

One might think that television and the press explain the internationalization of collective action's forms and rhythms. Certainly, demonstrations and distant rebellions become news rapidly and sometimes take the forms they do because of involvement by the media. It would be hasty, however, to confuse expanded media exposure with internationalization. A glance back at 1789 or 1848 will indicate how closely Europe's political centers connected with each other well before television or mass journalism provided their publicity. In 1789, English radicals and conservatives alike followed Parisian events day by day. The construction of "Parisian" barricades became standard practice in the Germany of 1848. Notice, however, what actually spread from place to place: not so much shared interests, awareness of oppression, or even models of collective action, rather information concerning changes in the vulnerability of authorities, the likelihood of international support, and the effectiveness of different known forms of collective action. If internationalization occurs, we should not imagine a wave of imitation but a change in the connections between the political situations of spatially separated actors.

Let me sum up. The origins of simultaneity in social movements that form in different countries lie in (1) alterations of the political situation that occur interdependently in the countries, as at the end of a war; (2) effects of political struggles on third parties, especially states, as when a revolution breaks alliances between the revolutionary state and others, and thus affects the prospects for revolution in the other states; (3) direct borrowing of collective action models, information concerning likely consequences of collective action, beliefs concerning legitimate ends of collective action, and expertise in action as such.

All these connections depend heavily on the history of relations among the countries in question. In the case of Europe in 1989, a common experience of Soviet hegemony created communication networks among Poland, East Germany, Czechoslovakia, and Hungary. Those networks reinforced the extreme sensitivity of those states to changes in relations of any one of them to the Soviet Union. The absence of Soviet reaction to the flight of East Germans to the West through Hungary and Czechoslovakia in 1989 rapidly lowered estimates of the probability of Soviet military intervention in that zone. Increased confidence in that regard allowed Czechoslovak activists to place at the top of their new regime the victim of the 1968 Soviet invasion, Alexander Dubcek, and a recently freed prisoner of the old regime, Vaclav Havel. Even in these times of chaos, the previously existing political structure unquestionably shaped political contention.

Recent work on new social movements in Western Europe teaches the same lesson. As it turns out, it establishes a correspondence between the structure of the state and the organization of activists. For example, the greater dispersion of activist organizations in federal countries (Switzerland and Germany) than in more centralized countries (France and the Netherlands) illustrates the influence of political opportunity structure. Groups that form to challenge state power take on its lineaments.

History intervenes at another level. Studies of collective action produced over the last twenty years or so have established a connection between two fundamental facts: First, that the means of popular collective action have altered since the time of Rough Music and grain seizures, giving way to such forms as the demonstration and the mass meeting; second, that the array of means for collective action actually available to any potential actor at a given time is very narrow as compared to what such actors might, in principle, be capable of doing. Collective action analysts have come to describe that situation in terms of collective action repertoires to underline the combination of constraint and learning with innovation that occurs chiefly at the edge of existing forms. Repertoires of contention do not belong to individuals or to groups, but to sets of political actors, for the set consisting of demonstrators, counterdemonstrators, and police. Such sets form and transform their repertoires as they interact.

Sidney Tarrow has observed how much the repertoires of the eighteenth and preceding centuries depended on particular circumstances of actors, places, and issues. Nineteenth-, twentieth-, and twenty-first-century collective action performances, in contrast, include much more portable, transferable forms such as strikes, demonstrations, and public meetings. Tarrow calls the latter forms "modular," noting how easily they move from group to group, country to country, and issue to issue. That modularity helps explain the more rapid recent generalization of movements. Through a basically historical and cultural conception—repertoires—we get a sense of interaction channeled not only by political structure but also by knowledge, belief, and communication lines. The same processes that help us explain the spread of social movement clarify the political changes of 1989.

9

Contentious Conversation

Ayodhya, India, long sheltered a sixteenth-century mosque, Babri Masjid, named for the first Mughal emperor, Babur. Ayodhya attracted worldwide attention on 6 December 1992, when Hindu militants destroyed Ayodhya's Muslim shrine, began construction of a Hindu temple on the same site, and launched a nationwide series of struggles that eventually produced some 1,200 deaths (Tambiah 1996, 251; Bose and Jalal 1998, 228; Madan 1997, 56–58; van der Veer 1996). But the campaign behind that newsworthy event began a decade earlier. During the 1980s, militant Hindu groups started demanding destruction of the mosque and erection of a temple to Ram, epic hero of the Ramayana. Just before the 1989 elections Bharatiya Janata Party (BJP) activists transported what they called holy bricks to Ayodhya and ceremoniously laid a foundation for their temple.

The following year, President Lal Advani of the BJP took his chariot caravan on a pilgrimage (*rath yatra*) across northern India, threatening along the way to start building the Ram temple in Ayodhya. Advani started his pilgrimage in Somnath, fabled site of a great Hindu temple destroyed by Muslim marauders. "For the sake of the temple," he declared en route, "we will sacrifice not one but many governments" (Chaturvedi and Chaturvedi 1996, 181–182). Advani's followers had fashioned his Toyota van into a simulacrum of legendary hero Arjuna's chariot, an image familiar from Peter Brook's film *Mahabharata*. As the BJP caravan passed through towns and villages, Advani's chariot attracted gifts of flower petals, coconut, burning incense, sandalwood paste, and prayer from local women. Authorities arrested Advani before he could begin the last lap of his journey to Ayodhya,

An earlier version of this chapter appeared as "Contentious Conversation," *Social Research* 65 (1998), 491–510. I have also included a few paragraphs from that article in chapter 5 of Doug McAdam, Sidney Tarrow, and Charles Tilly, *Dynamics of Contention*. Cambridge, England: Cambridge University Press, 2001.

but not before many of his followers had preceded him to the city. When some of them broke through police barricades near the offending mosque, police fired on them, killing "scores" of BJP activists (Kakar 1996, 51).

Both sides represented their actions as virtuous violence—one side as defense of public order, the other side as sacrifice for a holy cause. Hindu activists made a great pageant of cremating the victims' bodies on a nearby riverbank, then returning martyrs' ashes to their homes in various parts of India. Soon, the fatalities at Ayodhya became themes of widespread Hindu-Muslim-police clashes. Those conflicts intersected with higher caste students' public resistance to the national government's revival of an affirmative action program on behalf of Other Backward Classes (Tambiah 1996, 249). In Hyderabad, reports Sudhir Kakar,

> more than a thousand miles to the south of Ayodhya, the riots began with the killing of
> Sardar, a Muslim auto-rickshaw driver, by two Hindus. Although the murder was later
> linked to a land dispute between two rival gangs, at the time of the killing it was framed
> in the context of rising Hindu-Muslim tensions in the city. Muslims retaliated by stab-
> bing four Hindus in different parts of the walled city. Then Majid Khan, an influential
> local leader of Subzimandi who lives and flourishes in the shaded space formed by the
> intersection of crime and politics, was attacked with a sword by some BJP workers and
> the rumor spread that he had died. Muslim mobs came out into the alleys and streets of
> the walled city, to be followed by Hindu mobs in their areas of strength, and the 1990
> riot was on. It was to last for ten weeks, claim more than three hundred lives and thou-
> sands of wounded. (Kakar 1996, 51)

As his remarkable *Colors of Violence* unfolds, Sudhir Kakar seeks explanations for Hyderabad's 1990 violence by reporting discussions with some of the principals (including Majid Khan, still very much alive), reflecting on the identities involved, and reconstructing the psychological orientations that facilitate lethal violence. He establishes the deep grounding of ostensibly spontaneous intercommunal violence in everyday social relations and in the organization of such groups as the Hindu wrestlers-thugs-activists mobilized by local leaders, including Majid Khan.

Kakar does not, however, present his work as popular history or organizational analysis. On the contrary. Kakar, a professional psychoanalyst, deliberately sets his "primordialist" account of Hindu-Muslim conflict against the "instrumentalist" ac-counts he rightly sees as predominating in current social scientific explanations of ethnic and religious conflict. "There are many social scientists and political ana-lysts," he declares,

> who would locate the enhancements of ethnicity (cultural identity in my terms) in a par-
> ticular group not in social-psychological processes but in the competition between elites
> for political power and economic resources. In fact, this has been the dominant explana-
> tion for the occurrence of Hindu-Muslim riots. . . . Cultural identity according to this
> view is not a fixed or given dimension of communities but a variable one which takes
> form in the process of political mobilization by the elite, a mobilization which arises from
> the broader political and economic environment. (Kakar 1996, 149–150)

At length and through finely crafted vignettes, Kakar makes his case against such instrumental interpretations of cultural identity and his case for shared forms of consciousness based on common experience, reinforced by hostile interaction, and mediated by deep psychological mechanisms. He commits himself to phenomenological reductionism. That is his version of "primordialism."

Instead of choosing between starkly opposed instrumentalist and primordialist accounts, however, students of South Asia's Hindu-Muslim conflicts, of ethnic mobilization, of nationalism, indeed of contentious politics in general can adopt a third alternative: They can recognize the conversational character of contention. They can examine such a conversation's location in continuously negotiated interchanges among specific interlocutors, its constraint and mediation by historically accumulated understandings concerning identities and relations of the parties, its incessant modification of those identities and relations, hence its crucial causal contribution to interactions that instrumentalists explain on the basis of individual or collective interests and primordialists explain on the basis of deeply grounded individual or collective sentiments.

Sudhir Kakar shares with many canny observers a tendency favored by conversational convention: a propensity to shift from shrewd interactional observation into individualistic theories about what he has observed. That propensity extends to observations of his own observation processes. Sahba, his collaborator in many interviews, was a Muslim woman. "The Muslim *pehlwans* [strong men]," Kakar notes,

> had been open with Sahba but understandably guarded when I was also present. With Sahba they could express their bitterness and contempt for Hindus, show their pride in their role in the protection of the community from the Hindu enemy. In my presence, they became less Muslim and more inclined to express universal humanist sentiments. For instance, there was pious talk, not exactly reassuring, that if I were cut my blood would be exactly the same color as theirs. By the end of the interviews, though, all the *pehlwans* were perceptibly warmer. I like to believe that this opening up was because they sensed my genuine interest in them as persons rather than being due to any typical "shrink" "hmms," phrases, or inflections. I suspect, though, that their different—although, for my purposes, highly complementary—psychic agendas when talking to Sahba and to me were dictated by shifts in their own sense of identity. In other words, with Sahba, a Muslim, their self-representation was more in terms of a shared social identity. With me, a Hindu, once they felt reassured that the situation did not contain any threat, personal identity became more salient, influencing their self-representations accordingly. (Kakar 1996, 76–77)

Kakar is describing a process in which people's deployment of identities shifts as a function of their conversation partners and modifies as a consequence of conversation itself. Similarly, Kakar's vivid descriptions of interviews and events alike teem with interactions among participants in the course of which interpersonal negotiation transforms expressed identities and behavior attached to them. His subtle observations belie the individualized psychic gloss he gives them.

My point is not to carp at a brilliant analyst's logical inconsistencies but to underscore the conversational character of political contention. If we regard conversation as continuously negotiated communication and contention as mutual claim making that bears significantly on the parties' interests—which is how I propose we understand the two terms for present purposes—then the two social phenomena overlap extensively. They overlap in the zone we might call contentious conversation. Conversation is contentious to the extent that it embodies mutual and contradictory claims, claims that, if realized, would significantly alter the longer-term behavior of at least one participant.

Contentious conversation certainly activates visceral emotions, neurally processed cognitions, and individual anatomical performances. It also operates within limits set by historically formed conventions, with regard to collectively constituted interests, and in response to stimuli from leaders or bystanders. But it proceeds within a substantial, causally coherent realm we cannot explain away by referring either to individual psyches or to group interests. Contentious conversation follows its own causal logic.

Beth Roy's subtle study of ostensibly communal conflict of 1954 in a Pakistani village (Bangladeshi by the time she arrived there in the 1980s) identifies the significance of that causal logic. She shows how a local scuffle among farmers working adjacent fields escalated into a full-scale alignment of self-identified Hindus against self-identified Muslims. At the start, Golam Fakir (categorically Muslim) and Kumar Tarkhania (categorically Hindu) interacted as disputants over the fact that Fakir's untethered cow had eaten Tarkhania's lentils. The series of confrontations did not begin as communal mobilization, but it approximated increasingly to classic models of Hindu/Muslim strife as it grew in geographic scope and mounted the national administrative hierarchy.

In addition to its empathetic description and astute detective work, Roy's study fascinates by its patient unpacking of complexities in actors, actions, and identities. *Some Trouble with Cows* (the title echoes one of the first stories about the 1954 conflicts Roy collected) centers on questions of identity:

> When I consider stories of village communalism, I want to know how people saw their world, how they placed their own desires within it, and how their sense of political possibility was influenced by distant winds of change. It has become common to assert that the most intimate domestic behaviors are in fact socially constructed. Collective experience is translated into psychological reality through a web of ideas internalized as invisible assumptions about the world. To unravel the psychological realities of collective behavior, I believe we must look to shared areas of understanding and social location. For instance, group actions are formulated from the experience of identity, that is, the complex construction of an individual's location in the community and her ties with others. Similarly, the will to action is born of detailed ideologies that often are experienced as common sense or unexamined assumptions about rights and powers. (Roy 1994, 3)

In this introductory passage and throughout her superb reconstruction of old conflicts Roy exhibits ambivalence between two points of view, sometimes treating identity and action as individual mental realities multiplied, sometimes locating identity and action in social relations: "an individual's location in the community and her ties with others." She thereby pinpoints a major difficulty in contemporary studies of contentious politics (see Cerulo 1997, 393–394). Analysts of social construction have called attention to the difficulty, but have failed to resolve it.

Here is the difficulty: Humans live in flesh-and-blood bodies; accumulate traces of experiences in their nervous systems; organize current encounters with the world as cognitions, emotions, and intentional actions; tell stories about themselves in which they acted deliberately and efficaciously or were blocked from doing so by uncontrolled emotion, weakness, malevolent others, bad luck, or recalcitrant nature. They tell similar stories about other people. Humans come to believe in a world full of continuous, neatly bounded, self-propelling individuals whose intentions interact with accidents and natural limits to produce all of social life. In many versions, those "natural limits" feature norms, values, and scripts inculcated and enforced by powerful others—but then internalized by self-propelling individuals. Accounts in this vein adopt phenomenological reductionism. They reduce social life to states of individual consciousness.

Closely observed, however, the same humans turn out to be interacting repeatedly with others, renegotiating who they are, adjusting the boundaries they occupy, modifying their actions in rapid response to other people's reactions, selecting among and altering available scripts, improvising new forms of joint action, speaking sentences no one has ever uttered before, yet responding predictably to their locations within webs of social relations they themselves cannot map in detail. They tell stories about themselves and others that facilitate their social interaction rather than laying out verifiable facts about individual lives. They actually live in deeply relational worlds. If social construction occurs, it happens socially, not in isolated recesses of individual minds.

The problem becomes acute in descriptions and explanations of contentious politics. Political actors typically give individualized accounts of participation in contention, although the "individuals" to which they attribute bounded, unified, continuous self-propulsion are often collective actors such as communities, classes, armies, firms, unions, interest groups, or social movements. They attach moral evaluations and responsibilities to the individuals involved, praising or condemning them for their actions, grading their announced identities from unacceptable (e.g., mob) to laudable (e.g., martyrs). Accordingly, strenuous effort in contentious politics goes into contested representations of crucial actors as worthy or unworthy, unified or fragmented, large or small, committed or uncommitted, powerful or weak, well connected or isolated, durable or evanescent, reasonable or irrational, greedy or generous.

Meticulous observation of that same effort, however, eventually tells even a naïve observer what almost every combat officer, union leader, or political organizer acknowledges in private: that both public representations of political identities and other forms of participation in struggle proceed through intense coordination;

contingent improvisation; tactical maneuvering; responses to signals from other participants; on-the-spot reinterpretations of what is possible, desirable, or efficacious; and strings of unexpected outcomes inciting new improvisations. Interactions among actors with shifting boundaries, internal structures, and identities turn out to permeate what in retrospect or in distant perspective analysts call actor-driven wars, strikes, rebellions, electoral campaigns, or social movements. Hence the difficulty of reconciling individualistic images with interactive realities.

South Asia's Hindu–Muslim conflicts present that difficulty acutely. As Sudhir Kakar, Beth Roy, and many other recent students of South Asia have shown, analysts have readily available single-actor characterizations of Hindus in general, of Muslims in general, and therefore of their interaction as the inevitable consequence of contact between incompatible mentalities. But relations among persons who belong to the categories "Hindu" and "Muslim" take a wide range of forms, from avoidance to cohabitation. They frequently take place without reference to religious affiliation.

As Hyderabad's bloody contention of 1990 illustrates, furthermore, many confrontations that begin under other definitions eventually activate and receive coding as conventional expressions of communal hostility. We should notice the analogy to family disputes in which available epithets, memories, and lines of fractionation only enter the struggle as it escalates or as third parties enter the fray. Such phenomena provide empirical justification for the "instrumentalist" accounts of communal conflicts that Sudhir Kakar rightly challenges as sole explanations of the life-threatening interactions he studies. The effective response to instrumental reductionism, however, consists not of turning to phenomenological reductionism but of recognizing the conversational dynamics of such disputes.

The Hindu–Muslim conversation engages multiple interlocutors in varied settings. It therefore takes place in many modes. Majid Khan's interchanges with his counterparts who mobilize their own wrestlers–thugs–activists on behalf of Hindu causes differ greatly from the initial angry conversation between Golam Fakir and Kumar Tarkhania in the Panipur of 1954, which differ in turn from exchanges between high-caste Panipur resident Mr. Ghosh and the Muslim officials who came to Panipur when the local conflict started drawing in outsiders. More important, Fakhir and Tarkhania did not initially respond to each other as representatives of competing categories, but as multiply linked poor farmers within the same community. Only as their conflict escalated did they fall into ranks of self-identified Muslims on one side, self-identified Hindus on the other. Every pair of interlocutors has its own idioms and its own history, both of which frame their conversation. Which idioms they actually deploy and which histories they invoke, furthermore, varies with who else is participating. Because of learning and of constraint by relations to third parties, to be sure, conversations within similar and connected pairs share many properties. Yet, we must understand that contentious conversation proceeds through incessant improvisation within limits set by the previous histories and relations of particular interlocutors.

The conversational analogy applies to a wide range of political contention. We could pursue it across other instances of ethnic and religious conflict, expressions of nationalism, electoral campaigns, revolutions, parliamentary debates, industrial conflict, and much more. Let us, however, move the discussion onto familiar ground. In his analysis of thousands of demonstrations in Marseille, Nantes, Paris, and other parts of France between 1979 and 1993, Olivier Fillieule identifies the stylized but incessant interchanges that occur among demonstrators, spectators, police, officials, and other persons involved in any demonstration. Although observers, reporters, analysts, and critics often reduce such events to attitudes and actions of the persons who occupy the street with banners, chants, and other dramatizations of their demands, detailed accounts drawn from such sources as police blotters reveal continuous streams of mutual deliberations, taunts, threats, attacks, retreats, delegations, agreements, and much more—usually reported from a single viewpoint, but always reflecting participation in communicative interchange.

Consider the 1986 testimony of an experienced commander of riot police. When asked what would happen if he received contradictory orders from the local police commissioner and his own unit's superiors, he replied that it was unlikely, but added:

> At a moment like that I would probably decide for myself, as I actually once did for our buses. When we were setting ourselves up, the commissioner of the 16th [Parisian] arrondissement asked us, contrary to my view, to reinforce the street barriers with our vehicles. When I saw that the demonstrators were trying to set the barricades on fire, on my own initiative I had the vehicles moved to the middle of the bridge; my buses retreated. The other vehicles of the Parisian police that didn't retreat got burned. (Fillieule 1997, 257)

Torching buses and moving them back obviously constitutes a crude sort of dialogue. So do deploying shields against stone throwers, wading into a crowd with flailing clubs, or even receiving delegations from demonstrators at a minister's office. Yet, the dialogue involved is real and consequential. It engages two parties, or more. How one party responds to another affects what happens next. The conversation places unceasing improvisation within strongly defined conventions that mark the ongoing interchange as a demonstration rather than, say, a strike, a public meeting, an election rally, routine lobbying, or a coup d'état.

As with all conversation, contentious conversation has a delightfully paradoxical property: improvisation within constraints that produce order. Demonstrators, counterdemonstrators, police, authorities, and other participants in demonstrations improvise incessantly, jockeying for surprise, effect, and strategic advantage. If they simply repeated the routines they had followed during a previous encounter, they would resemble people who utter bromides; they would cede all strategic advantage to their partners and come off as dull automata. Yet, as compared with all the actions and interactions of which they are capable, they concentrate their efforts within a narrow range of symbols, utterances, and interactions. Demonstrators often march in ranks, display banners, shout slogans, and present petitions, but rarely carry machine guns, defecate in the street, strip naked, strangle spectators, sing nursery rhymes, stop to buy the day's groceries, or travel in taxis—except, of course, if they appear together as taxi drivers demanding protection from muggers. If participants in contentious conversation did not adopt recognizable idioms, they would undercut their own efforts to coordinate actions, convey messages, and influence objects of their claims.

As in less contentious forms of conversation, contentious conversation produces order by means of improvisation within constraints. At demonstration's end, marchers go off to their daily affairs, police take down their barricades, street cleaners sweep up debris, merchants unshutter their shops, reporters file their stories, officials deliberate on how, if at all, they will respond to the day's events, and politicians chat about what it all means for their causes. In the meantime, participants have broadcast messages to their various audiences: The regime is rotten, we deserve better treatment, proposal X is an abomination, everyone should adopt proposal Y, or something else along these lines. Members of audiences, furthermore, have started to form judgments about how effectively participants performed and how credible were their contentious claims.

We can capture the theatrical side of contention by speaking of *contentious repertoires* (Tarrow 1998, ch. 2; Traugott 1995). Any pair of interlocutors has available to it a limited number of previously created performances within which the people involved can make claims. That array of performances constitutes their repertoire. Seen from a distance, the same citizen–official pair that figures in demonstrations chiefly as claimant and object of claims also has available as claim-making vehicles petitions, elections, public meetings, lobbying delegations, bureaucratic letters, and other well-established performances; those vehicles form the big clumps within their repertoire. Seen from closer at hand, the demonstration itself displays the finer grain of deploying barricades, shouting slogans, making speeches from balconies, struggling for control of public spaces, and a dozen other variable elements.

Just as a company of actors deploys both a set of Molière dramas and a hardearned stock of two-line jokes, sword battles, pratfalls, gestures, embraces, double takes, and curtain calls, both the big claim-making routines and their fine, variable elements belong to their participants' contentious repertoire. The elements, after all, frequently recur from one kind of contentious performance to another, as when people voice the same slogans in demonstrations, pamphlets, petitions, and public meetings.

Like any other sorts of conversational forms, contentious repertoires embody history and culture. Participants and observers draw on previous experiences, incorporate readily available symbols, make selective references to shared memories, strategize as a function of what happened last time, notice the impact (if any) of their improvisations, compare notes after the fact. Repertoires matter to the course and outcome of contention for several reasons:

First, they incorporate scripts participants know to be performable, in which they know the parts and collaborative routines required, and of whose requisites and possible outcomes they share at least some awareness; all these features facilitate mobilization of participants for a new performance.

Second, they draw meaning and effectiveness in part from their connection with previous iterations of the same performances—our opponents' recent meetings or our own, the received history (however mythical) of previous demonstrations, and so on.

Third, they eliminate from consideration, and often from consciousness, a vast range of claim-making performances of which participants are technically capable, indeed may even undertake in other circumstances; thus, demonstrators besieging their city hall leave behind the prayers, confessions, rituals, and offerings by which they regularly ask their gods for favors elsewhere.

Finally, participants in contentious politics learn to grade, value, and contest the quality of performances, disputing how many people actually took part in a demonstration, arguing about how well the message got across, second-guessing the plans and strategies of the police, the mayor, or local leaders.

Struggle over contentious conversation therefore continues after the utterances in question cease. As Paul Brass puts it:

> The struggle among competing groups in society to capture the meaning of a violent incident or a riot, that is, for the right to *represent* it properly is far from a merely verbal game. It is also a struggle over resources and policy. If it is accepted that Russians attack Jews because Jews exploit them and because Jews set themselves apart, then measures need to be taken to prevent "Jewish exploitation" and to either promote their assimilation or separate them completely from contact with Russians by keeping them in the Pale of Settlement. Conversely, if Black ghetto violence is interpreted as justified rage against discrimination in white society, then policies and resources must be devoted to eliminating discrimination. If a riot is seen to arise out of justified mass resentment against a minority's exploitation of the majority or out of its alleged disloyalty to or betrayal of the country as in the case of Muslims in India, then measures to curb the minority's rights or demands and to put its members in their place will be the preferred response. Alternatively, if Hindu-Muslim riots are seen as a consequence of provocation of a harassed minority by militant Hindu nationalists, then measures to protect the minority and constrain militant Hindu groups are in order. (Brass 1996, 5)

Just as on the small scale we leave a contentious conversation asking, "What did they mean? Did we make our point? What's going to happen next?" a larger-scale confrontation's outcome stimulates acts of collective interpretation. The repertoire of performances activated in such a confrontation channels possibilities for subsequent interpretation.

In the BJP's approach to Ayodhya, we saw contentious repertoires in full action. The chariot pilgrimage, the ostentatious building of temples on sacred sites, the bloody encounter between demonstrators and baton-wielding police all form re-current performances of India's contemporary contentious conversation. The high stakes of such performances give us a salutary reminder not to take our theatrical metaphor as an indication of artificiality or triviality. In Ayodhya, Hyderabad, and elsewhere, these are deadly serious conversations.

Among other things, political identities are at stake. To continue with theatrical metaphors, claimmakers are acting out answers to the question "Who are you?" When contentious conversation arises in the course of routine social life, the an-swers are often obvious; we are whoever we were before the contention began, employees of a given company, purchasers in a weekly market, worshippers at a shrine, public officials doing public business, police officers patrolling their beats. Much of the time, however, identities remain unclear until participants dramatize them. All people have multiple identities at their disposal, each one attached to a somewhat different set of social relations: neighbor, spouse, farmer, customer, ten-ant, schoolmate, lover, or citizen. Some available identities appear in public only in-termittently, as is the case with many varieties of party affiliation, association mem-bership, and adhesion to social movements. In these circumstances, participants in contentious conversation regularly make a point of the capacities in which they are interacting, of the identities they are activating.

As in ordinary conversation, some performances actually center on the assertion of identities rather than the making of specific claims. One side says, "Recognize us as significant actors of a certain kind," while the other side accepts or contests that assertion of identity. Social movement activists often initiate performances whose central message declares that the activists and/or the constituency they claim to represent are WUNC: worthy, united, numerous, and committed. Demon-stration of worthiness varies by cultural setting, but often includes evidence of decorous self-control and standing in the community. Unity calls for moving in time, speaking together, broadcasting the same message, and collaborating in the same actions—even when the occasion calls for displaying how wide a range of community members support a given program. Numbers matter greatly, as fre-quent disputes among activists, observers, rivals, and police over how many people actually participated in an action indicate. Claims of numbers, however, may also refer to supporters as indicated by association memberships, financial contribu-tions, opinion polls, electoral results, or other quantitative signs. Commitment, fi-nally, comes across in evidence that participants are willing to bear costs and face risks on behalf of their common cause; the costs and risks can vary from laying down your life to coming from far away to join a collective action.

If any of the elements—worthiness, unity, numbers, and commitment—visibly falls to zero, a social movement loses credibility. Above the zero threshold, however, a high value on one element compensates a low value on another: people who show strong signs of commitment (for example, by taking life-threatening risks) need not be so numerous as those who merely show up for a rally. The notable presence of worthiness in the form of priests, dignitaries, prizewinners, and victims can easily make up for a certain disunity of voiced aims among other participants. The relative weight of worthiness, unity, numbers, and commitment defines rather different kinds of movements.

What's going on? Social movements link two complementary activities: assertions of identity and statements of demands. The two activities' relative salience varies from one phase of social movement activity to another as well as from one kind of social movement to another. As compared with strikes, revolutions, coups d'état, and many other forms of contentious politics, nevertheless, social movements stand out for their emphasis on identity assertion. They emphasize public assertion of identities whose possessors are worthy, unified, numerous, and committed. They do so because social movements grew up in the nineteenth century as means by which people currently excluded from political power could band together and claim that powerholders should attend to their interests, or the interests they represented.

Otherwise, the actions of social movement participants signaled, they had the capacity and will to disrupt and alter routine political life. Recognition of their claimed identities as wronged workers, dispossessed peasants, or persecuted religious minorities constituted them as political actors, but also drew them into bargaining collectively with existing holders of power. That stress on identity assertion persists in social movements, especially in their earlier stages, to the present day. Social movements continue to assert the right to respect and to a political voice for indigenous peoples, gays, conservative Christians, unborn children, laboratory animals, and even trees—the latter three categories through the mediation of their self-designated protectors.

Identity assertion in social movements has clear counterparts in everyday conversation. Effective conversation establishes in whose names and in what capacities the parties are speaking: Are we exchanging news as friends, neighbors, or business associates? Do I recognize you as a certified expert on our topic and myself as a grateful member of your lay audience? Are you speaking for your political constituency or simply on your own? Are we strangers on a train? The universal requirement for establishment of identities does not preclude error, dissimulation, contestation, or double entendre concerning the relationship among the parties. A friend can turn out to be a spy, while a sterile conversation for public consumption can carry erotic, subversive, or satirical overtones that bespeak a second relationship among the interlocutors. Conversation still proceeds on the basis of defined identities and often centers on establishing just what those identities are.

Whether contentious or otherwise, conversational conventions and the very course of conversation exert significant influence over their participants' behavior. Established identities and their associated social relations, for example, always make a difference to the course of interaction. In the extreme case of Hindu-Muslim massacres, Sudhir Kakar shows that neighbors of one faith often warned members of the other religious category of a coming attack, that in the heat of bloodshed Muslim households sometimes hid Hindus or vice versa, and that bands of killers ordinarily avoided bloodletting within their own neighborhoods; reduction of other people to nothing but their broadest public identities facilitated murder, while the presence of multiple ties and identities inhibited it. In the extreme reduction, extermination squads sorted potential victims by clothing or, for males, the condition of their penises, circumcision signaling Muslim identity, its absence Hindu identity.

Short of such an extreme, conversationally established identities always shape social interaction, including political contention. In Panipur, only as the struggle initiated by a cow's eating lentils came to be redefined as aligning Muslims in general against Hindus in general did armed combat among organized forces emerge as the mode of interaction. After the lethal confrontation of 1954, furthermore, most conflict took place on a smaller scale, under different auspices, with the blessing of a widely shared story about the ability of Panipur's diverse residents to live in harmony. Stories that people create in the course of contentious conversation themselves affect subsequent social interaction, both because they filter collective memory and because they build in commitments to behave consistently with those stories.

Let me state the point more strongly. Conversation in general shapes social life by altering individual and collective understandings, by creating and transforming social ties, by generating cultural materials that are then available for subsequent social interchange, and by establishing, obliterating, or shifting commitments on the part of participants. The same is true of contentious conversation, for the same reasons. In both noncontentious and contentious conversation, these processes work both through words and through a wide variety of nonverbal interchanges—not only gestures, body language, and deployment of physical objects, but also displays of symbols, spatial shifts, altered relations to physical settings, and interventions of third parties.

The crucial processes of contentious politics are not instrumental in the sense of proceeding directly from the self-centered competition of elites for political power and economic resources. They are not primordial in the sense of expressing deeply grounded individual phenomenology. They are conversational in the sense of proceeding through historically situated, culturally constrained, negotiated, consequential interchanges among multiple parties. Whatever else it requires, the explanation of political contention demands that analysts take mere speech acts and their nonverbal equivalents seriously.

10

Where Do Rights Come From?

Where do rights come from? We could ground this grand question in analytic philosophy à la Rawls, metaphysics à la Rousseau, or rational action à la Riker. I want instead to ground it in European political history. In this, I take my lead from Barrington Moore's *Social Origins of Dictatorship and Democracy* (1966), which repeatedly treats rights as historical products, outcomes of struggle. In particular, *Social Origins* argues that the creation of democracy—checking of arbitrary rulers, establishment of just, rational political rules, and influence of the "underlying population" in the making of such rules—entailed the making of rights. In that book, Moore grounded the crucial rights in Western European feudalism. "For our purposes," he argued,

> the most important aspect was the growth of the notion of the immunity of certain groups and persons from the power of the ruler, along with the conception of the right of resistance to unjust authority. Together with the conception of contract as a mutual engagement freely undertaken by free persons, derived from the feudal relation of vassalage, this complex of ideas and practices constitutes a crucial legacy from European medieval society to modern Western conceptions of a free society. (Moore 1966, 414)

Despite this passage's whiff of idealism, Moore's comparative history portrays those crucial rights as coming to fruition by means of revolution and class struggle;

An earlier version of this chapter appeared as "Where Do Rights Come From?" in Theda Skocpol, ed., *Democracy, Revolution, and History.* Copyright © 1998 by Cornell University. Used by permission of the publisher, Cornell University Press. The Vilhelm Aubert Memorial Symposium, University of Oslo, August 1990, heard a premature version of the paper and circulated that version slightly modified as a working paper in Lars Mjøset, ed., *Contributions to the Comparative Study of Development,* Oslo: Institute for Social Research, 1992.

he gave his opening chapter, after all, the title "England and the Contributions of Violence to Gradualism." My argument will diverge from Moore's in three directions: doubting the centrality of feudalism, downgrading the relative importance of ideas, and considering the crucial events to have occurred after the general dissolution of feudalism. It will nevertheless agree with Moore in two fundamental ways: by emphasizing resistance and struggle, by grounding rights in the specific histories of different European regions.

Grounded historically, the question about origins of rights becomes a naturalistic one: How have European people acquired enforceable claims on the states to which they were subject? More narrowly, how have rights of citizenship come into being? How did authorities come to owe goods, services, and protections to people merely on the ground of their belonging to a category, the category of people in the political community attached to a state? How did that political community expand to include most people, or at least most households, in the population at large?

Even more surprising, how did ordinary people get the power to enforce such weighty obligations? Vying in vain in a national arena, did Europeans instead wrest rights from local authorities and then see them eventually extended to a national scale? Or did benevolent despots first grant them to a small number of companions, and then, as enlightenment spread among rulers and ruled, extend them gradually to the rest of the population? Or did they emerge from struggle at a national scale?

My answer hews to the third alternative: struggle at a national scale. Rights, in this formulation, resemble what Amartya Sen calls entitlements: enforceable claims on the delivery of goods, services, or protections by specific others (Sen 1981). Rights exist when one party can effectively insist that another deliver goods, services, or protections, and third parties will act to reinforce (or at least not to hinder) their delivery. Such entitlements become *citizenship* rights when the object of claims is a state or its agent and the successful claimant qualifies by simple membership in a broad category of persons subject to the state's jurisdiction. I think that citizenship rights came into being because relatively organized members of the general population bargained with state authorities for several centuries, bargained first over the means of war, then over enforceable claims that would serve their interests outside of the area of war; bargaining enlarged the obligations of states to their citizens. The leverage broadened the range of enforceable claims citizens could make on states even more than it expanded the population who held rights of citizenship.

This answer emerges from the confluence of work on state transformation and work on collective action, two largely separate streams that, once joined, refresh our understanding. They clarify the paradoxical processes by which greatly unequal struggles produced mutually recognized rights: rights of citizens and groups of citizens with respect to states, rights of state officials (and even of states as corporate entities) with respect to citizens. From previous work on state transformation comes recognition of the extractive, repressive relationship of states to subject populations through most of history and wonder that they should ever concede extensive citizens' claims. From previous work on collective action comes a twofold model of struggle:

1. Struggle over demands made by states on their subjects, by subjects on states, or by subjects on each other
2. Struggle by specific groups of subjects to enter the polity (the set of persons and groups having routine, enforceable claims on the state), to help others enter the polity, to defend certain polity memberships, or to exclude others from the polity

In caricature, the argument says that rights of citizenship formed as the bargains struck in the course of both sorts of struggle, first chiefly in defense against invasive state demands for the means of war, later in the pursuit of a much wider range of collective action and state intervention.

This way of explaining rights is at once empiricist, speculative, and cynical. It is empiricist because it infers regularities from diverse experiences of Europeans over the last thousand years of state formation and transformation. It is speculative because no one, including me, has assembled the mass of comparative evidence its definitive verification or falsification requires. It is cynical because it assumes that whatever enforceable claims on states people acquired, however wrong they may now appear to be, constituted rights. It does not call "rights" only obligations of which I personally approve. In self-righteous retrospect, I do not like the legal support Prussian Junkers received from their state in making serfs out of free peasants, but for me the Junkers' enforceable claim to state assistance in apprehending rebels and runaways qualified as rights.

The Junker right to discipline rebels and runaways did not, however, constitute a right of citizenship. Citizenship rights belong in principle (if not always in practice) to everyone who qualifies as a full-fledged member of a given state; membership in the category suffices to qualify a person for the enforceable claims. These days citizens of European states typically have rights to vote in national and local elections, to engage in a wide range of collective action outside of elections, to receive a considerable number of governmental benefits and services, to move freely within the frontiers of their states, and even to receive the protection of their states when they travel or reside outside their frontiers; citizens can only lose these rights through a formal process of degradation, such as a criminal sentence or commitment to a psychiatric hospital; with respect to the same states, otherwise identical noncitizen neighbors do not generally share these rights.

EXPANSION OF RIGHTS, CREATION OF CITIZENSHIP

T. H. Marshall's classic formulation distinguished three elements of citizenship: civil, political, and social (see Barbalet 1988; Somers 1993; Turner 1990, 1993).

Civil rights comprised those protecting individual freedom, political rights those guaranteeing participation in the exercise of political power, and social rights those providing access to material and cultural satisfactions (Marshall 1965, 78). Thinking of England, Marshall assigned the definitive acquisition of civil rights to the eighteenth century, of political rights to the nineteenth, and of social to the twentieth. By the 1830s, he argued, "the civil rights attached to the status of freedom had already acquired sufficient substance to justify us in speaking of a general status of citizenship" (Marshall 1965, 78). In each case, Marshall conceived of the rights' extension as the almost–Hegelian realization of a principle in history. Characteristic common sense and fair play, it is true, implemented the English version of the Geist.

Although at times he recognized that labor fought capital and the state for its social rights, Marshall explicitly rejected my line of argument: "Rights are not," he declared, "a proper matter for bargaining" (Marshall 1965, 122). Despite recognizing that civil rights (protections of individual freedom) provided the frame for the other two, he did not see how the struggle for one in turn prepared claimants to struggle for the next. No doubt he resisted that line of argument because in 1946, when he wrote, it would have made the current struggle for social rights a matter of *rapport des forces* when he sought to prepare his audience for intervention in the order of social classes as a matter of unavoidable principle. However that may be, his otherwise perceptive analysis suffered acutely from historical foreshortening. We can place it in more adequate perspective by attempting to place the gain and loss of rights more firmly into history than Marshall did.

Citizens of European states now enjoy ipso facto rights to education, housing, health care, income, and a wide variety of political participation. Some resident noncitizens also have legal access to many of these benefits, but the enforceability of their claims remains limited and contested. If France grants the local vote to *ressortissants* of other states, the distinction will start to blur. When distinctions of this sort disappear, we have two linguistic choices: We can say that the rights attached to citizenship have diminished, or we can say that states have begun to equate citizenship with authorized long-term residence. In the case of Europe, a third choice may also apply: that citizenship rights have devolved to the European Union. The test will come with the treatment of nationals from outside the Union. In the meantime, citizenship makes a significant difference to the claims on a state any individual can enforce.

As the European Union's scope expands, one of the thorniest issues its members face grows on precisely that flowering bush: To what extent, in what ways, and with what sort of enforcement will citizenship rights become vested in the Union as a whole rather than in any particular state? To what extent will they become uniform and transferable among states? Instead of rebels and runaways, what about refugees? If one European state recognizes a set of people as political refugees who have high priority for citizenship, must all other members of the Union recognize those rights? Will the right of a newly unemployed worker to income, job placement, and retraining apply in the state to which he has migrated? Who will pay the benefits? When rights vary from state to state, will the lowest common denominator prevail throughout Europe? The average? The highest value anywhere? Similar questions face the rebuilders of political life in Latin America and Eastern Europe, as the decline of authoritarian regimes brings a new era of constitution making. The question of citizenship has become newly salient.

It has, in fact, remained prominent in Europe for about three hundred years, since the time when larger European states began building big standing armies drawn largely from their own populations—armies (and, for that matter, often navies as well) supported by regular taxation and state-funded debt. To be sure, long before the seventeenth-century expatriate European merchants formed "nations" in metropolises such as Constantinople and Rome, gaining a measure of self-government and of protection from their home states in return for policing their own members, assuring their own food supplies in times of subsistence crisis, and bearing negotiated shares of citywide expenses. No doubt the generalization of resident diplomatic missions in later fifteenth-century Europe entailed a certain mutual recognition of citizenship. For the burghers of city-states such as Florence and federations of city-states such as the Dutch Republic, membership in the financial elites and political councils of their own cities also qualified them for claims on their states long before the seventeenth century; in that limited sense, as Max Weber half-understood, Bürgerschaft anticipated citizenship.

Most European states and their subjects, however, did not begin bargaining out the rights and obligations of citizenship on a relatively large scale until the seventeenth and eighteenth centuries. Before then, unwritten constitutions frequently bound rulers to members of their ruling classes, but not to the ordinary population. Then rulers turned away from the episodic use of militias and mercenary forces for warfare, trying instead to staff standing armies from their own populations and to force the civilians in their own populations to pay for the armies routinely and well. Large, populous states thus gained the advantage over small, rich states, as a Venice or a Dutch Republic lost the ability simply to rent an army of poor foreigners and thereby to vanquish its neighbors.

FROM INDIRECT TO DIRECT RULE

That effort raised a critical problem: the transition from indirect to direct rule. Until the creation of mass national armies, all larger European states ruled indirectly, counting on the co-optation of various sorts of magnates who acted for the state and guaranteed the delivery of resources to it, but who also retained very large autonomy within their own reserved zones. Even France, that Tocquevillian model of centralization, relied heavily on hereditary governors, provincial Estates, and privileged municipalities until Richelieu (pressed for funds to join the widening European wars of the 1620s) improvised intendants to bypass stubborn regional magnates. Only

Mazarin and Colbert regularized intendants into direct and more or less subordinated regional executors of royal will. Even then the intendants spent much of their time negotiating with Estates, parlements, military governors, and other regional powerholders who had the power to block the crown's demands and sometimes to incite massive resistance against royal policy.

The dilemma had sharp horns: Relying on co-opted powerholders guaranteed a certain level of compliance so long as the crown limited its demands and respected the powerholders' privileges, but it reinforced the central authority's chief domestic rivals and most dangerous enemies; the installation of direct, centralized rule, however, was a costly, risky, time-consuming operation that often exploded in rebellion.

The expansion of armed forces impelled high officials of European states to undertake the cost, the risk, and the effort. In large states such as Prussia and Russia, reliance on powerful, partly autonomous intermediaries set a severe limit on the portion of national resources to which the central state could gain access, even if up to that limit it made the amassing of resources easier. Two of war's many unfortunate features are that (1) it really is a zero-sum game at best, and a negative-sum game much of the time: If one party wins, another definitely loses, often incurring penalties greater than the putative winner's gains; (2) within the limits imposed by declining efficacy as a function of the time and space separating antagonists, the party with the most effective armed force sets the terms; a state having small, very efficient armed forces sometimes loses wars with a state having large, inefficient armed forces and usually loses to a state having large, fairly efficient armed forces. As a consequence of these principles, the most effectively armed European states set the military terms for all the rest.

For several centuries before about 1750, the most effectively armed European states were those that could rent the most mercenary troops. Mercenaries—drawn especially from militarized and land-poor peasant regions such as Ireland, Scotland, Switzerland, Hesse, and Croatia—reached their European heyday in the sixteenth and seventeenth centuries, then began to lose ground in the eighteenth century, and became insignificant with the Napoleonic Wars. Mercenaries had the great advantage of being available rapidly for whoever had the necessary funds or credit. But they had dramatic disadvantages: They were expensive, unruly, unreliable if unpaid, and a great nuisance if not deported once a war had ended; unemployed mercenaries often became bandits, pirates, or the equivalent on a larger scale: warlords.

The old European alternatives to nationally recruited mercenaries had been urban militias, private armies of great lords, and various sorts of feudal levies; the three overlapped. From the perspective of rulers, these forces had the advantages of being cheap and disposable. But they were only available in limited numbers, for limited terms, in service whose conditions themselves generally had well-specified limits; what is more, their leaders and patrons had minds, interests, and ambitions of their own. Only the invention of mass national armies recruited directly from the subject population by the state and operated under control of the state's own officers overcame the clear disadvantages of mercenaries and of the older levies.

The creation of a large, durable national army recruited from the domestic population, however, posed one of those problems of consent, beloved of political philosophers. Supporting any army required large resources continuously over long periods: food, uniforms, weapons, transport, wages, and more. In the seventeenth century most states that hired mercenaries borrowed money from local capitalists in the short run, bought the requisites on well-organized markets in which state functionaries and capitalists collaborated, then taxed the general population in various ways to repay their capitalist creditors. A national army added the problem of soldiers, workers withdrawn from the households that would otherwise rely on them for support in present and future, workers who would now disappear from their households for years with the distinct possibility of returning useless or not at all and of remitting no income in the meantime. Entrepreneurs who knew how to deliver freely hired mercenaries did not necessarily know how to pry unwilling recruits from reluctant households. The enlarged numbers and continuity, furthermore, drove substantial increases in taxation at the same time.

How to gain consent? All army-building states turned to some combination of reliance on co-opted entrepreneurs, aggressive recruitment, impressment, and conscription. Even so, they faced widespread resistance to the increased burden of taxation and to the seizure of young men for the military. They bargained. They bargained in different ways: by sending in troops to recruit troops and collect taxes, by negotiating quotas for troops and taxes with the headmen of regions and local communities, by confirming the rights of existing assemblies (Parliament in England, Estates in France, Cortes in Castile, Corts in Catalonia, States General in the Dutch Republic) to legislate contributions to military budgets. Even bloody repression of rebellions typically involved bargaining, since authorities punished a few offenders spectacularly while pardoning others who would now comply with the state's demands, and stated in the rebellion's settlement the grounds and procedures for legitimate future remonstrance. White-hot bargaining forged rights and obligations of citizenship.

Attention! These days "citizenship" brooks few levels and exceptions; an economically unequal but politically egalitarian world abhors the maintenance of formal distinctions among classes of citizens. Old-regime European states took a much more differentiated and pragmatic approach. The partial truth in the old idea (promulgated more effectively by T. H. Marshall and Reinhard Bendix than by anyone else) of citizenship as episodic enlargement of participation in national politics lies precisely there: Nobles and clergy generally acquired the right of direct access to the sovereign long before bourgeois or, even more so, workers and peasants did.

The error lies in conceiving of the process as one of gradual enlightenment rather than continuous struggle, and in imagining that the same sequence of inclusion appeared everywhere that enlightenment spread. The implicit strategy of rulers was to grant national rights to the minimum set of persons that would guarantee the delivery of militarily essential resources to the state and to collaborate with citizens so privileged in exploiting and repressing the rest. Women and male servants, for example, only escaped from that collusion very recently. Indirect rule operated reasonably well with a small number of people having rights of citizenship—so few that in cases of indirect rule the word is more misleading than helpful.

CONTRASTING EXPERIENCES

The shift to direct rule did not immediately eliminate such distinctions. With whom rulers bargained varied according to their strategies for enlarging military force, which in turn depended on the social structures of the regions in which they based their states. Where rulers could co-opt well-established regional powerholders such as landlords who would guarantee a supply of troops and taxes to the state, nobilities and gentries flourished, distinctions actually increased, and citizenship in relation to the national state was slow to expand. Russia and Prussia followed that path, but not to a point that we could reasonably call direct rule, at least not until the twentieth century.

England came closer. There the state relied heavily on its squires and parsons to represent the state at the local level, but it also tolerated, however uneasily, considerable direct representation of parishioners, ratepayers, and freeholders vis-à-vis monarch and Parliament. Other states went even farther in the seventeenth and eighteenth centuries. Where rulers' agents bargained directly for resources with commercially active burghers or village elders, they had little choice but to concede claims on the state to large numbers of people, even if the consequence of those concessions was to reinforce the positions of those local elites within their own communities. Holland and Sweden followed different variants of that path.

In the process of building nationally based military forces and citizenship, indeed, Sweden was precocious. Sweden, poor in funds but rich in peasants, had recruited relatively large armies from its own population during its warlike sixteenth-century expansion; Gustav Vasa (1521–1560) and his successors had only managed to do so through a dramatic series of internal struggles and the steadfast collaboration of their now-Protestant and national clergy. Even Sweden, however, relied heavily on mercenaries during the Thirty Years War. Having discovered the limits of conquest by a small state, Sweden then became a pioneer in the creation of mass national armies.

Charles XI (1672–1697) took back crown lands his predecessors had been selling to pay for mercenaries and distributed much of the land to soldier-peasants who owed national military service in payment for their farms. The clergy and state bureaucrats, who created a system of local surveillance and control that rivaled the Chinese and Japanese systems of their time, became guarantors of state claims and peasant rights. Under that system, Sweden became one of Europe's most militarized states; in 1708, for example, something like 5.5 percent of its entire population was under arms. In the world of 1987 as a whole, about 0.5 percent of the population was in military service; in Sweden itself, the 1987 figure was about 0.8 percent. (By contrast, among the world's most militarized states Israel then had 3.2 percent of its population actively under arms, Syria 3.6 percent, Iraq on the order of 6 percent.) When 5 or 6 percent of a population is committed to military service, enormous burdens result. Sweden created an extraordinary state bureaucracy to distribute the burden.

Despite its deserved reputation as a sea power, the Dutch Republic built substantial armies in the seventeenth century, and maintained about 5.3 percent of its population under arms in 1700. Holland and its neighbors built their great seventeenth-century military force by means of a peculiar federal state in which mercantile municipalities held decisive power and the *stadhouder*, when he wielded power at all, did so by means of patronage and canny bargaining among the cities. Indeed, *stadhouders* actually received their appointments from individual provinces (which means in effect from the provinces' leading cities); provinces did not all necessarily name the same *stadhouder* and sometimes named none at all. On the whole, the state's armed forces actually consisted of troops and navies raised by the individual provinces, especially the disproportionately rich province of Holland. Provincial military forces were perpetually subject to withdrawal. The (contingently) United Provinces created very little central bureaucracy.

Prussia and Russia likewise turned toward their own populations for troops in the seventeenth century. Unlike Sweden, however, both states relied for recruitment and command on state-serving landlords who exercised great discretion within their own fiefs. Those great lords held the power to block excessive demands from the state. Thus, Prussia and Russia rebuilt indirect rule and the obstacles it set to centralized control.

The contrast between Sweden and Holland, on the one hand, and Prussia and Russia, on the other, is instructive. In Sweden, peasants acquired direct political representation on a national scale, even to the extent of having their own formally constituted Estate. In Holland and the other Dutch provinces, citizenship remained vested in municipal ruling classes until a series of struggles in the eighteenth century and the French conquest of 1798. In Prussia and Russia, peasants had practically no access to the national state except through the same landlords whose short-run interests lay in oppressing and exploiting them. Although no one should exaggerate the power of Swedish peasants or forget their subjection to clergy and bureaucrats, seventeenth-century Sweden had conceded a minimum set of citizenship rights to the population at large—or at least to the propertied—while its neighbors had granted none. On the contrary, as they built military power Prussia and Russia abridged the autonomies of merchants and villagers alike. The manner of recruiting soldiers made a large difference.

THE FRENCH REVOLUTION AND ITS AFTERMATH

Nevertheless, the decisive move to a model of mass national armies, direct rule, and extensive citizens' rights on a national scale came with the French Revolution.

Historians have the habit of thinking that revolutionary military activity was at first a byproduct of revolutionary enthusiasm, with the implication that the new forms of rule created the military transformation rather than vice versa. There is some truth in this sense of causal priority, since the political mobilization of 1789 to 1794 produced military forces of a tenacity and patriotism Europe had rarely seen, since revolutionary action against the Catholic Church, the nobility, and royalty surely brought France into conflict with its European neighbors faster and more generally than prudent temporization would have, and since the first steps French people recognized as revolutionary—notably the establishment of a National Assembly centered on the Third Estate—implied a considerable movement away from the old intermediaries and toward direct rule mediated by elected representatives of the population at large.

Yet, consider the importance of military changes in their own right: the crucial defection of French Guards in the Parisian revolution, the institution of citizen militias as a nearly universal feature of 1789's local revolutionary activity, the search for weapons to arm the new Parisian militia as the immediate incentive for breaking into the Bastille, the strong ties between military recruitment in 1791 or 1792 and support for the Revolution in general, the sale of Church and émigré property to finance the state's military efforts, the crucial place of military conscription in the widespread counterrevolutionary movements of 1793, the enactment of most instruments of the Terror in reaction to the double military threat from external enemies and domestic rebels, the organization of so-called Revolutionary Armies in the larger cities whose chief business was bending the people of their hinterlands (including peasants who were reluctant to deliver food) to patriotic action.

Consider furthermore that it was precisely the fiscal crisis stemming from the American war—a crisis set in motion not by the general inability of the French economy to absorb the cost but by the fiscal limits intrinsic to the French system of indirect rule—that led to the momentous convocation of the Estates General in 1789. In 1787, the state (guided by Calonne) attempted to bypass the limits of indirect rule in the *pays d'élection*—those regions lacking Estates to speak for regional privilege—by setting up representative assemblies and executive committees, but neither side invested enough power in its agents to produce effective bargaining of rights for fiscal cooperation.

Repeatedly, nevertheless, the effort to reorganize, enlarge, and finance the state's military activity led to bargaining with major sectors of the population, and thereby to the establishment or confirmation of enforceable claims such as the right to elected representation. Complaints about taxation—less its sheer bulk than the equity of its distribution—dominated parish, Third Estate, and noble *cahiers de doléances* prepared for the Estates General of 1789. What is more, the *cahiers* often linked citizenship directly to the payment of taxes (Markoff 1990, 413–454; see also Shapiro and Markoff 1998).

During the French Revolution, from the Declaration of the Rights of Man (26 August 1789) onward, bargaining that established citizenship rights took place right out in the open. The first revolutionary constitution (1790) installed a sharp distinction between "active" citizens (who paid the equivalent of three or more days' wages in taxes and had the right to vote) and "passive" citizens (who paid less or none and could not vote), with a secondary distinction of second-degree active citizens (who paid ten or more days' wages in taxes and could not only vote but also serve as electors and hold office)—a reasonable representation of the independent and propertied who had dominated the Third Estate of 1789. But for the elections of fall 1792, in the shadow of general war, the National Assembly decreed that almost all males twenty-five and over could vote; servants and other presumed dependents still lacked voting rights.

Advocates of the expanded electorate argued specifically that men who could fight for the *patrie* should also be able to vote for its governors. Unwilling conscripts of March 1793 often turned the argument around, declaring that they would be ready to serve if the government also drafted the officeholders who were receiving military exemptions.

On 23 June 1793, in the midst of war, insurrection, and bitter struggles over the food supply, the Convention abrogated martial law (including the Le Chapelier law forbidding private associations such as guilds) yet authorized severe price controls. The next day it voted a new constitution as well as a new Declaration of the Rights of Man and the Citizen. While outlawing slavery (the black insurgents of Saint-Domingue had finally received a hearing), they guaranteed not only manhood suffrage, but also the rights to rebellion, to education, to public welfare, to property, and to subsistence. True, the legislatures of Thermidor and thereafter abridged citizens' rights dramatically; manhood suffrage did not reappear in France until the Revolution of 1848. But by 1793 the French had clearly established the category of citizen as well as the principle and practice of negotiating the rights and obligations attached to that category in elected national assemblies. Their military conquests and their example spread category, principle, and practice throughout much of Europe.

The citizenship that emerged from the French Revolution and Napoleonic Wars was exiguous by today's standards, although from an eighteenth-century perspective it was thick indeed. It consisted of property-restricted rights to vote for legislative assemblies, veterans' benefits, limited protection for political associations, relative freedom of movement within national boundaries, a measure of religious toleration, and not much more. The array obviously varied from country to country within Europe; Russia in 1815 was far from granting anything resembling national citizenship, while in Great Britain even ambitious rulers did not dare to abridge the prerogatives of a Parliament chosen by an amalgam of electors, the general right of religious association (political and economic association remained much more fragile but never nonexistent), freedom to assemble for peaceful purposes (although which purposes were peaceful likewise remained open to negotiation and official interpretation), or the right to petition national authorities. Nevertheless, through much of Europe it meant that the capitalists who were so crucial to state finance had obtained political position and freedom of action they had not enjoyed in most places during the eighteenth century.

WHAT HAPPENED, AGAIN?

In a long, uneven first phase, the creation of mass national armies created the rudiments of national citizenship in European states. Then between the eighteenth century and the recent past, the rights attached to membership in the national category of citizen expanded dramatically. Why and how? It happened in two further phases, a second of a bourgeois-led drive for civil and political rights, a third in which workers, petits bourgeois, and peasants bargained more autonomously with the state.

In the second phase, negotiation over the making of war continued to play a central role. General war among European powers diminished for a century after 1815, but Europeans maintained nationally recruited standing armies and exported war to the rest of the world in the form of imperial conquest. The greatly increased military budgets empowered the bourgeois- and landlord-dominated legislatures that had taken shape during the French wars and never quite disappeared after they had ended; they now became the loci of struggle over government expenditure, the gateways through which ministers and kings had to pass on their way to military expansion. But to balance their aristocratic counterparts in the legislature, fragments of the national bourgeoisie commonly formed coalitions, implicit or explicit, with unenfranchised but increasingly organized workers and petty bourgeois. Within limits, the same civil rights that advanced the bourgeois position supported the organization of workers and petty bourgeois. As they pushed for freedom of association, freedom of assembly, freedom of the press, and related liberties, they willy-nilly promoted the mobilization of poorer, less powerful members of their commercial world.

Let me not exaggerate. The famous British Reform Act of 1832 slammed shut in the faces of organized workers a door they and the bourgeois who benefited from the act had battered open together; the workers' consequent sense of betrayal helped motivate the great Chartist Movement that followed almost immediately. Its relation to the coalition breaking of 1832 and the recognition of political advantages industrial masters drew from it explains to a considerable degree the surprisingly political program of Chartism; one might have expected impoverished and browbeaten workers to emphasize wages, employment, and working conditions rather than annual meetings of Parliament. Not until 1867 did substantial numbers of British workers begin to vote in national elections. European bourgeois of the post-Napoleonic period found themselves in the ambivalent position of enjoying the sharp political distinction between themselves and workers or shopkeepers while wanting workers and shopkeepers as counterweights against their powerful political rivals. Nevertheless, the net effect of their action was to enlarge the zone of civil rights and to make the state more vulnerable to workers', shopkeepers', and peasants' demands for political rights.

In the third phase, promoted by the bourgeois-worker-peasant coalitions of 1848 revolutions, the chief beneficiaries of expanded civil, political, and social rights began to mobilize and act more autonomously than before. If Marshall was right to name the twentieth century as the great age for social rights, the nineteenth century laid the foundations in two important ways: by providing workers, shopkeepers, and peasants with the space to organize legally and state their demands forcefully, by initiating a three-way process of negotiation among workers, capitalists, and the state over state-enforced limits on exploitation and over the minimum material benefits to which all citizens were entitled. Under Bismarck, the newly formed German state preempted the negotiation by installing a remarkable social contract top-down (Steinmetz 1993). But to some degree most European states found themselves intervening in the organization of production and distribution under pressure from increasingly organized workers and consumers.

With the later nineteenth century arrived the age in which military expenditure and debt service for past military expenditure no longer dominated European state budgets, as they had ever since distinct budgets had started to form in the sixteenth century. Wars began to matter chiefly as times when state powers and budgets expanded, and ends of wars began to matter as crucial times of political mobilization; the widespread adoption of female suffrage after World War I illustrates those effects. But much more than suffrage was at stake. Social rights to public services—education, health, and welfare—became major businesses of government. Many European states became welfare states, states committed to providing services and guaranteeing income to large categories of their citizenry.

What of the next phase? If the effect of Europeanization is to displace resources and power toward larger compacts, including the European Union, the displacement should equalize rights among the citizens of different states, vest many rights in greater entities than states, diminish differences between national citizens and European foreigners within any particular state, and therefore narrow the scope of national citizenship. We might schematize the phases as in figure 10.1. The diagram portrays a movement chiefly of inclusion for persons in the early phases, a movement chiefly of the range of entitlements in the later phases. If there is something to my argument, we should discover some version of this question-mark curve in Europe as a whole over the last three or four centuries, but also in smaller areas of Europe at different times depending on the timing of military expansion and bourgeois strength.

Need I recall how empirical, cynical, and speculative my account of citizenship rights is? Rather than a general theory stating the principles by which rights should form, I have offered a quick gloss on European historical experience. Rather than drawing out the noblest principles in which the process might be wrapped, I have insisted on the struggle, self-interest, and inadvertence involved. Rather than basing

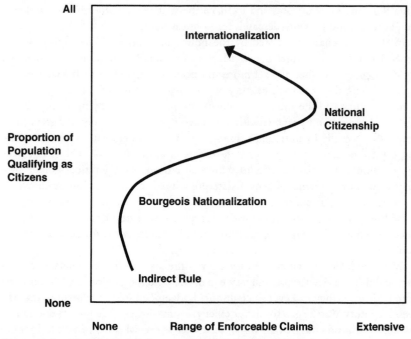

Figure 10.1   Hypothetical Trajectory of National Citizenship in Europe

my analysis on close, well-documented comparison, I have ridden high and fast across three or four centuries of history. The chronology itself requires enormous qualifications: formally designated serfs, for example, still existed in the Russia of 1860, but had disappeared from England and the Netherlands four or five centuries earlier; even today, rights of free speech vary enormously from Albania and Turkey to Norway and Finland. Most European states have found it expedient at some times in the twentieth century to define some putative citizens—Communists, Fascists, Gypsies, Jews, homosexuals, collaborators—as undeserving of their rights. A full theory of citizenship rights would account for these variations as well as broad trends over the whole continent. Please treat my account exactly as it deserves: as a provocative, historically grounded, theoretical sketch that invites confirmation, refutation, modification, and extension.

EXTENSIONS AND APPLICATIONS

This product of empiricism, cynicism, and speculation applies most surely to the creation of citizenship rights on a national scale during the emergence of consolidated states in Europe. Considering how shakily it walks its own terrain, perhaps we should simply leave the model there, and see if it gets anywhere. Nevertheless, it should be at least instructive to generalize from the specific historical terrain. The model says in general that rights—enforceable claims—arise from the repeated making of similar claims under certain conditions: (1) The claimant and the object of claims each can reward or punish the other in some significant way; (2) they are in fact bargaining over those rewards and punishments; (3) one or both also bargains with third parties who have an interest in the claims being made and will act to enforce future granting of the claims in question; (4) the three or more parties to the claims thus constituted have durable identities and relations with each other.

This is not, I submit, a bad model—and there are many bad models—of how states become legitimate: not because citizens believe in rulers' virtue, divinity, or traditional authority but because third parties—especially powerful parties such as the rulers of other states—step in to support citizen–ruler bargains, particularly when the disputed matter concerns states' demands of citizens rather than the other way round. A legitimate state is one whose domestic demands the rulers of most other states will support. Again, the model applies nicely to the way workers' rights vis-à-vis employers come into being, with the relevant third parties often being labor unions and the state. More generally, it provides a plausible account of how what James Coleman calls "disjoint constitutions" come into being: arrangements in which individuals transfer to some collectivity the rights to control some of their actions and accept the establishment of procedures to implement those rights, together with sanctions to enforce the norms and rules, when the people ceding such rights differ, to some degree, from those whom the cession benefits (Coleman 1990). The model tells us that disjoint constitutions result from coercive, unequal bargaining with third-party ratification.

The model also suggests how rights disappear. If any of the four founding conditions—claimant and object controlling relevant rewards and punishments, actual bargaining, interested third parties, durable identities and social relations—weaken significantly, so will rights. In the case of European citizenship, third parties to rights of religious diversity weakened significantly with the peace settlements of 1648, which ratified the establishment of Protestant or Catholic state religions and denied rulers the rights to change them. With that arrangement, the chances that princely members of a sect would intervene in another state on behalf of their religious brethren diminished significantly, and the path to persecution of religious minorities widened. The rights of religious minorities declined through much of Europe, as rulers sought the organizational advantages of cultural homogeneity and exemplary intolerance. Although during the eighteenth century a number of states came to tolerate and to accept payoffs from formally proscribed minorities, no major changes in religious *rights* occurred until the French Revolution. This model of rights as the product of interest-driven bargaining looks at least as plausible as the common notions that rights derive from mentalities, *Zeitgeisten*, general theories, or the sheer logic of social life.

11

Power—
Top Down and Bottom Up

German foresters of the later eighteenth century took a leaf from Frederick the Great. They replaced diverse woodlands with militarily aligned columns of a single tree species, thus assuring precision, uniformity, and efficiency in the wood harvest. German mathematicians supported their foresters by producing tables of wood yields for tree size and age under specified conditions of production. Those tables built on the conception of a standardized tree (*Normalbaum*), and foresters did their best to reproduce just such a tree. A regimented forest had the advantages not only of being easy to manage and harvest but also of being legible—readily subject to patrolling, to inspection, to planning, to taxation, and to estimates of yield. After a century and a round of replanting, however, German specialists began to speak of *Waldsterben*, forest deaths: Over the long run, uniform planting depleted the soil, disrupted working ecosystems, and provided splendid environments for pests specializing in the favored species of tree.

The importance of this tale, remarks James Scott, "is that it illustrates the dangers of dismembering an exceptionally complex and poorly understood set of relations and processes in order to isolate a single element of instrumental value" (Scott 1998, 21). For Scott it serves as a parable of the destruction wrought by heedless imposition of standardizing schemes in the interest of maximizing some narrow outcome. For more wood at less cost, read well-being as seen from the seats of power. James Scott's *Seeing Like a State* (1998) warns us of the reckless damage inflicted by top-down power.

Scott was not the first to notice how regularly coupling of high-minded standardization with overweening state power produces enfeebled progeny. In the

An earlier version of this chapter appeared as "Power—Top Down and Bottom Up," *Journal of Political Philosophy* 7 (1999): 330–352. Reprinted with permission of Blackwell Publishing, Ltd.

interests of very different causes, Frederick Hayek, Hannah Arendt, Michel Foucault, and Lewis Mumford have long since issued that eugenic warning. Conservatives have often cautioned against interfering with nature or its proxy, the market, while anarchists and syndicalists have identified states as inseparable friends of capital, hence undying enemies of labor. Still, *Seeing Like a State* identifies origins and consequences of unbridled top-down interventionism with exceptional force.

Scott writes as a veteran political ethnographer who has spent most of his career examining relations of farmers and villagers to local authorities and to local representatives of national or international authority. He has often noticed outsiders making demands on the locals that ignore or threaten the very bases of local survival. Why does that happen? Sometimes, Scott tells us, powerful authorities aggressively seek intelligibility and manipulability of the resources, activities, and people under their control. Sometimes they actually succeed in imposing some sort of new order. When they do, Scott argues, their interventions generally inflict violence—virtual or physical—on life's particularity and interdependence.

That is likely to happen, according to Scott, when four circumstances coincide: an authoritarian state, administrative ordering of nature and society, high-modernist ideology, and prostrate civil society. In the long run, local complexity subverts all such efforts to render life legible. But in the meantime damage accumulates on the scale of China's Great Leap Forward, Tanzania's ujamaa villages, or Brazil's Brasilia. Forests of Normal Trees, after all, lasted a century before disintegrating.

Of Hayek, Arendt, Foucault, and Mumford, Scott's reasoning comes closest to that of Lewis Mumford. In such works as *The City in History* (1961), Mumford argued that below some minimum concentration of production and of power no cities, hence no civilization, ever existed. But the band of tolerability remained narrow: Great concentration of production brings us the filth and degradation of Coketown, great concentration of political power brings us the autocratic excesses of the Baroque city, and great concentration of both brings us the urban Armageddon that Mumford saw fast approaching in North America. Scott says little about concentration of production except as an auxiliary of political aggrandizement. He follows Mumford, however, in stressing the corruption that results from unchecked power. For both of them, corruption includes megalomaniac plans in the style of Le Corbusier, better designed for surveillance, discipline, and massage of architects' egos than for human well-being.

Scott then departs from Mumford's analysis. He strikes off in two important directions. First, instead of assuming a more or less automatic translation of scale into tyranny, he specifies conditions under which tyrannical master plans flourish and how they collapse. Second, instead of proceeding from a general conception of human needs, he explicitly takes account of the particularity, contingency, and interdependence of routine life that provide both the incentives and the obstacles to imposition of master plans. (Scott waxes eloquent on the indispensability and toughness of the local, particular, practical, experience-driven knowledge he calls *metis*.) In both regards, Scott aficionados will hear echoes of such earlier Scott classics as *Weapons of the Weak* and *Domination and the Arts of Resistance*.

Instead of stalking Scott's argument and evidence from page to page, this chapter examines his analysis of top-down power, complains about his failure to integrate that analysis firmly with his earlier bottom-up studies, then connects elements of Scott's analysis with work by three other authors who have dealt creatively with those elements: Eric Wolf on authoritarian states and their administrative ordering, Alain Desrosières on high-modern ideology (in his case as represented by statistics), and Viviana Zelizer on American popular responses to top-down imposition of uniform legal tender (as a comment on Scott's condition of "prostrate civil society"). From confrontation among the authors the chapter draws four conclusions:

- All four scholars are dealing in complementary ways with the top-down imposition of rationalizing schemes on the recalcitrant complexity of local social life.
- Neither Scott nor these other scholars have fashioned an adequate theory of interactions between top-down and bottom-up power.
- Zelizer's analysis of American popular responses to monetization contains the kernel of a rich theory in that regard.
- Integration of Scott's early treatments of resistance with his current analysis of state control points in the same direction.

The discussion therefore closes with an inventory of causal processes that such a theory must take into account.

SCOTT'S QUEST

Scott veered into his new inquiry from an attempt to trace and explain why expanding states so regularly struggle with mobile populations they find roaming their territories—nomads, Romany, hunter-gatherers, swidden agriculturalists, transhumant herders, and others (see Huggins 1985, 1998; Lucassen 1996). He noticed how regularly those struggles intensified as states shifted from indirect to direct rule, from making accommodative deals with selected representatives of local populations to the imposition of centralized administrative hierarchies and uniform regulations on most of their subjects. He accumulated increasing doubts about conventional high-modernist explanations of struggle and failure in such cases: that the plans or their implementation were technically deficient, given insufficient means, and/or subverted by unforeseeable accidents and unenlightened opponents (see Hall 1981).

If Scott had stopped there, he would simply have added one more account (no doubt subtler and differently documented, but still familiar in many regards) to the already abundant literature on state transformations. He might then have fruitfully joined his insights to those of G. William Skinner, whose influential model of imperial Chinese social structure treats it as a dynamic product of variable intersections between the top-down structure of the empire and the bottom-up structures he identifies with markets (Skinner 1964, 1985; for a recent synthesis, see Pomeranz 2000 and Wong 1997). Or he might have integrated his analysis with Robert Dodgshon's argument that the spatial variability and embeddedness of social practices and organizations introduces inertia into all large-scale processes of social change (Dodgshon 1998).

Integrated into the literature on state transformations in one of these ways or some other, *Seeing Like a State* would add to existing accounts of extraction and repression both a refined analysis of the circumstances favoring statist excesses and an alternative to treating such excesses as straightforward expressions of ruling class self-interest. In that light, the book's greatest weaknesses are an undeveloped conception of civil society, a thin account of the process translating crazy ideas into implemented master plans, and (most surprisingly) near silence on how tyrants and bureaucrats actually work their will at the local level.

Seeing Like a State invests little energy, however, in revision of existing ideas about routine state transformations. Most states committed only small versions of the large outrages that caught Scott's attention: death and destruction on the scale of Soviet collectivization or what he calls high-modernist agriculture in East Africa. (His other major instances include high-modernist practices of city planners and revolutionaries, forcible agricultural reorganization in Asia, and, in a chapter excised from the book but still casting a shadow on its pages, the Tennessee Valley Authority.) Scrutinizing the cases at hand, Scott concludes that such outrages generally occurred after large shocks to existing social arrangements promoted coincidence of his four crucial conditions: high-modernist ideology, administrative ordering of nature and society, an authoritarian state, and prostrate civil society. Without such an extraordinary and tragic coincidence, he implies, *metis* would have prevailed.

Or would it have? In a chapter on practical knowledge, Scott tells a luminous story about a Malaysian village neighbor who used his deep practical knowledge of entomology and ecology by inducing black ants to colonize a mango tree infested with mango-eating red ants, soon to drive out the red ants and save the mango crop (Scott 1998, 333). But Scott concludes that the growth of state and market power inevitably smothers this sort of local knowledge: "The reduction or, more utopian still, the elimination of *metis* and the local control it entails are preconditions, in the case of the state, of administrative order and fiscal appropriation and, in the case of the large capitalist firm, of worker discipline and profit" (335–336).

In this strong version of Scott's argument, it begins to look as though states and capitalist markets ineluctably erode practical knowledge, a process which in turn favors the prostration of civil society. The conjunction of high-modernist ideology, administrative regularization, authoritarian state power, and prostrate civil society remains exceptional, but becomes a more likely consequence of modernization than Scott's initial focus on social disasters leads us (and perhaps him) to believe. The undoubted benefits of uniformity and legibility entail the undoubted costs of authoritarianism. The strong version of Scott's thesis binds him more closely to angry or fearful critics of modernism than does the weak version.

Either version of Scott's argument raises difficulties for analysts of state formation who have seen ordinary people as often promoting state expansion by demanding services and protection from rulers, or at least bending state power to their own advantage—as in the case of old-regime families that actually requested *lettres de cachet* for the incarceration of their unruly members (Lis and Soly 1996). Either version raises even greater troubles for theorists of democracy, troubles reaching back past Edmund Burke to Aristotle's fear that democracy would give way to demagoguery. Scott's challenge to democratic theory is twofold: first, that the indispensability of particular local practices and knowledge to routine social life appears to conflict with the desirability of uniformity in the production of equality before the law; second, that substantial state capacity seems necessary for protection and for guarantees of well-being while the very processes that create substantial state capacity also facilitate abuses of central power. In his characteristically concrete way, Scott is addressing deep questions of political philosophy.

PRACTICAL KNOWLEDGE

Take the idea of *metis*—practical knowledge of contingent, variable, local, and interdependent processes. On the whole, Scott opposes *metis* to abstract reason, which he sees searching for uniformity behind every complexity, and dismissing the residue as error. In a sinewy chapter called "Thin Simplifications and Practical Knowledge: Metis," he makes the case that capping oil well fires, Bugis navigation, folk medicine, craft production, and a host of other skilled activities depend precisely on knowing how such local residues work and how to compensate for them. Considering the ways that effective industrial workers adapt, and must always adapt, the plans devised for their operations by engineers, Scott hints at deep incompatibility between abstractly conceived plans and practical knowledge. In so doing, he challenges every recommendation to improve human life (or, for that matter, the cosmos) through the development and application of abstract reason.

There Scott falls victim to his own reasoning. For he works with a single continuum featuring *techne* at one end and *metis* at the other: "[W]e can find in the Greek concept of *metis* a means of comparing the forms of knowledge embedded in local experience with the more general, abstract knowledge deployed by the state and its technical agencies" (311). On such a continuum, each increment of abstract knowledge constitutes a decrement of practical knowledge.

In fact, the two vary in partial independence, and in partial reinforcement, of each other. Watch a talented child go from violin novice to violin virtuoso: At the start, barely able to match fingering on a string to notes on a page, she displays neither abstract nor practical knowledge. She passes through a subtle negotiation between increasing musicological sophistication and growing adeptness at reading, memorization, fingering, bowing, interpretation, recollection of previous interpretations, and adaptation to local conditions of memory, metabolism, muscle tone, instrument, temperature, humidity, acoustics, and accompaniment. Now she corrects or covers her inevitable errors with finesse. In full maturity, our virtuoso is not choosing between abstract and practical knowledge, but merging them in *tours de main* that take our breath away.

To be sure, activities vary in the extent to which they emphasize one sort of knowledge or the other; despite its deep dependence on shared understanding of scripted harmony, melody, and rhythm, a jazz group's improvisation on "Autumn Leaves" emphasizes practical knowledge relative to abstract knowledge, while a string ensemble's first reading of Bartok's fifth quartet relies more heavily on abstract knowledge. What follows? Not that practical and abstract knowledge contradict each other, but that many logically possible combinations of the two either never occur or cause dissonance when they do. Scott has selected his social disasters—which are, indeed, disasters—from the high abstraction/low improvisation corner of a two-dimensional space.

Thus interpreted, Scott's argument gains heft: In the absence of vigorous, vibrant civil society, it indicates, the conjunction of high modernism with an authoritarian state and its administrative ordering of nature and society tends to produce aggressive promotion of highly abstract programs that disregard practical knowledge, a form of top-down intervention which in turn makes disastrous consequences likely. In the argument's weak version, this sort of intervention simply becomes more likely if and when authoritarian rulers and modernist ideologues collaborate in the absence of civil counterweights. In the argument's strong version, growth of state power and capitalist production inexorably undermines both local control and practical knowledge, which increases the likelihood of disastrous modernist interventions. Hesitating between the weak version and the strong version, Scott relies on superbly narrated case studies to show that in the relevant circumstances disasters do, indeed, occur.

Despite all the richness and intelligence of Scott's case studies, experienced students of experimental or comparative methods should hesitate to take his conclusions, whether in the strong version or the weak version, as proven. In either version, he is claiming to specify necessary conditions for an unusual outcome. Logically, one might therefore expect him to search for disconfirming cases. Those would be cases of catastrophic large-scale planning in the absence of the four crucial conditions: Do pyramid construction in Egypt, vast irrigation projects in China, and the gigantic Angkor temple complex in Cambodia refute Scott? To the extent that we read Scott to be identifying sufficient conditions, we might also expect him to look for conjunctions of the four circumstances in which catastrophic large-scale planning did not emerge. He does neither.

The chief alternatives to the search for necessary and/or sufficient conditions would be (1) to identify the causal processes linking high-modernist planning to its disastrous outcomes or (2) to investigate the dynamics of administrative ordering, modernist ideology, authoritarian states, and civil society separately before examining their interactions and joint effects. Later I explore some ways of thinking about those alternatives. Scott himself would surely deny the intent or the responsibility—perhaps the very possibility—of proving his analysis's general applicability. Given his stress on *metis*, he might well regard such an effort as a contradiction in terms. But his own analytical forcefulness poses that challenge for his readers.

Rather than a sedulous survey of evidence pro and con, however, I want to take a different departure from Scott's provocative thesis. Let me point to three important recent studies that have pursued one version or another of Scott's problem, reflecting on their implications for steps beyond *Seeing Like a State*. Those studies are Eric Wolf's *Envisioning Power* (1999), Alain Desrosières's *The Politics of Large Numbers* (1998), and Viviana Zelizer's *Social Meaning of Money* (1994). Wolf's book addresses the operation of authoritarian states, Desrosières's the character and genesis of high-modernist schemes, Zelizer's the forms of popular response to such schemes.

ERIC WOLF ON POWER

In substance, Wolf's book comes closest to Scott's. Like Scott, the late Eric Wolf spent a career integrating small-scale ethnography with large-scale analyses of social processes. In *Envisioning Power*, Wolf reflects on three instances in which political and economic power spun out of control with devastating results for ordinary people: Kwakiutl villagers in the time of giant potlatches, Aztecs in the time of human sacrifices, and Nazi ascent to control of Germany. Having endured Nazi seizure of the Sudetenland as a youth before escaping to England and the United States, Wolf has firsthand experience with tyrannical power in the pursuit of megalomaniac plans.

As in such previous books as *Peasant Wars of the 20th Century* (1969), Wolf lays out his cases in their own terms one by one, then offers concluding reflections. This time, however, he precedes the case-by-case analysis with a long, wise review of anthropology's intellectual heritage in regard to power, ideology, and culture. Wolf follows Norbert Elias (whom he heard lecture on the subject in an alien detention camp near Liverpool in 1940) in treating power as "an aspect of all relations among people" (1999, 4). Wolf distinguishes four different modalities of power: as individual capability, as X's ability to influence Y's action, as control (individual or collective) over access to contexts of social interaction, and as deployment and allocation of social labor within those contexts. He calls the fourth *structural power*. After careful parsing of the relevant intellectual history, Wolf defines *ideology* as "a complex of ideas selected to underwrite and represent a particular project of installing, maintaining, and aggrandizing power in social relationships" (55). Culture then becomes the stock of material inventories, behavioral repertoires, and mental representations available to various interacting parties within a given population.

Unlike *Peasant Wars*, Wolf's new book requires a conceptual introduction because his argument employs highly contested terms. Situations of intense social stress, according to Wolf, promote the linking of ideology to structural power, thus facilitating oppression through the reorganization of social labor. For the Kwakiutl of the late nineteenth century, in Wolf's account, stress took the form of forced incorporation into a subordinate niche of the Canadian economy and polity. For fifteenth-century Aztecs, stress took the form of famine, natural disasters, and defeat in war. For the Nazis, Wolf highlights not the loss of World War I or the economic crisis of the 1920s, but "a century in which the Germanies underwent a convulsive transition from local artisanry to industrial capitalism and an abrupt political unification whereby multiple, socially distinctive local and regional entities were brought under the aegis of a militaristic and bureaucratic Prussia" (1999, 278).

In such stressful circumstances, runs the argument, segments of Kwakiutl, Aztec, and German society fused mobilizing ideologies with new forms of structural power, and thereby created unprecedented oppression. Kwakiutl leaders began using the potlatch and access to it brutally in defense of inequality. Aztecs engaged in increasingly widespread human sacrifice. Nazis waged war against much of Europe and against whole categories of the population within the territories they controlled.

Broad similarities between Wolf's analysis and Scott's strike the eye immediately. Substitute *totalizing ideology* for *high modernism* and recognize that Scott is restricting his attention to relatively strong, fully constituted states; with those qualifications, the causal accounts resemble each other. Both are describing and explaining pathologies of top-down power. Differences between Wolf and Scott lie in two realms. First, for Wolf when ideology and power converge ideology tends to drive power, while for Scott ideology comes closer to being an instrument of power. Second, Scott provides a much fuller account of resistance before, during, and after implementation of high-modernist schemes; Wolf concentrates almost exclusively on origins. Yet these differences amount to no more than variations on common themes.

ALAIN DESROSIÈRES ON STATISTICS

At first it seems a great leap to the world of statistical reasoning analyzed by Alain Desrosières in *The Politics of Large Numbers*. In fact, a short path through a dense thicket leads directly from Scott and Wolf to Desrosières. His book confronts a paradox: Statistics comes into being by means of conventions that treat disparate, lumpy events as precisely comparable; yet statistics gains its authority from the claim to describe its objects more exactly than ordinary observation. Beginning with the simple construction of tables that cross-classify objects by rubrics—

whether entries in the tables' cells are numerical or qualitative—statistics rests on the very claims of equivalence, of commensurability, to which Scott worriedly calls our attention. To that extent, statistics embodies a quintessential modernist scheme.

The word *statistics,* through no accident, has two significantly different denotations: (1) measurement and numerical representation of comparable phenomena; (2) analysis of those numerical representations by means of mathematical models. The two enterprises have partly independent histories, with the measurement side arising largely as an auxiliary to public administration and the analytic side frequently the domain of theorists outside of public administration. As the derivation of the word *statistics* from the German *Staat* suggests, administrative practice most often met analytic theory in the state's shadow.

Desrosières explores both the contradiction and the intersection of statistics 1 and statistics 2. His declared aim

> is to study how the tension between the claim to objectivity and universality, on the one hand, and the powerful conjunction with the world of action, on the other, is the source of the very dynamics of science, and of the transformations and retranslations of its cognitive schemes and technical instruments. Linked successively to the domestication of risks, the management of states, the mastery of the biological or economic reproduction of societies, or the governance of military and administrative operations, the history of probability calculus and statistics teems with examples of such transformations. (1998, 7)

Desrosières seeks to demonstrate how measurement techniques, statistical models, and reifications of social processes reinforced each other until in our own time the only choices seem to be (1) accept without cavil the value of statistics in getting at systematic realities, or (2) reject the whole statistical enterprise on the ground of social reality's chaotic unknowability. Gently, he prods his readers toward a third alternative: (3) treat processes of measurement and analysis as objects of systematic study, then incorporate the results of that study into efforts to describe and explain social processes.

Beginning in the seventeenth century, Desrosières reconstructs the interacting histories of statistics 1 and statistics 2 in Germany, Great Britain, and, especially, France. He detects strong effects of political regimes, with Prussian administrators actively inventing categories for uniform reporting to the central administration without investing much energy in techniques of measurement, Britain's political arithmeticians analyzing bills of mortality and other registrations of vital events without being able to promote national surveys, Louis XIV's representatives patching together surveys (some of them in numerical form) for the enlightenment of particular administrators including the king, and the French Revolution producing a spectacular convergence of counting and making uniform (see also Meinzer 1992).

Although a census mandated by the Constitution and first conducted in 1790 provided a partial exception, the United States characteristically relied on state, local, and specialized federal services to produce public statistics until well into the twentieth century and did not establish national statistical services similar to those of Western Europe until the 1930s—that is, until the expansion of the federal bureaucracy that accompanied the New Deal and World War II (for more historical detail on national statistic services, see Alonso and Starr 1987; Brian 1992; Crosby 1997; Curtis 2001; Linder 1994; Lorwin and Price 1972; Mols 1954–56, Schröder 1994; Wachter 1988; Willigan and Lynch 1982; Wilson and Parker 1997; Wrigley 1972).

In all these countries, statistics in both senses of the word eventually became a project of high modernism. Both the collection of uniform observations and the establishment of regularities through statistical analysis deeply concerned statisticians. An ancient quarrel took a new form: Do aggregates of objects, as represented by statistical summaries of individual measurements, possess a reality independent of the individual objects? Do birth rates, population densities, business cycles, income distributions, and similar aggregates obey laws that are not reducible to individual behavior?

The frequency with which different attributes varied among individuals in conformity to one of a limited number of statistical distributions—say, a logistic or a bell curve—encouraged proponents of lawful aggregates. Belgian astronomer Adolphe Quetelet developed and publicized an influential idea: The bell curve, he claimed, centered on an average that was not simply a statistical device but a model in a strong sense of the word. The Average Man represented a kind of central tendency determined by the nature of the generating process; individuals approximated that central tendency with varying degrees of error. (The Normal Tree grew nearby.)

This line of thought opened up a furious debate. Quetelet and his followers distinguished among the following:

- A mere arithmetic mean calculated over some set of objects without regard to establishing the laws of its generation
- A subjective mean computed from an aggregate of imperfect observations matched to a model
- An objective or true mean belonging to the underlying phenomenon itself

Expert statisticians should, in this view, avoid mere arithmetic means and compute subjective means only in the effort to approximate the objective mean. But such distinctions revived deep epistemological and ontological controversies about the nature of statistics in senses 1 and 2: Properly speaking, to what degree do the numbers represent lawful phenomena that are (1) aggregate in character and (2) separable from the perceptions of the persons who devised, collected, and analyzed them? Opponents of the Quetelet view insisted that statistics must and should concern subjective estimates by individuals, without claims concerning regularities external to those estimates. The Quetelet view, however, won out.

Do these refined philosophical controversies distract us from the subject of power and high modernism? Listen to Desrosières:

Among the traits characteristic of the historical line of research begun during the 1930s by the *Annales* school, reference to statistical objectifications has been significant. From this point of view quantitative history has inherited, via Simiand, Halbwachs, and Labrousse, elements of the Durkheimian school and, even closer to the source, of the mode of thinking centered on averages engendered by Quetelet, who opposed macrosocial regularities to the random, unpredictable, and always different accidents of particular events. It sought, by this technique, to overcome individual or factual contingencies in order to construct more general things, characterizing social groups or the long run, depending on the case. (323)

Macrosocial regularities, in this reading, predominate over mere local events. We can hear Scott snort or sigh.

Desrosières goes on to argue that the state's construction of public statistics did not merely facilitate the search for true reality by more refined means, but made it possible for statisticians and their public to believe in an objective, lawful world concerning which statistics provide imperfect evidence, but better evidence than common sense. John von Neumann's great collaborator Oskar Morgenstern offered inadvertent confirmation of Desrosières's arguments in his rich *On the Accuracy of Economic Observations* (1963, first published in 1950), which might better have been titled *On the Inaccuracy.* . . . After three hundred alternately appalling and hilarious pages enumerating egregious errors in collecting, aggregating, and interpreting economic statistics, Morgenstern concludes hopefully:

Eventually a new generation of economists will have learned to live with data of widely differing quality and how to improve their observations. In that they will emulate the physicists who have created a magnificent and terrifying theory though their data range in accuracy from better than 10^{-8} to only 50%—that is, when they can measure at all. In appreciating the true condition of the data, economists cannot fail but to develop economic theory in conformity with the high scientific standards set in the physical sciences. (Morgenstern 1963, 305–306)

Morgenstern's sunny high-modern confidence is infectious, but it completely ignores the processes of construction that Desrosières stresses.

Desrosières takes up a great many other issues, notably the debate between conceptions of probability as a feature of minds (hence measures of uncertainty or subjective likelihood) or as features of external phenomena (hence measures of risk, distributions, or objective likelihood) and the shift from central tendencies to distributions in the characterization of populations, which facilitated such means of comparison as the IQ and the income percentile, not to mention the introduction of sampling as a device for describing large populations. In all these cases and more, Desrosières argues forcefully that conventions of measurement, representation, and analysis rest on strong presumptions concerning the nature of social reality, but

once in practical operation those conventions transform social life. He therefore
pleads first for recognition of the social construction that shapes statistical analysis
and argument, then for integrating accounts of such constructive processes into
theories of social reality, finally for debate about accepted conventions as an opening to social change.

VIVIANA ZELIZER ON MONEY

Connections of Viviana Zelizer's work to that of Scott, Wolf, and Desrosières are
not immediately obvious, but they are profound. In a series of books concerning
life insurance, valuation of children, and money in American life, Zelizer has striven
repeatedly to show that what appear to be narrowly rational economic transactions
actually result from pursuit of meaningful social relations. Hence, she observes, fears
that monetization and commodification are desiccating social life have their causality backward.

In fact, argues Zelizer, people constantly rework standardizing systems until they
serve the creation and maintenance of meaningful social relations. Markets and
monies certainly exist, but they rest on webs of shared understanding and facilita-
tive social interaction. Expansion of markets and money surely transforms social
life, but it does so by means of incessant negotiation between their agents and ordinary people. The treatment of money as an unstoppable instrument of rationality and an implacable enemy of social solidarity recurs from Karl Marx to Georg
Simmel to Jürgen Habermas, but it tells only the top-down half of the tale. As
compared with the lines taken by Scott, Wolf, and Desrosières in the books under
discussion, Zelizer attributes much more creativity to ordinary people.

In *The Social Meaning of Money*, Zelizer examines the monetization of American
life in three main areas: domestic money, gift money, and various forms of charity.
In each area, she documents how ordinary Americans resisted the state-backed
high-modernist program of uniform, completely fungible currency by earmarking,
segregating, and channeling legal tender into distinguishable streams, by creating
their own currencies outside the realm of legal tender, and by assiduous matching
of monetary transactions to social ties. Although with great effort the American
state finally came close to monopolizing production of legal tender within its territory, Americans proliferated new media and, especially, new ways of conducting
monetary transactions that distinguished meaningfully different social relations
from each other. "Therefore," remarks Zelizer, "the forms of monetary earmarking
multiplied just as official money became *more* uniform and generalized" (17).

As husband–wife relations shifted in the United States, Zelizer shows, so too did
the storage, labeling, transfer, and expenditure of domestic money. As monetary
gifts became more common, Americans expended great ingenuity on distinctions
among different sorts of tips, bribes, charitable contributions, religious donations,
ritual prestations, declarations of commitment, and love tokens, as well as separat-

ing them carefully from established forms of entitlement and compensation. Bitter struggles over proper forms of public aid to poor families pivoted less on how much to spend than on what relation to establish between client and public agency. The contest over relief in cash or in kind, for example, engaged competing donors and competing recipients for decades. Public disagreements pivoted on varying judgments of the capacity of poor people to handle money on their own, but those judgments rested in turn on contradictory ideas of actual and proper relationships between donors and recipients as well as between recipients and their families. Meanwhile, recipients fought for means of relief that would sustain their daily lives and social ties. It is, in short, "very hard to suppress the active, creative power of supposedly vulnerable social relations" (35).

Without equating the U.S. government's monopolization of legal tender with Nazi terror or the Great Leap Forward, we can see that Zelizer is analyzing from the bottom up American variants of processes like those that Scott, Wolf, and Desrosières examine from the top down. Earlier in their careers, indeed, both Scott and Wolf rightly gained fame for their bottom-up analyses of power struggles, for their sensitive portrayals of how ordinary people create space for themselves either by rebellion or by negotiation with powerful agents of large-scale structural change.

Although she studies no large rebellions, Zelizer continues to analyze resisting and reshaping as seen from below. In that regard, she resembles those specialists in Soviet social life (e.g., Feige 1998; Ledeneva 1998; Solnick 1998) who point out that the Soviet Union's vast system of centralized planning, rationing, and distribution only worked at all because subordinate members of the system figured out how to fill quotas, meet bureaucratic demands, perform ritual activities, yet survive by fashioning semilegal or illegal arrangements of stockpiling, barter, influence, protection, and private supply.

As it happens, Scott's obiter dicta and rich footnotes in *Seeing Like a State* often describe accommodations of this very sort, as assembly-line workers and members of collective farms fiddle with the specifications handed down from above to make them viable without too obviously challenging the intelligence or authority of management. Although a zero-sum conception of exploitation and resistance generally informed such earlier Scott works as *Weapons of the Weak* and *Domination and the Arts of Resistance*, in those analyses as well he occasionally identified compromises: "performances that are not bad enough to provoke punishment but not good enough to allow the enterprise to succeed" (Scott 1990, 192). Closer examination of those situations will lend insight into both conflicts and accommodations between top-down and bottom-up exertions of power.

CONFRONTATIONS AND RECONCILIATIONS

At first reading, Scott, Wolf, Desrosières, and Zelizer offer competing accounts of relations between top-down standardizing processes and bottom-up everyday practices.

For Scott, we have moments of social aberration in which ideologues and tyrants not only join hands but succeed in entangling whole populations under their heavy, ill-fitting nets. For Wolf, we have threatened or ascendant powerseekers generating their own inhumane worldviews. For Desrosières, we have unwitting conspiracies taking place at the edges of power. For Zelizer, we have ordinary people coping and surviving by reweaving strands of any net cast down upon them. Can they all be right?

Let us proceed dialectically. Our thesis will offer a superficial reconciliation of the four views by means of an old trope: Pieces of the Elephant. Our antithesis will reply that all four authors have misrepresented the interplay of top-down and bottom-up power. Our synthesis will reprieve the condemned four by declaring that they provide us with elements of a superior theory.

Thesis. Scott, Wolf, Desrosières, and Zelizer are simply palpating different parts of the same old pachyderm. All are examining how power intersects everyday practice, but from different angles. Scott singles out potent but ultimately unusual moments when what he calls a "prostrate civil society" offers perpetrators of large-scale standardizing plans opportunities to implement their destructive programs. Wolf wonders how ordinary people could ever assent to the implementation of dehumanizing worldviews, finally concluding, "The ideologies in all three cases focused explicitly on matters of life and death, and they imparted to the holders of structural power a superhuman aura of involvement with them" (Wolf 1999, 290–291).

Desrosières concentrates on the work of intellectuals, giving only secondary attention to their collaboration with holders of power, concluding wearily, "I would like the reflection offered in this book on the relationships between statistics and the public sphere to help clarify and analyze these spaces of durably solidified forms, which must simultaneously remain undebated so that life may follow its course, and debatable, so that life can change its course" (Desrosières 1998, 337). With Desrosières, Zelizer is observing normal times rather than the extraordinary moments revisited by Scott and Wolf; "To the extent that money does become more prominent in social life," she concludes, "people will segregate, differentiate, label, decorate, personalize it to meet their complex social needs" (Zelizer 1994, 216). Thus, our four authors walk off the same stage in different directions.

Antithesis. Surprisingly for Scott and Wolf, less surprisingly for Desrosières and Zelizer, our four authors misrepresent the interplay of top-down and bottom-up power. The surprise is greater for Scott and Wolf because both of them once wrote brilliant, influential analyses of bottom-up power. Scott has certainly not forgotten his earlier analyses, on which his rich discussions of practical knowledge draw repeatedly. But he cannot escape the contradictions among thinking that *metis* is stronger than abstract rationality, that states and markets smother *metis*, and that the planning disasters his book records only occurred because of exceptional circumstances.

In general, our authors fail to recognize the incessantly negotiated character of power. Power is an analyst's summary of transactions among persons and social sites: We can reasonably say X has power over Y if in the course of a stream of interaction between X and Y (1) a little action from X typically elicits a large response from Y, and (2) their interaction delivers disproportionate benefits to X. Because Y always has access to local ties, resources, and knowledge that are unknown or unavailable to X, however, even very asymmetrical exercises of power entail negotiation based on practical knowledge.

Equally important, struggles *generate* practical knowledge, as apparent victims use what Scott once called "weapons of the weak" to create new means of accommodation while preserving valued social ties. The daily improvisations with monetary transactions described by Zelizer (whether small-scale adaptations or open struggles) transform social relations, practical knowledge, and the character of money itself. As Arthur Stinchcombe (1996) has pointed out for Caribbean slavery, even extremely asymmetrical power relations involve bargaining and adaptation on both sides. The lesson applies to intersections between modernizing schemes and everyday experience.

MEDIATING MECHANISMS

Synthesis. Since I have used the four authors' own words against them, it is only fair to concede that they generally recognize their analyses' limits and further implications. Where do those analyses invite us to go next? Toward, I think, specification of the recurrent causal processes that govern intersections between abstract, centrally promoted plans and social life on the small scale. To illustrate this intellectual strategy, let me pluck just five such processes from the four books at hand: polyvalent performance, accommodative bargaining, category formation, intellectual brokerage, and improvisation.

Polyvalent performance involves individual or collective presentation of gestures simultaneously to two or more audiences in ways that code differently within the audiences. Polyvalent performers often send supplementary signals—winks, grimaces, shrugs, and their collective equivalents—to one side or another, thus reducing the likelihood of miscoding on that side. Erving Goffman (1971) offered superb examples of polyvalent performances, but compromised his explanations of them by assuming that one side was authentic and the other artificial as well as by ignoring the conversational character of such performances; they always include some interaction, however asymmetrical, with their audiences, and that interaction always modifies the performances. Similarly, James Scott's own famous distinction of hidden transcripts from public transcripts (1990) attributes greater authenticity (at least from the perspective of subalterns) to the first than to the second.

Of course, many social situations require people to fake or fabricate emotions (Hochschild 1983), and inside jokes often consist of gulling one audience while making derisive signals to another. The effectiveness of polyvalent performance does not, however, depend on its masking of genuine feelings. In the language of multilevel games, what matters is whether simultaneous, identical moves on two or more boards constitute recognizable, effective maneuvers in each setting.

Sometimes, indeed, players on both sides recognize their participation in a double game, but maintain their relations by refusing to acknowledge that duality openly. The polyvalent performance of working by rule to undermine overzealous bosses gains its effectiveness precisely from resonance in two registers, both of them audible to each side. In a striking example, Thomas Barfield (1989) has examined the actual exchange of goods in the regular performances by which Mongol leaders paid homage to Chinese emperors, discovering that over long years those threatening northern warriors were receiving a substantial net return from China; in effect, Mongols were receiving payoffs from a protection racket (cf. Stanley 1996).

Polyvalent performances affect relations between top-down standardizing processes and bottom-up everyday practices. To the extent that local social relations and the demands of standardizing authorities contradict each other, polyvalent performance becomes a valuable means of mediating between them: giving census enumerators acceptable answers to their surveys without revealing the presence of illegal residents, reporting dutifully for military service but giving evidence to your dissident peers that you do so reluctantly, speaking of democracy with sufficient vagueness that one side hears equality and another liberty. In the statistical world described by Desrosières, specialists often make public presentations of data whose fragility is the everyday concern and dirty secret of the other specialists on hand.

Eric Wolf gives us the apposite example of the Kwakiutl Winter Ceremonial, in which "a spirit kidnaps and consumes the initiand, and in so doing grants him supernatural powers; it then releases him back into normal life as a person transformed by that experience" (Wolf 1999, 105). Later, Wolf draws from Susan Reid the insight that

> the novice undergoes the experience of death and release at the hand of the Man-Eater but also discovers that the experience is stage managed. In his resocialization after the experience, he learns that he must accept the simulation as part of his return to the society of humans. Acceptance is "helping the novice to find his way out of the myth." Yet more is involved, I believe, than a simple acceptance of a human lot. Since the initiate will return to society as an aristocrat or chief, he will also qualify for that position by the political knowledge that it takes stage management to project reality. (Wolf 1999, 109–110)

Audiences on the sides of aristocrats and commoners read the performance differently, and its very polyvalence reinforces the distinction between them. That distinction then subtly mediates the intersection between top-down schemes and local knowledge.

Accommodative bargaining could be a redundant phrase, since the word *bargaining* implies give and take on each side. I adopt the cumbersome term to emphasize the multiple relations among parties (and not just the immediate bargainers) engaged by most exercises of power. Even in the case of brutal conquest, as Machiavelli remarked a half millennium ago, conquerors face the problem of ruling, or at least withdrawing safely with their booty, after a successful siege ends. When French regional governors of the seventeenth century faced rebellions against new or increased royal taxes—which often happened into the 1670s—they generally routed whatever rebel forces had assembled, rounded up a few ringleaders, gave them spectacular public executions, held drumhead trials for some lesser participants, but simultaneously worked out settlements with regional and local leaders; in addition to guaranteeing renewed flows of revenue, those settlements confirmed the identities of authorities who had the backing of royal power and stated the proper conditions for future fiscal demands. Although over the long run taxes per capita rose through such settlements as well as through day-to-day pressure from tax farmers and officials, each side accommodated to the other. They even tolerated a little graft on one side and a little tax evasion on the other, just so long as those practices did not become too visible and too disruptive to local social relations.

In another instance of prolonged accommodative bargaining, Zelizer calls attention to burial insurance as a practice over which high-minded charity workers and their poor clients often clashed from the later nineteenth century to the 1930s. Quoting studies from 1898 and 1910, Zelizer summarizes:

> Why, then, the battle against industrial insurance? It was partly a matter of control; insurance monies escaped the monitoring web of charity workers. By paying their premiums, the poor purchased the right to subsidize their own version of a "good death," spending in ways that often violated middle-class notions of a proper funeral. To the dismay of charity workers, insurance premiums were directly and almost exclusively converted into funeral fees, paying not only for a "costly casket" but also, in some cases, for an "imposing cortege" of carriages (including a special one to display flowers) and sometimes a band to head the procession. If any money was left, it went for mourning garments. (Zelizer 1994, 181)

Yet after decades of haggling with clients over the question, charity workers came to accept the purchase of burial insurance, and of insurance in general, as part of sensible household management. Charity workers got their household budgets, but households got their respectable funerals. They had negotiated a new interface between universalizing schemes and local practices.

Category formation belongs even more visibly to the causal processes by which top-down and bottom-up power interact. Categories consist of boundaries and defined relations both within and across those boundaries. To classify someone as female, for example, both distinguishes that person from all males and defines relations to (1) other females, (2) males (Connell 1995; Kessler and McKenna 1985). Similarly operating distinctions relate different grades of citizens and noncitizens, professionals to nonmembers of their professions, and officially designated races to each other. People build such boundaries and attendant relations into a wide variety of organizations, often reinforcing inequality as they do so (Tilly 1998). Yet away from the boundary plenty of room exists for gradations, ambiguities, and further classifications.

Among our authors, Desrosières deals with category formation most directly. As he reports:

> On the one hand, as tributaries of administrative records, [later statisticians] worked on constituting and defining categories and on encoding singular cases, in a perspective that shows some affinity with that of legal or administrative specialists (the word "category" itself derives from the Greek term *kategoria*, connected with judgment rendered in the public arena). But on the other hand, as interpreters of their own productions they tried to infer, on the basis of ever more complex mathematical constructs, the existence of underlying categories revealed by statistical regularities or by particular forms of distribution, notably the law of errors or the binomial law (the future normal law). Later on, the factor analysis of psychometrists—detecting a "general intelligence"—or the methods of classification resulting from data analysis would be situated in this same general trend. (Desrosières 1998, 238)

Category formation created social realities, for example, by dividing workers among retired, proprietors, employed, and unemployed, with different rights and obligations attached to membership in each category (Keyssar 1986; Salais, Baverez, and Reynaud 1986; Topalov 1994). But, of course, the categorized fought back, with capitalists, workers, economists, and politicians wrangling over who belonged to which category and what membership in each category entailed. Thus, category formation combined with accommodative bargaining in fashioning new articulations between state-driven high-modern schemes and local practices.

Intellectual brokerage also figured importantly in those articulations. Intellectual brokerage is the linking of two or more previously unconnected ideas, thinkers, or bodies of thought. It may seem the innocent pastime of intellectuals, but it affects both the structure of standardizing schemes and their intersection with worlds of everyday practice. Powerful examples come from the history of nationalism, where the conjunction of nation with state only firmed up with the ostensibly liberating conquests of French armies under the Revolution and Napoleon (Tilly 1995b). From that point on, the claim to be a state implied the right to impose a certain set of cultural forms on citizens of that state, while the claim to be a nation implied the right to acquire your own state. In a world where languages, religions, kinship systems, trading networks, and migration streams actually overlapped and intertwined, conjunction of the ideas nation and state caused the same sorts of terrible troubles that Scott documents for imposed projects of high modernity.

Scott, a sheep farmer himself, offers us the vivid example of Soviet collectivized agriculture. There, agronomists (both Russian and American) joined the idea of communism with the idea of large-scale mechanized agriculture. In 1928, American agronomists M. L. Wilson, Harold Ware, and Guy Riggin responded to a Soviet invitation by gathering in a Chicago hotel room to make plans for the world's biggest mechanized wheat farm. Soviet authorities actually created the farm under American guidance:

The giant *sovkhoz*, named Verblud, which they established near Rostov-on-Don, one thousand miles south of Moscow, comprised 375,000 acres that were to be sown to wheat. As an economic proposition, it was an abject failure, although in the early years it did produce large quantities of wheat. The detailed reasons for the failure are of less interest for our purposes than the fact that most of them could be summarized under the rubric of *context*. It was the specific context of this specific farm that defeated them. The farm, unlike the plan, was not a hypothecated, generic, abstract farm but an unpredictable, complex, and particular farm, with its own unique combination of soils, social structure, administrative culture, weather, political strictures, machinery, roads, and the work skills and habits of its employees. (Scott 1998, 201)

Although this high-modern project failed visibly, collectivization and the installation of large-scale high-tech farm management accelerated during the 1930s, with devastating results for displaced peasants but some success in providing food for Soviet cities. Scott's explanation of that partial success echoes our earlier review of accommodations between high modern and local:

That collectivized agriculture persisted for sixty years was a tribute less to the plan of the state than to the improvisations, gray markets, bartering, and ingenuity that partly compensated for its failures. Just as an "informal Brasilia," which had no legitimate place in official plans, arose to make the city viable, so did a set of informal practices lying outside the formal command structure—and often outside Soviet law as well— arise to circumvent some of the colossal waste and inefficiencies built into the system. Collectivized agriculture, in other words, never quite operated according to the hierarchical grid of the production plans and procurements. (Scott 1998, 294)

Here we see intellectual brokerage initiating a process that eventually engaged polyvalent performance, accommodative bargaining, and category formation as well.

It also engaged incessant *improvisation*. As a whole family of causal processes, improvisation covers a wider range of social activities than the other causal processes we have reviewed. I single it out because short-term creation of new forms of action and interaction in response to errors, environmental changes, unanticipated consequences, unexpected obstacles, new opportunities, strategic interaction, or sudden inspiration—which is what I mean by improvisation—plays a central part in the articulation of standardizing schemes with local knowledge. Under the Scott-like title *Working Knowledge*, Douglas Harper (1987) meticulously describes the daily improvisations of a veteran automobile mechanic in rural upstate New York who works among the carcasses of Saab automobiles, scavenging parts when he can, making new parts when necessary, refashioning metal, glass, and plastic before he returns cars to their owners as recognizable Saabs. Harper's mechanic mediates between standardizing Saab engineers and locally available materials. He can serve as a metonym for improvisers on all sides of the momentous political processes analyzed directly by Scott and Wolf, less directly by Desrosières and Zelizer.

Why does improvisation matter so much? First of all, because in general the scripts available for social action and interaction would never work without nudging, bending, and moment-to-moment modification. That is why working by rule is an effective bargaining strategy, why ostentatiously precise following of instructions makes people laugh, and why the effort to specify precisely how a worker or spouse should behave in various circumstances leads with high probability to ever-greater elaboration of rules for unforeseen cases or to an explosion. Improvisation matters because it always takes place within limits set by existing social relations and locally shared understandings, then modifies existing social relations and locally shared understandings.

Improvisation also matters as the site of durable incremental changes and innovations—the latter being a name for those improvisations that stick and achieve some sort of recognition as such. Most of all, improvisation matters (at least for present purposes) because it blunts the edges of great standardizing projects, opens up space for the exercise of *metis*, and thereby articulates the large scale with the small (see Schlumbohm 1998). States do not always, *pace* Strong Version Scott, benefit from uniformity, since diversity enriches their resource bases and improvisation permits otherwise impracticable central plans to survive. In the closer examination of improvised articulation lies the synthesis between top-down and bottom-up conceptions of power.

Why, then, do great planning disasters ever occur? My gloss on Wolf, Desrosières, Zelizer, and Scott suggests looking for processes that undermine, counter, or render pernicious the sorts of interactive mechanisms that usually mediate uniform schemes and local practice: polyvalent performance, accommodative bargaining, category formation, intellectual brokerage, and improvisation. When they involve encounters between local and large scales, these mechanisms are most likely to fail or to generate destructive incompatibility where little previous communication between local and large scale has occurred, where local connections and resources have diminished, where time horizons have shortened, and where authorities are responding to serious struggles with their own peers or predators rather than to relations with their subordinates. Since our contemporary world frequently generates changes of exactly these kinds, *Seeing Like a State* implicitly broadcasts a worrisome message: Yes, alas, it can happen again.

Part IV

POLITICAL CHANGE

12

States and Nationalism
in Europe, 1492–1992

As an independent state, Romania has not been around much more than a century. Wallachia and Moldavia only acquired autonomy as coupled principalities under Ottoman sovereignty in 1861 and only became an independent kingdom in 1881. The kingdom of Romania, furthermore, only annexed Bessarabia, Bukovina, and Transylvania—more than half of its maximum territory—after astute switching of sides during World War I. In the absence of a Romanian state, nevertheless, Romanian chroniclers of the seventeenth century propounded three theories of their ethnic origins, Latinist, indigenist, and mixed: first, that a homogeneous people descended from the Roman legions and colonists established in the new province of Dacia after the emperor Trajan conquered the region in A.D. 105–106; second, that a likewise homogeneous people sprang from the highly civilized Dacians already on the spot whom the Romans integrated into their empire; third, that Romans and Dacians not only mixed, but selectively assimilated some later migrants into the region.

All three theories, especially the first two, made Romanians an ancient, self-contained population, clearly distinct from the Turks who ruled them, as well as prior to the Germans, Jews, Slavs, and Hungarians who now shared the territory with them. As a British historian of the region remarks, dryly, of the ninth century A.D.:

> The ethnic appurtenance of the then inhabitants of Transylvania is acrimoniously disputed between Roumanian [sic] and Hungarian historians, the former maintaining that a Roman, or alternatively, Romanised Dacian, population had survived the Dark Ages, the latter pointing to the fact that all the pre-Magyar place-names of Transylvania are

An earlier version of this chapter appeared as "States and Nationalism in Europe, 1492–1992," *Theory and Society* 23 (1994): 131–146. Reprinted with permission from Kluwer Academic Publishers.

Slav, except four river-names, which are not Latin; also that the first mentions of "Vlachs" in Hungarian documents comes in the thirteenth century, when they figure only as roving shepherds, and not numerous. (Macartney 1962, 5)

I need hardly add that Romanians and Hungarians dispute not only the ancient history, but the present nationality, of Transylvania, which houses many speakers of Hungarian but since World War I appears on maps as part of Romania.

In a Balkan region splintered by hundreds of ethnicities and subject to the incessant competition of Russian, Habsburg, and Ottoman empires, the Roman and Dacian myths voiced claims to autonomy and coherence. Russian rulers of the eighteenth century who ground away at Ottoman territory reinforced the myths by trying to establish a distinct Dacian state as a buffer between Ottoman and Russian territories. Only during the nineteenth century, however, did the Latinist, the indigenist, or the mixed theory of Romanian origins begin to command wide popular support. In general Romanian nationalists then argued some variant of the proposition that a distinctive Romanian people had long existed, still maintained a coherent, contiguous, common life, and therefore deserved its own sovereign state.

Hence, an irony: The first elected prince of Wallachia and Moldavia was the bourgeois Moldavian nationalist Alexander Cuza, who faced severe political problems precisely because he already had strong connections in the region; he fell to a coup five years after taking office. The relatively successful prince who followed him and eventually became King Karol I was not Romanian, but a member of the Prussian royal family, Karl of Hohenzollern-Sigmaringen.

Eric Hobsbawm has already had a lepidopterist's field day pinning up the butterflies of nationalist fantasy (Hobsbawm 1990). His net moves fast; I will not compete with him on that ground. Instead, let me lay out some observations on connections between changes in the European state system and the evolution of nationalism in Europe and elsewhere. In a few pages I can do no more than sketch a line of inquiry, illustrating it very sparsely. In this day of apparently resurgent nationalism in Eastern Europe and elsewhere, I aim to demonstrate that a proper understanding of the past does illuminate the present, or even the future, and to suggest that what we loosely call nationalism waxes and wanes with the manifest value and feasibility of ruling your own state.

My very schematic survey will provide few clues as to the reasons why nationalism took different forms, intensities, and social bases in, say, Norway and Bohemia (see Hroch 1985). Nor will it dare to explain the content of nationalist ideas or the mechanisms of their diffusion in the style of a Benedict Anderson or a Liah Greenfeld. Instead it will seek insight into the remarkable historical timing of nationalist demands.

When and how did ethnic multiplicity become a political problem? For most of world history, after all, thousands of peoples claiming distinctive identities have coexisted with and within states that managed some form of indirect rule (Armstrong 1982). More states resembled the Austro-Hungarian Empire than emulated Sweden. Those states have usually favored some identities over others, but neither homogenized their populations nor faced serious threats that subject peoples would rebel in the name of their distinctness. Only late in the eighteenth century did nationalism become a salient force in European politics.

To be precise, two different phenomena acquired the name "nationalism." We might call one top-down nationalism, the other bottom-up nationalism. In *top-down nationalism*, rulers aggressively pursued a defined national interest while successfully making demands on a broadly defined citizenry in the name of the whole nation and in exclusion of other loyalties those citizens might have. In *bottom-up nationalism*, representatives of some population that currently did not have collective control of a state claimed a distinctive political status, or even a separate state. The two sometimes merged in irredentism, the demand that the territories occupied by related populations in adjacent states be attached to a putative mother state.

In any case, the two phenomena linked in their insistence that states ought to correspond to homogeneous peoples, that homogeneous peoples had distinctive political interests, that members of homogeneous peoples owed strong loyalties to the states that embodied their heritage, that the world should therefore consist of nation-states having strongly patriotic citizenries. Over the roughly ten thousand years that states have existed somewhere in the world, such ideas have been rare, their actual realization in states exceptional. I do not mean to deny Spartan patriotism, Jewish captivity, or ancient hatreds of Armenians and Turks. I mean to say that only during the last two hundred years have the two specific forms of nationalism become staples of national and international politics.

Not that homogeneous nation-states suddenly became dominant in Europe. On the contrary: Even during the last two nationalistic centuries, only a tiny proportion of the world's distinctive religious, linguistic, and cultural groupings have formed their own states, while precious few of the world's existing states have approximated the homogeneity and commitment conjured up by the label "nation-state." Within Europe itself, perhaps twentieth-century Portugal, Albania, Greece, Austria, Finland, Norway, Sweden, and Denmark all approached the mark at one moment or another. Despite much mythmaking to the contrary, however, such large states as France, the United Kingdom, Germany, Italy, and Spain all hosted visibly, vigorously heterogeneous peoples (see, for example, Noiriel 1988).

Should we therefore conclude with Hobsbawm that we are tracking a chimera? No, because from 1789 onward European rulers *did* make larger demands on their citizens in the nation's name while insisting that citizens themselves give their nation priority over other interests, states did commonly adopt programs of normative indoctrination designed to homogenize their subject populations and to activate their national commitments, cultural uniformity within states did increase, the cultural distinctiveness of states likewise increased, and spokesmen for national minorities did demand distinctive political treatment or separate states far more often than before 1789. What is more, political doctrines came to assume that the homogeneous and connected population of a nation-state not only existed but enjoyed

rights of citizenship rights by the very fact of its existence. "Just as the Greeks," remarks Robert Dahl, "took for granted that the proper scale of democracy, or for that
matter any decent political system, was necessarily extremely small—a few tens of
thousands of people—so since the late 18th century advocates of democracy have
generally assumed that the natural locus of democracy is the nation-state or, more
generally, the country" (Dahl 1989, 4).

Large groups of people acted on similar beliefs, demanding rights on the base of
citizenships real or imagined. Although we think of the century and a half after
1789 as the age par excellence of class revolutions, for example, even then the majority of forceful seizures of state power took place in the name of oppressed cultural minorities (Luard 1986, 54–58).

Why did those things, the very integument of nationalism, occur? Because in the
face of wars that demanded far more men, supplies, and funds from national populations than ever before, those women and (overwhelmingly) men who ran European states laid claim to and bounded a much wider range of resources than before, found it advantageous to homogenize and commit their populations, took
steps to do so, allied with segments of the bourgeoisie that shared an interest in ad-
vancing their own definitions of national identity over and against parochial identities, diminished the leverage of cultural brokers as such, and thus increased the
difference in power between those whose culture predominated in an existing state
and those whose culture did not.

Why did war matter? After a few seventeenth-century experiments, the eighteenth century saw the definitive decline of mercenary armed forces in favor of
large standing armies and navies recruited or even conscripted almost entirely from
national populations and financed chiefly by taxes on those same populations; the
French *levée en masse* of 1793 marked a major moment in that change. Except
where invasion loomed, ordinary people resisted press gangs and conscriptions
fiercely. Nevertheless, states beat down that resistance. Once France, Prussia, and a
few other powers were fielding massive armies and navies in this way, the market
for mercenaries collapsed in most of Europe, and every state that claimed a military presence followed the great-power suit.

The formation of such vast military forces in this peculiar way had a whole series of unintended but fundamental consequences: involving rulers in extended
struggle and bargaining with their subject populations, expanding definitions of
citizenship, forwarding ideas and practices of popular sovereignty, generating enforceable claims of subjects on states in such forms as rights to petition and associate, reinforcing various kinds of representative institutions, inflating central state
bureaucracies, moving states from indirect toward direct rule, extending state controls over stocks and flows of labor, capital, commodities, and money within and
across increasingly well-defined national borders, enlarging state obligations to military veterans and their families, constituting military veterans and their families as
collective political actors, and forwarding shared experience through military service itself. In Great Britain, for example, the war years from 1792 to 1815 saw not

only massive increase in armed forces and taxation, substantial growth and centralization of the national state, and a large increase in the powers of parliament, but also a great mutation of popular collective action toward associational bases, national issues, and claims on parliament (Tilly 1982, 1995b, 1997a).

Two linked features of these momentous processes deserve special attention: circumscription and central control. First, circumscription. All states exercise priority within relatively well-defined territories; that is one way we know they are states, not lineages, gangs, churches, corporations, or something else. Nevertheless, they vary widely with respect to how contiguous and sharply bounded those territories are and in regard to how deeply they exercise control at and within their boundaries.

In eighteenth-century Europe, larger states generally maintained lax controls over ill-defined and enclave-ridden borders; within those borders, furthermore, either they did not penetrate very deeply or they left that penetration to largely autonomous intermediaries. Migrant workers, merchants, goods, and money confronted many bandits and tollgates, but otherwise moved easily and without state monitoring within and across frontiers. Few states, furthermore, maintained effective systems of registration for property or persons; witness the rarity of national tax assessments and the surprise occasioned by the results of nineteenth-century censuses. Even obligatory military service, where it occurred, depended on local knowledge of the eligible males and was therefore highly vulnerable to local mystification.

What of central control? With the growth of massive national armed forces and the attendant growth of state budgets, almost all states erected wider, deeper, more direct systems of control. Central control extended, obviously, to property, production, and political activity; rulers stopped relying on highly autonomous magnates and pressed toward direct rule, toward the creation of administrations extending directly from the central power down to individual communities and households. It emphatically included *cultural* control, the singling out or creation of a single linguistic, historical, artistic, and practical tradition from all those present within the national territory. States began as never before to create national educational systems; to impose standard national languages; to organize expositions, museums, artistic subventions, and others means of displaying cultural production or heritage; to construct communications networks; to invent national flags, symbols, anthems, holidays, rituals, and traditions.

As a result, national populations did finally become less heterogeneous, even though few of them ever approximated the homogeneity of the ideal nation-state; the homogenizing effect extended to such profound matters as demographic behavior (Watkins 1990). National bourgeoisies and intelligentsias commonly collaborated in the effort, which in its early phases often discredited the exclusiveness and self-interest of the aristocracy, sometimes of the crown itself. Once begun, the process perpetuated itself, for the advantages of speaking a national language and adopting a national style rather than continuing to live within a shrinking, stigmatized pool became more and more manifest.

Cultural control benefited from the existence of a well-defined other; the alien enemy within or without magnified the value of assimilation, even for members of that alien enemy. Anti-Semitism had this force through much of Europe, but anti-German sentiment reinforced the desirability of becoming very French, as anti-French, anti-Polish, or anti-Russian feeling reinforced the desirability of becoming very German. The same dynamic operated within plural empires; once Austria and Hungary became well-defined separate spheres within the same empire after 1866, for example, the many German speakers of Budapest felt intense pressure either to leave or to Magyarize.

The process of circumscription helps explain a surprising feature of European nationalism: the relative unimportance of religious identification in the continent's top-down and bottom-up movements. More so than language or everyday practices, religion served for centuries as the prime symbolic bond among European peoples in those encounters that transcended strictly local ties (Armstrong 1982). The relative absence of mobilization based on shared religion after 1750, furthermore, contrasts sharply with the savage salience of religious boundaries during the Reformation and the various wars that followed up to the settlements of 1648. On the whole, religious identities became salient in two circumstances: (1) where the dominant class belonged to a distinctly different faith from their subjects, as in the Ottoman Empire, or (2) where (especially in the course of the Reformation) the state had managed to establish its own church, as in England, Scotland, and Sweden. Outside of these circumstances, religion had the troublesome consequence of identifying populations within one state with confessional cousins who inhabited quite different, and even rival, states.

Not that rulers never tried: Louis XIV's expulsion of Huguenots and his subsequent scorched-earth wars against Camisards supported his claim to be Europe's principal defender of the Catholic faith as well as weakening autonomous bases of power within his kingdom; even there the crown eventually settled for accepting payoffs from the remaining Protestants of the Midi. French revolutionaries and their successors tried first to capture the French Catholic church, then to suppress it, then to establish their own church, then to work out a modus vivendi with a church recognized to be multinational. From that point onward, language and presumed common origin constituted much more powerful bases of European nationalist demands than did religion. During the very period (say 1780–1830) in which anti-French nationalism was swelling in England, its rulers were dismantling the religious monopoly of public office they had erected with the Glorious Revolution of 1688.

This vast top-down process constituted top-down nationalism, making it seem normal politics in a world that had only recently experienced a quite different politics of dynastic interest, indirect rule, virtual representation, brokerage among multiple ethnicities, and extensive particularism. But it also increased the incentives and opportunities for bottom-up nationalism. To understand the connection, we must be clear about the constitution of ethnic groups and must avoid the presumption that they are primordial, unchanging entities that lie dormant for long periods and then express themselves when the time is ripe.

An *ethnic group* is a set of people who publicly claim a common origin and kinship that distinguishes them from other members of the same population. Ethnic groups form where and when the members of at least two well-connected networks defined by claimed origin and kinship begin competing for the same social niches; they form as ethnic groups rather than castes, classes, or local communities to the extent that (1) they coincide with systems of migration and (2) members define their ties as those of kinship. Entire ethnic groups almost never mobilize or act collectively, but ethnic groups serve as bases for mobilization and collective action when the actions of outsiders either threaten to exclude them from shared and collectively controlled opportunities or open up new niches to collective competition; ethnic entrepreneurs (who are often professional brokers such as intellectuals and politicians) play exceptional parts in such mobilizations.

Leaders and mobilized members of ethnically defined populations make strong claims for control over autonomous states or subdivisions of states under two conditions:

1. When competitors begin to make claims for statehood that would exclude and/or subordinate the ethnic group in question
2. When the agents of a state to which the population is already subordinated begin to threaten (a) the group's distinctive identity and/or (b) its shared access to advantageous niches

They actually acquire states of their own when they and their coalition partners, if any, both amass greater force than their competitors can assemble on the same territory and gain recognition from the rulers of other states that wield power in their region. Claims for statehood thus come in bunches and escalate to the point where one of the contenders has established priority in each territorial subdivision.

Top-down nationalism activated the formation, mobilization, and claim making of ethnic groups. It did so by legitimating the potent principle of correspondence between people and state, by greatly increasing the advantages to any group of controlling its own state (not to mention the disadvantages of *not* controlling its own state), by more frequently situating cultural minorities within one state adjacent to cultural majorities in neighboring states, by diminishing state toleration of distinctive cultural enclaves, and by attempts at forced assimilation of minorities, which in their turn threatened the positions of regional intelligentsias and bourgeoisies as cultural brokers. Only after 1790, for example, did any substantial number of Hungarian nobles start demanding that a standard Magyar, instead of Latin, become the language of administration and public life in polyglot Hungary; popular mobilization around that demand only occurred many decades later. But Hungary enjoyed a dual monarchy with Croatia, where the Hungarian demand stimulated first a defense of Latin and then a call for Croatian (which was then even less standardized than Magyar) as the "national" language. In the process German, which had served as a major lingua franca throughout the Habsburg domains, became much more clearly identified with Austria, as the ethnic Germans who had so long served as merchants and middlemen everywhere in the empire faced sharpened political choices.

The exact modalities of mobilization and resistance varied with the national population's class composition, urbanity, extent and multiplicity of cultural cleavage, and aggressiveness of attempts at assimilation. Throughout Europe, nevertheless, as those groups that controlled the state apparatus pursued campaigns of homogenization and assimilation they faced not just widespread resistance but newly mobilized demands for political autonomy, even for independence.

What, then, is happening today in the former Soviet Union and former Yugoslavia? Are we simply witnessing the explosion of bottled-up bottom-up nationalism? Not exactly. Although Russians certainly moved into positions of power in the Soviet Union's non-Russian sections and Serbs took advantageous positions within Yugoslavia, both states offered considerable latitude to ethnic minorities and enclaves. In both cases, however, the weakening of the central power forwarded a quasi-revolutionary situation that introduced uncertainty into each particular compact between a recognized group and the center.

As in the surge of claim making that occurs early in revolutions when everyone's rights and privileges become uncertain, both locally dominant ethnic groups and their threatened neighbors began jostling each other for position at the next settlement. But the tearing of the Iron Curtain and the rapt attention of states outside of Eastern Europe made possible two outcomes that were unthinkable a few years before 1989: (1) the formation of firm, independent alliances between segments of the old composites such as Estonia or Slovenia and states outside the zone of state socialism; (2) the application of the principle one people: one state within that zone. The likelihood that Western powers would facilitate those outcomes without fear of attack from the Soviet military opened entirely new opportunities.

Despite the recent surge of bottom-up nationalism, nevertheless, a number of changes point toward a longer-term *decline* in nationalism. The most important is the shrinking capacity of European states to sustain the dramatic circumscription of capital, labor, goods, services, money, and culture that began occurring so widely two hundred years ago. After two centuries in which they did succeed remarkably in monitoring, capturing, and storing resources within well-defined borders, Western states in general are finding it increasingly difficult to maintain control of migrant workers, capital, drugs, technologies, and money.

The European Union is compounding that difficulty for its members by actually promoting free movement of capital, commodities, and labor, establishing a common currency, and pressing them toward uniform welfare policies. In the longer run, these pressures will undermine the autonomy and circumscription of individual states, make it extremely difficult for any state to carry on a separate fiscal, welfare, or military policy, and thus reduce the relative advantage of controlling the apparatus of a national state. It is quite possible that the many activities states bundled together in the era and aftermath of the French Revolution will again separate, with capital, for example, operating rather independently of any particular state's interests.

If this happens, the incentives to both top-down and bottom-up nationalism will decline rapidly. A conceivable result, ironically, is a proliferation of cultural particularisms, now freed from the burden of challenging state authority and seeking political autonomy. In the future, cultural pluralism may well become compatible with the devolution of economic and political power to very large units, no longer identical and no longer consolidated states as we have known them for two hundred years. What some people see as an age of renewed nationalism may well preface an age of its utter decline.

13

The Time of States

Born in 1921, my late friend and collaborator Stein Rokkan died in 1979, well before his time, and well before his wide-ranging view of political processes could take the hold it merited in comparative politics and macrosociology. Rokkan was a visionary virtuoso, a complex thinker who frequently incorporated new perspectives into his work only to discard them later as unhelpful. Anyone who tries to summarize the new directions his work was taking in the late 1970s therefore runs the risk of mistaking small waves for high tides. Let me take the risk, inviting refutation but also exploring possible extensions of his oeuvre. For most of his career, Rokkan treated time and space as he treated so many other factors that entered his explanations of political processes: as two among many dimensions of variation whose causal relations remained uncertain. For the Rokkan of *Comparative Research across Cultures and Nations* (1968), furthermore, time and space resembled each other in having little content, in mattering chiefly because they contained or represented other variables such as class, religion, or national culture.

Here he followed the intuitions of his friends the survey researchers, who normally take variation in space and time as challenges to discover the deeper variables that presumably underlie them, rather than historians, who commonly believe that (because experiences connect and accumulate) time and place themselves affect how things happen, even why they happen. For survey researchers, time and space are usually *thin*, transparent media carrying more substantial causes. For historians, time and space are usually *thick*, drenched with causes that inhere in sequence, accumulation, contingency, and proximity. The difference in conception

In October 1993, an audience at the University of Bergen heard the earliest version of this chapter as the Stein Rokkan Lecture. A later version appeared as "The Time of States," *Social Research* 61 (1994), 131–146.

has repeatedly led social scientists to the mistaken conclusion that historians are particularizers while social scientists are generalizers, hence that only social scientists can discern profound patterns in the facts about particular times and places historians so obligingly gather for them.

As I read Rokkan's late papers, his predilections changed during the 1970s; he moved toward a thicker conception of time, if not of space. He became more of a historian. In both his successive conceptual maps of European political history and his examination of citizenship's varying courses among Scandinavian countries, he began to reflect on what economists now often call path-dependency: on the idea that the order in which things happen affects *how* they happen, that the trajectory of change up to a certain point itself constrains the trajectory beyond that point, that choices made at a particular moment eliminate whole ranges of possibilities from later choices. Thus, in his unpublished draft of *Economy, Territory, Identity* (chapter 2) completed shortly before his death, Rokkan outlined a "four-step model" for the interaction of politics, economy, and culture in the production of distinctive language patterns in peripheral regions.

The four "steps" included medieval geoeconomic position, commercial expansion cum early urbanization, timing of the Industrial Revolution, and changes in the peripheral economy. In each of the first three steps, according to the model, timing made the difference: early versus late territorial unification, early versus late alphabetization, early versus late standardization of printing, and so on. Not only timing but sequence, in this scheme, deeply affected the paths and outcomes of linguistic transformation. Rokkan's conceptual maps applied parallel reasoning to the formation of different kinds of states.

So far as his published bibliography reveals, Rokkan never wrote a sustained analysis of time. Assuming that is correct, let me once again take up a subject that Rokkan opened but did not close: the time of states. The phrase has three different meanings, all of them germane to the history of European states. The first refers to the *era* in which consolidated states—powerful, sharply bounded, relatively centralized coercion-wielding organizations—dominated the European landscape, which started about two centuries ago and is now ending. Looking back from A.D. 2100, I suggest, Europeans will consider the twenty decades in question as the lost heyday of state power, the Time of States.

The second refers to the changing *medium* of time in which states lived, the diverse temporal organizations of other actors with which agents of states had to contend. I will claim that military reorganization and the growth of capitalist discipline both marked the medium deeply. The third meaning refers to the *influence* states exerted by ordering their citizens' time. I will argue that after 1800 or so agents of states themselves imposed new forms of time discipline on their citizens, to the point of making a version of astronomical time seem universal, natural, and fundamental. If time is a sea, the era is the course of consolidated states' voyage upon it, the medium is the sea's condition as such states steamed through it, and influence is the effect on the sea of the vessels' passage.

THE PLACE OF TIME

What sort of sea is this, anyway? For present purposes, let us adopt a *relational* conception of time. Time is an invention, the humanly negotiated concordance of two or more sequences, any sequences whatsoever. No single sequence establishes a time, and no time exists outside of human convention. Despite its appearance of superhuman reality, time reeks of culture; it centers on shared understandings about relationships among sequences. Time therefore changes as shared understandings and choices of sequences change.

This conception obviously sidesteps the important philosophical question of whether some absolute superhuman time exists against which we could or should calibrate all other times and the important sociobiological question of whether genetically grounded physiological rhythms provide the unconscious model for most or all human times. It also neglects the obvious bonding of time with space in order to emphasize the social plasticity of times. It took a great deal of effort to establish what most Westerners now take for granted: the priority of links to astronomical sequences (for example, the earth's rotation around the sun) over local events and cycles as "real" time. Once people start relating the histories of their own bodies to the succession of seasonal cycles or connecting their workday routines to the routine tolling of church bells, however, they have already invented nonastronomical times.

Many times therefore exist simultaneously, and most people spend their lives maneuvering among multiple times: family times, work times, church times, commercial times, transport times, and many more, only some of them closely coupled to astronomical sequences. The intersection of those times produces further times, some of them individual and some of them collective. To the extent that it involves negotiated connections with other sequences, a person's daily schedule incorporates many times, only some of which the person can control; the same is true of an organization's daily schedule.

Social events (bounded interactions) and processes (sequential relations among events) vary in texture and meaning as functions of their connections to different times. "Socially expected times," for example, define otherwise similar events as desirable or undesirable depending on where within a well-known sequence they lie (Merton 1984). In contemporary America, the birth of a first child to a couple in their twenties is a burden, but it fits with relative ease into existing schedules of work, school, and recreation; a comparable birth to a couple in their fifties, however gratifying to them personally, becomes an anomaly that disrupts the times of friends, relatives, work associates, and children of previous marriages.

Many features of life vary significantly as a function of prevailing times. The readiness of people to make long-term investments in friendship, parenthood, education, real estate, agriculture, and politics depends heavily on the shared commitment of other parties to continuous, enduring times. Douglass North (e.g., in North 1990) has argued persuasively that states promoted capitalist entrepreneurship by guaranteeing individuals' property rights; those property rights linked present investment with future return through the protection of ownership over long periods. Democracy crumbles without the assurance that those who lose in the current round of decision making will have a fair chance to win in the next; that assurance depends on the institution of a historically peculiar time, continuous and permanent but punctuated by incessant collective choices. Ambient times shape the linking of causes to effects, of rights to obligations, of pasts to futures.

This chapter makes no effort to explain in general how people conceptualize, experience, and organize time, or how temporal conceptualization, experience, and organization have changed in general over the last few centuries. Classical questions about the nature of time only enter the discussion insofar as they help us understand the impact of changing state activity on the public organization of time. Our subject is the time of states. Nevertheless, that subject requires a few general observations.

Ronald Aminzade has usefully singled out four temporal features that affect the social meanings of events and processes: pace, duration, cycles, and trajectory. These are not features of times as such, but of events' *situation* in time. Aminzade reluctantly concedes to Fernand Braudel and other macrohistorians the existence of "objective temporalities" in the long run, but insists on their problematic relation to the "subjective temporal orientations of social actors" (Aminzade 1992, 470; see also Abbott 2001b). We can therefore generalize Aminzade's analysis by pointing out (1) that the so-called objective temporalities are not actually natural, but result from negotiated concordances among sequences many people have simultaneously accepted as given, (2) that the so-called subjective temporal orientations consist of other times, often grounded in smaller populations and more local routines, (3) that intersections among the two categories of time therefore constitute new times, and (4) that pace, duration, cycles, trajectory, and texture in general assume different meanings and effects depending on the times in which they are embedded. That is why the same event—for example, a funeral—can be long or short, slow or rapid, repetitive or unique for different participants, depending on their own temporal frames.

As a medium for social life, an existing time constrains the choices of individuals and groups. If other people use certain sequences as major points of reference in their own lives, a person wanting to enter those lives must take the sequences into account, or even adopt them as reference points. G. William Skinner showed, for example, that in China the market schedules of adjacent centers dovetailed in a way that permitted merchants to make the rounds over regular cycles. Market areas thus delineated became effective units for marriage, social mobility, and regional politics as well (Skinner 1964, 1985). In Europe before the metric system, measures of cultivated land area usually referred either to the amount of seed it required (e.g., the *boisselée* for one bushel) or the amount of time it took to plow (e.g., the *journal* for a day's plowing); thus, people made the organization of time, space, property, and labor intersect (Kula 1986; Pro Ruiz 1992). In company towns, schools, military bases, monasteries, and other loci ordered by a single dominant time, activities such as gossip, flirtation, drinking, personal care, and fighting unintentionally but almost inevitably take their own sequences from those of the dominant time; they take place in the interstices offered by that time. In all these regards and more, established times constrain social action.

In similar ways throughout the world, existing sequences order a wide range of social behavior. Let us concentrate on the ways that states and political authorities intervene, intentionally or otherwise, in the sequences that prevail within their domains. Political authorities shape prevailing times in three different ways:

1. By preempting and ordering citizens' time directly, as in government employment, conscription, or obligatory voting
2. By absorbing portions of citizens' times indirectly in such activities as earning to pay taxes, answering official inquiries, or attending political meetings
3. By establishing their own inescapable temporal references: clock times, calendar times, schedules of school and work, cycles of military service, and so on

To the extent that citizens adjust other times to those reference points, states influence their citizens' time even when they do not command it directly. Direct command, in any case, need not involve minute-by-minute scheduling; on the average, microscopic supervision costs authorities more effort than do well-managed incentive systems and the building of self-directed loyalty, both of which often command large commitments of time and energy. By no means, furthermore, is all state influence on time nefarious; for many groups and individuals, the creation of common times affords possibilities of coordination and communication they would not otherwise enjoy. Precisely because it produces collective bads and goods, state intervention in time becomes an object of political contention. Sunday closing laws, curfews, regulation of workweeks, obligatory school attendance, setting of holidays, scheduling of transportation, parking rules, and publicly mandated pensions mark some of the more obvious regards in which state regulation of time affects widespread interests and therefore stimulates contention.

Times vary in many respects: continuity, repetitiveness, precision, and much more. Here, we can conveniently posit just two continua: from weak time to strong time and from particularized time to generalized time. *Weak time* links relatively reversible sequences, as in the correspondence between a series of musical notes and a series of dance steps, while *strong time* links relatively irreversible sequences, as in the attachment of human aging to the accumulation of solar years; the comment "Your child is big for his age" invokes just such a strong time. (Sequences of strong time need not, however, lodge chiefly in nonhuman processes; the binding of national histories by means of dynasties and heroes' lives also produces relatively strong times based primarily on human convention.) *Particularized time* applies to a limited range of circumstances, at the limit just one, while *generalized time* applies to a wide range of circumstances, at the limit all; two acrobats

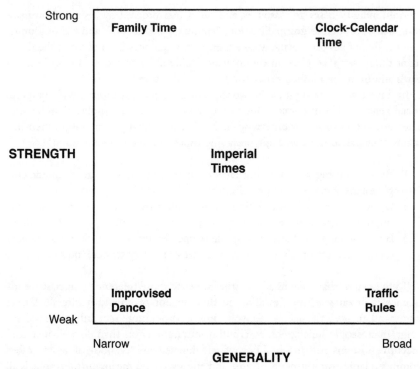

Figure 13.1   Varieties of Time

coordinate their sequences of gymnastics in a particularized time, while calendars announce generalized times. (Not all generalized times, however, are strong; traffic rules, for example, apply quite widely but involve mostly reversible sequences.)

Within the space defined by the two continua, as figure 13.1 indicates, many distinct times survive. *Family time* remains strong but particular, since such processes as fertility, mortality, nuptiality, and aging produce irreversible sequences whose concatenation uniquely defines the histories of particular families. *Imperial time* refers to the intersection in empires of the sequences imposed from the center of military power—for example, the annual exaction of tribute by Mongol khans— with the multiple sequences of tributary populations. We could, if necessary, distinguish other times—religious times, market times, school times, and many more—none of them precisely coordinate with astronomical time.

If a single irreversible sequence such as the history of the universe pairs with many reversible or less clearly irreversible sequences, nevertheless, it tends to become the *numéraire* of a generalized strong time. Powerful states promoted generalized strong times; they promoted the substitution of a small number of strong times for the enormous variety of weaker times by which most people organize their lives. Eventually they converged on the generalized strong time we now in-scribe on clocks and calendars, a time tied closely, albeit imperfectly, to astronomical sequences. State-designated fiscal years, for example, not only set the rhythms of government agencies but also affect the timing and sequence of tax-related expenditures and other activities among the general population of taxpayers. States inadvertently imposed generalized strong times on their citizens as state agents undertook sequences of action (first, mainly war, later, a much wider variety of activities) that demanded new resources and activity from the citizenry at each step of their realization.

More generally, two centuries ago or so militarily and economically induced changes in time as a *medium* helped bring Europeans into the *era* of strong states, which in turn produced new forms of *influence* over time. For two exceptional centuries European states and their extensions elsewhere succeeded remarkably in circumscribing and controlling the resources within their perimeters, employing various forms of time discipline as major elements of that mastery. But in our own era worldwide alterations in time as a medium are undermining that once-enormous control of states over their citizens' time. In consequence, at least in Europe, the era of strong states is itself now ending. So, in capsule, runs the series of speculations, conjectures, and hypotheses that informs my inquiry into time.

THE ERA OF STATES

In analyzing the time of states, we are talking about strong times, times involving irreversible sequences, but at several different scales: the scale of centuries, the scale of decades, the scale of years, the scale of weeks, for state employees and politicians, the scale of days, hours, and minutes. First, however, the large scale. States are organizations distinct from households and kinship groups that control the principal concentrated means of coercion and exercise priority over other organizations within substantial delimited territories. By this definition, states of some description have existed somewhere in the world for about eight thousand years. In the more urban parts of the world, they have exerted more power than other kinds of organizations over most of the last five thousand years. Even in Europe, which remained peripheral to the world's major systems of trade and empire until six or seven hundred years ago, states of some sort have wielded substantial power for two millennia or so. But only in the last two centuries did the sort of state that Europeans now take for granted assume recognizable shape.

Before the eighteenth century almost all European states above a very small scale were *segmented* in one of two senses; either (1) consisting of a small unit such as a seagoing city and its immediate hinterland or (2) governing a composite of many segments, each enjoying considerable autonomy and distinctness. Empires, federations, city-states, and dynastic composites all deserve the label "segmented." To the segments corresponded separate times, separate concordances of political sequences with the biographies of citizens, groups, and dominated regions.

After 1750 Europe produced *consolidated* states: large, differentiated, ruling heterogeneous territories directly, claiming to impose uniform fiscal, monetary, judicial,
legislative, military, and cultural systems on their citizens. Europeans mapped almost
all of their continent (and eventually much of the world beyond it) into mutually
exclusive territories each dominated by a single consolidated state. They created the
powerful idea, although rarely anything like the reality, of the nation-state: the coherent, homogeneous people matched to its own state. With that idea arrived the
troublesome doctrine and selective practice of national self-determination.

The times of ostensible nation-states were more uniform, more often astronomical, than those of segmented states. State times, to be sure, had their limits, especially limits set by competing generalized strong times. The French revolutionary calendar, which prevailed for about ten years, expressed the will of France's new
rulers to impose a state-defined time. In the Year VI/1798 the republican government made a serious effort to require citizens to time weddings, festivals, and days
off to the new calendar. At least in Marseille, and to a lesser extent in Provençal villages, the calendar's imposition did alter the rhythms of both public and private life
(Meinzer 1992, 77–156). But the new time did not survive the Napoleonic
regime's reconciliation with the Catholic Church, purveyor of its own version of
astronomical time.

In Europe after 1750, large states finally intervened directly and continuously in
the daily lives of their citizens instead of relying on privileged, autonomous intermediaries. In a wide variety of spheres—production, employment, welfare, education, public morals, transportation, income—state intervention displaced or subordinated particularized times to relatively general, strong state times. Recruitment
of large standing armies from the national population, it seems to me, played the
major part in these transformations; only during the nineteenth century did the
obviously augmented power of states regularly generate struggles through which
nonmilitary interests and issues became dominant in governmental affairs.

Increases in war's expense and scale outran the capacity of many states to employ mercenaries, who dominated European warfare from the fifteenth through
the seventeenth centuries; states turned to the creation of domestically recruited
standing armies, which generated national fiscal apparatuses, supply systems, and
field administrations, bypassed or co-opted previously autonomous local and regional powerholders and suppliers of troops, subordinated municipal finances more
completely to national finances, and engaged agents of the state in extensive, sometimes bloody, bargaining with leaders at all levels from village to nation, bargaining
that committed leaders and followers to the military effort but also gave them new
rights vis-à-vis national authorities. The wars of revolutionary and imperial France
seem to have been crucial both as models of military-political organization and
through France's deliberate imposition of new governmental forms in conquered
areas.

Many scholars doubt my strong emphasis on military transformation (Downing
1992; Gorski 1993; Lachmann 1987, 1989a, 1989b). They insist on the influence of

religious traditions, previous constitutions, geopolitical positions, elite kinship systems, and other "variables" that would no doubt have occurred to Stein Rokkan as well. They may well be right. Certainly, the exact process of consolidation varied greatly across Europe as a function of the relative predominance of coercion and capital in a region, the presence or absence of powerful empires, and the extent to which governmental change occurred through conquest. Fortunately, all we need to believe for present purposes is that consolidated states, for whatever reasons, became dominant in Europe after 1750 or so. As that happened, Europe—and eventually the whole world—entered the era of states.

The era of states made a profound difference to the world's experience. War, for example, reached previously unimaginable deadliness. The world death rate for war ran around 90 per million population per year during the eighteenth century, 150 per million during the nineteenth century, over 400 per million during the twentieth century. (Without the Napoleonic Wars, the nineteenth century would look less violent than the eighteenth, as the excision of the two World Wars would greatly diminish the twentieth century's increase in violence; but those wars did happen in those centuries.) Because consolidated states forwarded the principle of national self-determination, nationalism became a much more widespread basis of revolution, rebellion, and civil war. Although the Chinese state and major Christian churches had something to teach the Europeans about bureaucracy, lay Westerners encountered bureaucracies as never before.

That was not all. Policing shifted from reactive to proactive, from the apprehension and exemplary punishment of some criminals after the fact to patrolling, surveillance, and other measures designed to prevent and channel illegal activity, including illegal collective action. Elections, plebiscites, politicized media, and political parties began to affect the distribution of power on a national scale. Ordinary citizens found their rights, obligations, opportunities, threats, and interests so heavily tied up in states that state personnel and performance came to concern them greatly, even to generate mass claim making. On the average, European states moved toward incomplete forms of democracy: broader and more equal citizenship, greater citizen control over state personnel and policies, more extensive protection of citizens against arbitrary action by state agents. For better *and* worse, the era of states created popular politics at a national scale.

Need I recall how much my dates resemble the panels of cartoons? Of course, Maurice of Nassau organized military drill in his Dutch armies during the sixteenth-century war against Spain; of course, conquering Gustavus Adolphus was consolidating the Swedish state of 1632 in ways that I have consigned to the period after 1750; of course, the Ottoman Empire remained segmented to its very demise in World War I; of course, the Thirty Years War was deadly. Nevertheless, over most of Europe the trend toward consolidated states and their concomitants grew much stronger and more unitary after 1750. That acceleration and generalization ushered in the Time of States.

THE CHANGING MEDIUM

In the realms of both coercion and capital, between the sixteenth and nineteenth centuries Europe made major moves from particularized weak times to generalized strong times. Before then religious institutions, agricultural cycles, and sequences implied by a demographic regime pairing high fertility with high mortality had all imposed particularized times of at least moderate strength within their own zones, but nothing like the generalized strong times that emerged after 1500 or so. The reorganization of military force and the expansion of capitalist production promoted parallel changes in the organization of time. In the realm of coercion, European states effected widespread disarming of their civilian populations, greatly sharpened the distinction between military and civil force, created extensive markets for military supplies, and built armies remarkable for their discipline at levels from the drilling company to the maneuvering regiment. The process also generated civilian bureaucracies devoted to financing and supplying those armies. All these efforts involved time discipline on a scale unprecedented in European experience, although no doubt rivaled by Chinese imperial armies. All of them relied increasingly on scheduling and timing, on astronomically based clock time, without which money and supplies would be lacking at crucial moments, distinct military units would fail to meet, and the rate of infantry fire would fall so low as to subject whole companies to annihilation.

Crucial alterations occurred in the recruitment of military force. In general, rulers in regions of great landlords such as Russia, Lithuania–Poland, Castile, and East Prussia relied longer and more extensively on the calling up of private armies whose commanders integrated them into national forces contingently by the campaign, while urban-commercial areas relied longer and more extensively on partly autonomous militias and mercenaries likewise hired by the campaign. With that crucial qualification, we can break European military history of the last eight centuries or so into three broad phases: (1) a period dominated by levies and militias, up to the fifteenth century, (2) a period of mercenaries, especially from the fifteenth to seventeenth centuries, (3) a transition to nationally recruited standing armies, from the eighteenth century onward. (Focusing on the great European military powers, John Lynn distinguishes a full seven phases from A.D. 800 to the present, but his overall sequence dovetails with this one; Lynn 1993.) During the intermediate mercenary period, the export of mercenaries became a major source of revenue for such energetic suppliers as Switzerland, Hesse, Ireland, and Croatia. On the sea, parallel processes brought privateers and pirates onto the oceans.

Although freebooting nobles played an important part on land and sea, the entire system depended on military entrepreneurs, men who could not only recruit good soldiers but also find enough capital to supply them, equip them, transport them, and pay them until monarchs or conquered areas refilled the coffers. Capitalist risktakers on a grand scale, entrepreneurs such as Wallenstein grew rich and powerful by assembling and hiring out military force; for their time, they became quintessential capitalists. It was they especially who applied time discipline to military organization on a large scale. The application of generalized strong time to military activity, in its turn, first promoted the rise of consolidated states, then permitted the rulers of consolidated states to command increasing destructive power.

Parallel changes occurred in the realm of capital. Europe's consolidated states grew up in a world of expanding capitalism, the system in which people who control capital make the major decisions concerning the combination of capital, labor, commodities, technology, and land in production of goods and services. To the extent that capitalists chose to produce on their own premises rather than purchasing other people's production for further processing or resale, they tied up capital on whose continuous and rapid deployment their profits depended. Capitalism generated wage labor, that historically peculiar arrangement in which for a payment stipulated in advance and within conventional or contractual limits workers subject their labor power to a capitalist's control, expending it on means of production owned by the capitalist. Although some capitalists paid by results in piecework, task work, or commissions, and although capitalists long acquired much of their labor power through subcontracting rather than direct supervision, most capitalist wages stipulated time: hour, day, week, month, or year. The formula

$$(\text{Work time} \times \text{Wage per unit time}) \, / \, \text{Prices} = \text{Real income}$$

came to define a household's capacity to acquire the goods necessary for its survival. This fact sensitized proletarian housekeepers exquisitely to triangulation among work time, wages, and prices. Capitalists were creating new versions of time as a medium.

To be sure, European monasteries, ships, armies, and scientists had already invented their own disciplined times well before the eighteenth century; capitalists adapted those times by means of such devices as chronometers, starting bells, lunch hours, and penalties for missed work time. But industrial capitalists generalized the practice of time discipline, scheduling and supervising their employees' work closely. They thus created such recurrent conditions as rush hours, when many people were traveling between home and workplace because multiple firms summoned and dismissed their workers simultaneously.

Railroads thrived on the combination of pocket watch and telegraph, which made it possible to establish simultaneity over large distances, therefore to schedule movements along great lengths of track. By 1837, Great Britain had established uniform time throughout its railways, a move that cascaded to businesses and households relying on railways, thence to the whole country. After railway-inspired Americans forwarded worldwide unification by establishing time zones for their broad continent in 1883, European states bargained out their reckoning of time from Greenwich in 1884. (Proud France, however, held to its own time until 1911.) Later, telephone and radio hugely extended the range of simultaneity. Thus, most of the world fell subject to a strong, generalized time, largely inspired by capitalists but promoted and enforced by states. Advocates rationalized the uniformity as scientific, natural, or even universal time.

Capitalist work generated such devices as the watchman's clock (in which keys located along a route the watchman is supposed to patrol leave timed marks to indicate when the guard actually arrived at each post) and the redundantly named time clock (in which workers insert their "time cards" for stamping when they start and leave work), not to mention the more recent closed-circuit television and computer surveillance of performance. They created time-and-motion studies as a means of maximizing production per unit of time. Later capitalists followed the same line in engineering telephone-mediated electronic mail and satellite-mediated television.

In imposing time discipline, capitalists unintentionally stimulated new forms of time-tuned resistance such as goldbricking, working by rule, signaling the approach of supervisors, restricting output, sabotaging production lines, and stretching authorized breaks. The well-timed firm-by-firm strike itself gained effectiveness from the reliance of firms on tight schedules and continuous production. Scheduling and time discipline became crucial components of capitalist work, to such an extent that capitalists came to believe in them as personal virtues and to deplore the lax time sense of ordinary workers. "Time is money" epitomizes this mentality.

The texture of time as a medium for states therefore altered significantly during the nineteenth and twentieth centuries. Military conscription, for example, now threatened to disrupt the operation of large, capital-concentrated organizations whose owners wielded considerable political power; that led to negotiation over who should be eligible for the draft. The schedules of government services, surveillance, schools, military movements, careers, pensions, purchases, payments, and tax collections all impinged on the times of powerful organizations and individuals outside the state, and therefore became objects of political struggle. Reciprocally, the expansion of capitalist time induced changes in policing, officially declared holidays, information gathering, and so on through a wide range of state activity. When Lenin and his fellow Bolsheviks founded the first socialist state, as they reorganized labor processes in manufacturing they turned to Taylorism, a quintessential application of capitalist time discipline.

STATE INFLUENCE OVER TIME

Since state agents interacted incessantly with other political actors, my discussion of time as a medium has inevitably drifted into observations of state influence over time. But states did much more than I have said so far. The displacement of segmented states by consolidated states forwarded two related aspects of state power we can call circumscription and central control.

Circumscription refers to the increasing capacity to regulate stocks and flows of resources within and across national frontiers. To a previously unimaginable degree, European states began regulating the accumulation, movements, and transfer of ideas, technologies, goods, persons, and capital, with sufficient effectiveness that they could intervene deliberately in money supply, technological innovation, investment, and employment. They started to require passports for entry and exit, to restrict the passage of all sorts of resources across frontiers, therefore to regard international enclaves and regions under the jurisdiction of multiple states as undesirable anomalies.

Central control refers to the state's penetration of existing groups and activities at all levels by means of command, coordination, and surveillance. States began to exercise unprecedented control over working conditions, transportation, education, urban form, and much more. Central control included the reshaping of culture: shared understandings and their objectifications. During the nineteenth and twentieth centuries, state-directed schools, museums, festivals, and publications all favored nationally defined self-identifications, histories, languages, and creeds, labeling their rivals as inferior, primitive, mistaken, or even subversive. Each such nationally promoted culture involved an irreversible story of origin and destination; the attachment of linguistic, cultural, and social histories to a political narrative produced a strong national time. National narratives, furthermore, situated their states with respect to other times, claiming a place for Russians or Norwegians in the history of Europe as a whole. Wherever the idea of the nation-state and its priority over other political forms came from originally, cultural control cemented it in place.

Although the time of states first centered on military activity, the extension of circumscription and central control spread state capacity into widening circles of social life, made access to state power a prize for many groups having little direct involvement in military affairs, generated struggles whose settlements established civilian claims on the state, and thereby enormously broadened the scope of civilian politics at a national scale. Organized claimants—communities, employers, workers, kin groups, religious congregations—found themselves willy-nilly embedding their privileges and rights in the state. As a consequence, the range of activities and social relations influenced by state time underwent a huge expansion.

State circumscription and central control intervened in the subject population's conception and allocation of time in three related ways.

First, states acquired greater power to define the date and the time within the day, eventually assuming the authority to manipulate the clock by such devices as daylight saving time. Within limits set by international compacts, they came to own definitive answers to the questions "What day is this?" and "What time is it?"

Second, states instituted direct controls over the timing of a whole series of activities: long-distance travel, crossings of frontiers, acquisitions of citizenship, payments of taxes, attendance at school, military service, hours of work, holidays, openings of public monuments, museums, and parks, terms of office, mail delivery, availability of other government services, and much more.

Third, their expanded demands for resources preempted citizens' time—directly in the form of government employment and military service, indirectly in the form of work time devoted to generating the money to pay taxes. In Great Britain, for example, the total tax burden per capita, computed as equivalents of a laborer's daily wage, came to 12 days in 1758, 14 in 1789, 32 in 1815, with a postwar recession to 23 by 1827 before a resumption of increases in the 1840s, but nothing like a return to prewar levels; the great French wars almost tripled the time a hypothetical average British worker devoted to earning tax money (computed from Lindert and Williamson 1983; Mitchell and Deane 1971; Wrigley and Schofield 1981).

The state's three great interventions in time—establishing official clocks and calendars, controlling the time of multiple activities, and preempting citizens' time for state service—altered popular time horizons, for example, by favoring incremental political activity that could cumulate to a change in state policy or personnel at the next scheduled election.

Just as the institution of capitalist times opened up various time-tuned forms of resistance and claim making to workers, the institution of state times promoted time-tuned forms of resistance and claim making among citizens. Once governments operated on regular schedules for tax collections, military conscription, censuses, registrations of property, voting, and any number of other interventions to gather essential resources or information, they became vulnerable to collective control of the time in question by opponents or competitors—churches, labor unions, revolutionary conspiracies, political parties, separatist groups, or other governments. Boycotts, damage to registers or other instruments of surveillance and control, collective blockage of governmental agents, flight, hiding of desired resources, even the mass display of intent and capacity to undertake any of these actions all became more disruptive to the extent that (1) other governmental activity depended on the results of the challenged interventions and (2) the effectiveness of the interventions themselves depended on their timing and on the collaboration of citizens with state-prescribed times.

One remarkable consequence of state time's expanding influence was therefore a transformation of popular collective claim making. We know more about Western Europe, where scholars have spent greater energy cataloging forms of contention than elsewhere in Europe. There predominant eighteenth-century forms of collective claim making included land invasions, group hunting on posted land, attacks on customs barriers, rituals shaming ostensibly immoral persons, seizures of grain, expulsions of tax collectors and other unwanted officials, displays of hostile symbols during public ceremonies and festivals, orderly destruction of houses, mutinies, resistance to arrests, trade-wide turnouts, and similar forms of action. During the nineteenth century, as these contentious forms receded over much of Western Europe, others took over: public meetings, electoral rallies, demonstrations, parades, firm-by-firm strikes, and related forms of action. Generally speaking, social movement logic came to prevail.

From the perspective of time, this transition from one repertoire to another has three noteworthy features:

First, the far smaller array of new forms often occurred more or less simultaneously according to similar routines in multiple locations, connected by networks of activists and political entrepreneurs. They responded to coordinated timing.

Second, while the older forms of action generally relied on times that belonged to interconnected local routines—markets, holiday assemblies, the rhythms of agricultural work, and so on—the newer ones created their own times, deliberately disrupting or at least diverting daily routines of assembly and dispersion.

Third, on the average their temporal logics differed greatly. "Eighteenth-century" actions could, if successful, often accomplish their objects within the course of a single gathering: the destruction of a toll barrier, the lowering of prices in the market, the ejection of an obnoxious official, and so on. That was almost never the case with the "nineteenth-century" forms; in their very logic, they belonged to accumulations of displays, of statements of support for or opposition to programs on which someone else—parliaments, rulers, capitalists—might act.

Comparing social movement politics with such insider activities as lobbying and party politics, twentieth-century observers (e.g., Flacks 1993) have often thought that the essence of such movements is direct action—action that often breaches political rules and conventional norms. As compared with their predecessors, however, the meetings, marches, and rallies of social movements proceeded quite indirectly. They assumed a Great Scorekeeper who somehow computed for each gathering the multiple of worthiness, unity, number, and commitment manifested by the supporters of one program or another, then summed all gatherings program by program.

The shift from one form of claim making toward the other therefore imposed a series of costs on leaders of collective action and their associations: the burden of exerting significant control over their members' times, the burden of articulating the connection between the particular action and goals that could only be accomplished by means of cumulation across many actions, the burden of foregoing short-run satisfactions in favor of long-run discipline. They succeeded, where they did, to an important degree because the transformation of state and capitalist times deprived the older claim making of its efficacy and because the new times made the influence of national actions by state agents and capitalists on the fates of ordinary citizens more visible. In Great Britain and France, the two countries where I have studied changing repertoires carefully, parliamentary time clearly became more pivotal; political entrepreneurs and social movement activists tuned their claim making increasingly to recent or impending decisions of legislatures whose powers had greatly expanded through the fiscal negotiation entailed by major wars. Even in popular politics, then, the state's influence over time greatly increased.

THREATS TO STATE TIME

Consolidated states grew preeminent through their capacity to circumscribe and control a wide variety of resources in time and space. But in our own days flows of the crucial resources have enormously expanded in geographical extent, rapidity, and volume. Capital, labor, technology, information, goods all move with remarkable ease from country to country and continent to continent. Although wars civil and international continue to generate and to disrupt these movements, increasingly they travel not on the time of European states but on the times of world capital and of international compacts among states.

This liquidification of resources has, I suggest, two significant impacts on states. First, it undermines the capacity of any particular state to pursue monetary, welfare, investment, employment, and other policies that depend on the relative containment of the relevant resources for considerable time spans. Second, it encourages the best-positioned participants to create organizations at a scale far larger than the individual state—especially economic and political organizations in the form of multinational firms, common markets, and the like. In both cases, the state ceases to be an effective organizer of its citizens' time; at larger–than-national scales, new times emerge and new simultaneities result.

Consider the European Union. Civil wars, pressures for immigration, and demands or opportunities for investment along its perimeter could slow the advance of collective arrangements among its members and thus maintain their autonomies longer than seemed likely before the disintegration and economic contraction of socialist states that occurred after 1989. Eventually, however, the Union will surely resume steps that subvert both circumscription and central control at a national scale: not only the widely accepted euro, but also mobility of capital, free movement of labor, enhanced flow of communication, ready transfer of technology, coalescence of educational systems, and similar forms of pooling mandated by the Maastricht pact. In all these regards, the influence of individual state actions on the overall timing of activity will greatly diminish.

At a world scale, furthermore, other forces are pushing in the same direction. Multinational corporations and worldwide financial markets are facilitating the worldwide mobility of capital with attendant movements of information, technology, and labor. Rising international inequalities of income are raising the pressure for migration from poor countries to rich; employers of cheap labor and members of international migration chains who have already established themselves in rich countries are collaborating implicitly or even explicitly to spirit low-wage workers past border controls. Capitalists are dissolving the Fordist logic that gave priority to career employment to full-time workers, especially adult males. The increasing prevalence of civil war among military conflicts is generating refugees at an unprecedented rate. Informal and underground economies are proliferating. These changes, too, undermine state circumscription and central control, diminishing the influence of state time on the rhythms of employment, investment, schooling, and technical innovation.

The question remains, however: What new times will emerge? I see three possibilities. First, my analysis may be mistaken, for any of several reasons, with state or national times turning out to be more durable than I have said. Second, today's trends may actually be extending those of the last two centuries to a larger scale, so that superstates and supermarkets (the European Union among them) will displace national states and markets as the world's great timekeepers. Third, the long movement toward strong, generalized times may reverse itself as people come to live in multiple times—separate times for protection, production, consumption, procreation, recreation, friendship, worship, and other zones of activity, each individual and group knotting them together in their own distinctive times. Far from the gray, clocked uniformity that critics of modernity have so often feared, we could be approaching lives and times of unparalleled diversity.

14

Processes and Mechanisms of Democratization

Aristotle described democratization as a perversion. In a constitutional government, when the majority substituted its particular interest for the community's general interest, self-serving rule of the many—democracy—resulted. In his analysis of political forms, Aristotle went on to specify processes promoting a majority's pursuit of its narrow interest; for example, the rise of demagogues and the increase of a polity's size beyond the limits of mutual acquaintance. He also allowed that revolution could convert a tyranny or an oligarchy (his names for degenerate forms of monarchy and aristocracy) directly into a democracy. Aristotle's *Politics* does not offer a causal theory sufficient to specify the process by which today's Uganda or Uzbekistan could become democratic. It does, however, provide an exemplary model of theoretically coherent explanation. It goes far beyond mapping the initial conditions and sequences of events that constitute paths to democracy. It actually features causes and effects.

Explicitly identified causes and effects, in contrast, rarely grace recent discussions of democratization. Instead, analysts of democratization favor path tracing. No doubt detecting a path's existence makes a crucial move toward learning how to walk it. But even an excellent map does not teach plodding urbanites how to climb mountains. A commendably earnest search for visibly viable paths to democracy has skewed recent investigations away from causes to necessary and sufficient conditions. By now we have a plethora of conditions that someone has found to be associated with the onset of democracy and precious little idea of causal processes that generate such associations.

As a preliminary effort, to be sure, a search for conditions under which democratic polities emerge (or, for that matter, disappear) forwards the explanation and

An earlier version of this chapter appeared as "Processes and Mechanisms of Democratization," *Sociological Theory* 18 (2000): 1–16.

production of democratization. It helps specify exactly what investigators must explain. If, for example, democratization always occurs in the company of widening splits within ruling oligarchies (that is, such splits are active candidates for necessary conditions of democratization), a valid causal story will most likely connect democratization with such splits. Search for closely associated conditions also rules out many bad explanations simply by showing that they are incompatible with existing cases; if, for example, a population's generalized trust often rises from very low to very high after democratization begins, then previously existing high levels of generalized trust lose credibility as general causes of democratization. Specifying what must be explained and ruling out bad explanations contribute significantly to any explanatory inquiry. But they do not in themselves constitute explanations.

What does? Explanation requires identification of recurrent causal mechanisms that democratize a polity, plus specification of conditions that affect emergence and concatenation of those mechanisms. This chapter grows out of an effort to specify the various conditions and processes that promoted or blocked democratization in different parts of Europe between 1650 and the present. The chapter identifies possible mechanisms in democratization, then specifies likely conditions affecting their emergence and concatenation. It concentrates on relational mechanisms and processes, those connecting citizens with each other and with agents of government. It works its way backward through the broad causal sequence schematized in figure 14.1. Read forward, the diagram says the following:

- A variety of changes here bundled together as "regime environment" activate mechanisms that in turn generate incremental alterations in public politics, inequality, and networks of trust.
- Changes of inequality and of trust networks have independent effects on public politics.
- Regime environment also produces occasional shocks in the form of conquest, confrontation, colonization, or revolution.
- Such shocks accelerate the standard change mechanisms, thus causing relatively rapid alterations of public politics, inequality, and networks of trust.
- Whether incremental or abrupt, those alterations interact.
- Under rare but specifiable conditions those alterations produce democratization.
- Democratization is a special condition of public politics.

The point of the chapter is to unpack, clarify, and make plausible such an argument.

The argument proceeds on six fundamental assumptions: (1) If democratization occurs, the process does not take place on the scale of millennia (with the implication that it can only happen in places that have accumulated a favorable environment very gradually) or on the scale of months (with the implication that canny social engineers can build it rapidly almost anywhere), but at a scale in between, most likely over years or decades; (2) prevailing circumstances under which

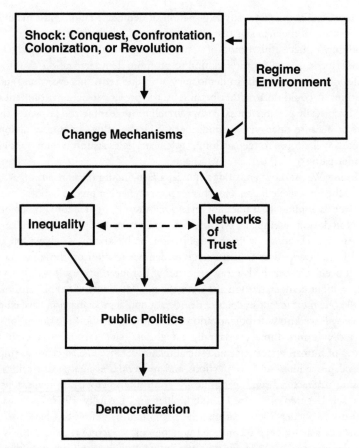

Figure 14.1   Casual Sequences in Democratization

democratization occurs vary significantly from era to era and region to region as a function of the international environment, available models of political organization, and predominant patterns of social relations; (3) not just one, but multiple paths to democracy exist; (4) most large-scale social environments that have ever existed and the majority of those that exist today contain major obstacles to democracy; (5) yet such obstacles diminish rapidly under specifiable circumstances; (6) democratization has rarely occurred, and still occurs rarely, because under most political regimes in most social environments major political actors have strong incentives and means to block the very processes that promote democratization.

If all six of these assumptions hold, attempts to specify universally applicable necessary and/or sufficient conditions for democratization will invariably fail. In that case, our best alternative is to look for widely applicable democracy-promoting causal mechanisms, then to identify variable conditions for their emergence and concatenation. In this view, any explanation of democratization must include a serious account of mechanisms that reduce the standard obstacles.

Ironically, a successful version of such an inquiry could plausibly produce a single prescriptive model for intervention to promote democratization, thus fostering the illusion of a single path to democracy, a unique set of necessary and sufficient conditions. It could do so either because in the present social environment one of many historically possible causal paths is much more feasible and attractive than the others or because once-viable conditions for all the others have now disappeared. Few of us will choose to reenact long, violent struggles against tyranny or oligarchy if gentler paths to democracy have opened.

Warning: We are now embarking not on a fact-finding mission but on a conceptual and theoretical excursion. This chapter presents neither precise hypotheses nor evidence for its arguments. It does not review the vast recent literature on democratization. Nor does it attempt to synthesize arguments or findings in that literature. It makes rash declarations without qualification or illustration. It draws on insights gained in my own effort to make sense of democratization on those rare occasions when it occurred over the last four centuries of European history. It sketches a way of thinking about democratization and states the case for a different explanatory strategy from the one most recent students of democracy and democratization have employed.

How will we know democratization when we see it? Working definitions of *democracy* divide into three overlapping categories: *substantive* criteria, emphasizing qualities of human experience and social relations; *constitutional* criteria, emphasizing legal procedures such as elections and referenda; *political-process* criteria, emphasizing interactions among politically constituted actors (for reviews and critiques, see Bermeo and Nord 2000; Collier and Levitsky 1997; Dawisha 1997; Heller 2000; Sheller 2000; Warren 1999). Substantive definitions have the inconvenience of leaving deeply contested whether any concrete regime actually qualifies as democratic, and if so, for whom. Constitutional definitions have the inconvenience of raising questions about discrepancies between official rules and their practical enforcement. Political-process definitions have the dual inconveniences of unfamiliarity and complexity, hence of greater distance from the everyday discourse of politicians and citizens.

Shouldering the inconveniences, my own preferred definition falls squarely within the political-process category. For present purposes, *a regime is democratic insofar as it maintains broad citizenship, equal citizenship, binding consultation of citizens at large with respect to governmental activities and personnel, as well as protection of citizens from arbitrary action by governmental agents.* I prefer such a political-process definition on the grounds that (1) it captures much of what theorists of democracy from Aristotle onward have been trying to describe without the usual inconveniences of substantive and constitutional definitions; (2) it clarifies causal connections between popular struggle and democratization, a much misunderstood but crucial relationship; and (3) it locates democracy within a causally coherent and more general field of variation in characteristics and practices of regimes.

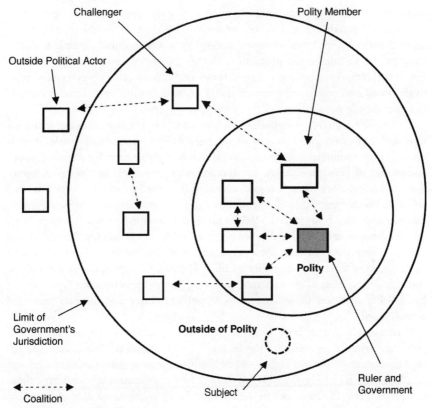

Figure 14.2   A Static Regime Model

Let me excavate the political-process definition of democracy to expose its foundations. Regimes, as schematized in figure 14.2, consist of governments and their relations to populations falling under their claimed jurisdictions (Finer 1997). Singling out constituted collective political actors (those that have names, internal organization, and repeated interactions with each other), we can distinguish *agents of government, polity members* (constituted political actors enjoying routine access to government agents and resources), *challengers* (constituted political actors lacking that routine access), *subjects* (persons and groups not currently organized into constituted political actors), and *outside political actors,* including other governments. Public politics consists of claim-making interactions among agents, polity members, challengers, and outside political actors.

Regimes vary, among other ways, in *breadth* (the proportion of all persons under the government's jurisdiction that belong to polity members), *equality* (the extent to which persons who do belong to polity members have similar access to governmental agents and resources), *consultation* (the degree to which polity members exercise binding collective control over governmental agents, re-sources, and activities), and finally *protection* (shielding of polity members and their constituencies from arbitrary action by governmental agents). Breadth, equality, consultation, and protection change in partial independence of each other; authoritarian populist regimes, for example, have commonly created rela-tively broad and equal polity membership in combination with limited consul-tation and little protection.

To simplify matters, nevertheless, we can combine breadth, equality, consulta-tion, and protection into a bundle of variables we call *protected consultation*. (Read-ers who prefer numerical formulations can think of it this way: We standardize our assessments of breadth, equality, consultation, and protection on the full range of historical experience in each regard, assigning 0 to the lowest value ever observed and 1 to the highest value, then multiply the four ratings into a single score that will likewise vary from 0 to 1.) When protected consultation reaches high levels (say, 0.8 on our combined scale), we begin to speak of democracy. Strictly speak-ing, then, democratization is not a consequence of changes in public politics but a special kind of alteration in public politics. Figure 14.1 represents public politics and democratization as two separate boxes simply to stress the causal problem at hand: What produces those alterations of public politics that increase protected consultation?

If democracy entails high levels of protected consultation by definition, as a practical matter it also requires the institution of citizenship. Citizenship consists, in this context, of mutual rights and obligations binding governmental agents to whole categories of people who are subject to the government's authority, those categories being defined chiefly or exclusively by relations to the government rather than by reference to particular connections with rulers or to membership in categories based on imputed durable traits such as race, ethnicity, gender, or reli-gion. (Thomas Janoski reaches for a similar conception in defining *citizenship* as "passive and active membership of individuals in a nation-state with certain uni-versalistic rights and obligations at a specified level of equality" [1998, 9].) At higher levels of protected consultation, we begin speaking of democratization. *De-mocratization* means any net shift toward citizenship, breadth of citizenship, equality of citizenship, binding consultation, and protection.

Our analytic problem, then, is to discover how and why regimes make net moves toward protected consultation, especially those net moves that bring them into the narrow zone of citizenship and democracy. Since many regimes that edge toward democracy later veer away, we can hope that solution of our primary analytic prob-lem will also help explain why de-democratization occurs.

One last definitional matter. *Governmental capacity* is the extent of governmental agents' control over changes in the condition of persons, activities, and resources within the territory over which the government exercises jurisdiction. Beyond a very small scale, no democracy survives in the absence of substantial governmental capacity. That is true for both internal and external reasons. Internally, maintenance of protection, consultation, equality, and breadth against the maneuvers of powerful domestic actors who have incentives to subvert them rests on substantial governmental capacity.

Externally, governments lacking substantial capacity remain vulnerable to subversion, attack, or even conquest by bandits, rebels, guerrilla forces, and outside governments. From the perspective of its large noble class (although certainly not from the perspectives of its merchants and peasants), eighteenth-century Poland's government glowed with protected consultation. It notoriously lacked capacity, however, so much so that rebellions of Cossacks and others from within its perimeter and conquest by Russia, Prussia, and Austria from without choked off its existence as an autonomous state from 1795 to World War I.

Figure 14.3 schematizes a line of reasoning that follows. Where low governmental capacity and little protected consultation prevail, political life goes on in

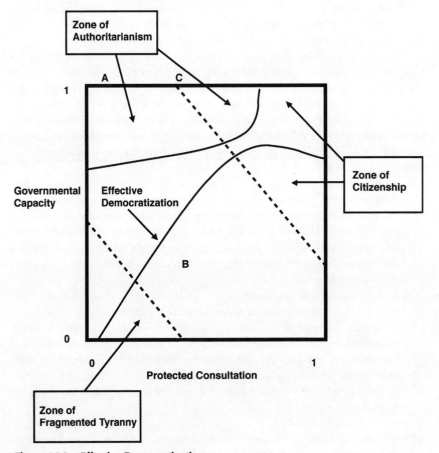

Figure 14.3   Effective Democratization

fragmented tyranny: multiple coercive forces, small-scale despots, and competitors for larger-scale power, but no effective central government. The diagram's opposite corner contains the zone of citizenship: mutual rights and obligations binding governmental agents to whole categories of people who are subject to the government's authority, those categories being defined chiefly or exclusively by relations to the government rather than by reference to particular ties with rulers or membership in categories based on imputed durable traits such as race, ethnicity, gender, or religion.

At point A of the diagram's triangular citizenship zone, a combination of little protected consultation and extremely high governmental capacity describes a regimented state, one we might call totalitarian. Nazi Germany illustrates political processes at that point. At point B, protected consultation has reached its maximum, but governmental capacity is so low the regime runs the risk of internal and external attack. Nineteenth-century Belgium never reached that point, but veered repeatedly toward it (Deneckere 1997). Point C—maximum governmental capacity plus maximum protected consultation—is probably empty because of incompatibilities between extremely high capacity and consultation.

This line of reasoning leads to my sketching a zone of authoritarianism in the diagram's upper left, overlapping the zone of citizenship but by no means exhausting it. It also suggests an idealized path for effective democratization giving roughly equal weight to increases in governmental capacity and protected consultation up to the point of entry into citizenship, but then turning to deceleration, and ultimately mild reduction, of capacity where protected consultation has settled in.

Figure 14.4 sets limits on real histories of democratization by sketching two extreme paths:

A strong-state path, featuring early expansion of governmental capacity, entry into the zone of authoritarianism, expansion of protected consultation through a phase of authoritarian citizenship, finally, the emergence of a less authoritarian, more democratic, but still high-capacity regime; in European historical experience, Prussia from 1650 through 1925 came closer to such a trajectory than most other states.

A weak-state path, featuring early expansion of protected consultation followed only much later by increase in governmental capacity at the large scale, hence entry into the zone of effective citizenship from below; although few European states followed this trajectory very far because most of them that started succumbed to conquest or disintegration, Switzerland—shielded from conquest by mountainous terrain, rivalries among adjacent powers, and a militarily skilled population—came closer to this extreme than most other European regimes.

All real European histories fell within the extremes, most described much more erratic courses with reversals and sudden shifts in both dimensions, and the vast ma-

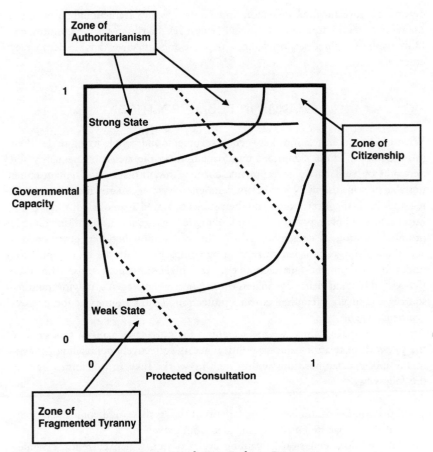

Figure 14.4   Strong-State versus Weak-State Paths to Democracy

jority entered or approached the zone of authoritarianism at one time or another. The schematic map simply makes it easier to describe the concrete paths of change we are trying to explain.

Where should we look for explanations? Democratization, I argue, emerges from interacting changes in three analytically separable but interdependent sets of social relations: public politics, inequality, and networks of trust. In the course of democratization, the bulk of a government's subject population acquires binding, protected, relatively equal claims on a government's agents, activities, and resources. In a related process, categorical inequality declines in those areas of social life that either constitute or immediately support participation in public politics. Finally, a significant shift occurs in the locus of interpersonal networks on which people rely when undertaking risky long-term enterprises such as marriage, long-distance trade, membership in crafts, and investment of savings; such networks move from evasion of governmental detection and control to involvement of government agents and presumption that such agents will meet their long-term commitments. Only where the three sets of changes intersect does effective, durable democracy emerge.

CHANGE IN PUBLIC POLITICS

What of changes in relations between governments and people living under their jurisdictions? Without significant transformations in the arenas of inequality and networks of trust strictly governmental changes toward democracy remain either unstable or nonexistent. Nevertheless, democratization necessarily includes shifts in relations between governments and their subjects, as well as among constituted political actors in public politics. We are looking for change mechanisms that directly promote creation of citizenship as a distinctive relation between governmental agents and subjects; broaden citizenship by comparison with the total population under the government's jurisdiction; equalize citizenship among those who qualify; expand binding claims by citizens over a government's agents, activities, and resources; and finally, strengthen citizens' protections against arbitrary action by governmental agents.

Broadly speaking, then, we are searching for causal mechanisms that enlarge the network of relations among political actors collectively controlling governments and equalize positions within such networks. Likely mechanisms include the following:

- Coalition formation between segments of ruling classes and constituted political actors that are currently excluded from power
- Mobilization-repression-bargaining cycles during which currently excluded actors act collectively in ways that threaten survival of the government and/or its ruling classes, governmental repression fails, struggle ensues, and settlements concede political standing and/or rights to mobilized actors
- Extraction-resistance-bargaining cycles in which governmental agents demand resources currently under control of nongovernmental networks and committed to nongovernmental ends, holders of those resources resist, struggle ensues, and settlements emerge in which people yield resources but receive credible guarantees with respect to constraints on future extraction
- Central co-optation or elimination of previously autonomous political intermediaries
- Bureaucratic containment of previously autonomous military forces
- Dissolution or segregation from government of nongovernmental patron–client networks
- Imposition of uniform governmental structures and practices throughout the government's jurisdiction

Each of these mechanisms poses further explanatory problems—for example, what processes dissolve nongovernmental patron–client networks, and why. But this inventory of proximate causal mechanisms in itself clarifies how and why broad, equal citizenship with binding consultation and protection come into being. All of them promote establishment of categorically defined rights and obligations directly connecting citizens to agents of government. Most of them also inhibit the pursuit of control over governmental activities, resources, and personnel by other means than those categorically defined rights and obligations.

CATEGORICAL INEQUALITY

Changes in categorical inequality require a bit more conceptual discussion than does the familiar topic of governmental change. Social categories consist of a boundary and a set of relations across that boundary; for example, the boundaries and relations that define such pairs as women/men, whites/blacks, or citizens/foreigners. Boundaries are usually incomplete, and areas away from boundaries, ill-defined; while at the frontier the distinction Arab-Jew takes on great salience and defines relations stringently, there are plenty of circumstances when it doesn't matter, and away from the point of confrontation it becomes less clear which people really qualify as Arabs (what about Arab Christians?), which people really qualify as Jews (what about Ethiopian adherents to Judaism?).

When relations across the boundary in question regularly produce greater advantages or fewer disadvantages for the parties on one side, we can speak of categorical inequality. The extent and character of categorical inequality in the population subject to a given government's jurisdiction significantly affects prospects for democratization. Where the limits of citizenship correspond to a widely operating categorical boundary (for example, an ostensibly racial boundary), that fact in itself constitutes a major obstacle to democratization. Widespread categorical inequality within the subject population, furthermore, increases incentives and capacities of participants in favored categories to turn the governmental apparatus to their own private ends, thus promoting the perversion of aristocracy that Aristotle called oligarchy.

Inequality can coexist with democracy just so long as it remains outside the sphere of public politics. Today's parliamentary monarchies often sustain relatively democratic institutions despite their categorical separation of royal families and aristocracies from the rest of the population. Conversely, inequality threatens democracy to the extent that its categorical relations reproduce themselves as divisions within public politics. Deep material inequality with respect to gender, race, lineage, or age usually translates into political inequality and thereby hinders democratization. But moderate levels of categorical inequality remain compatible with democratization so long as substantial insulation between public politics and other areas of life exists.

Four very general mechanisms interact to produce categorical inequality: exploitation, opportunity hoarding, emulation, and adaptation (for extended discussion, see Tilly 1998). Exploitation involves capturing control over a value-producing resource, imposing a distinction between owners and nonowners of the resource, enlisting the effort of nonowners in the production of use value by means of that resource, and yielding to those who contribute their effort less than the value the effort in question adds. Opportunity hoarding likewise involves capturing a value-producing resource, but excluding others from access to it, and collecting rents from that control. Emulation is borrowing of organizational forms, in the present case organizational forms that already have categorical inequality built into them.

Adaptation, finally, is alteration of social routines and relations in ways that depend on the presence of unequal categories and presume their persistence. Exploitation establishes inequality between owners and nonowners, opportunity hoarding creates inequality between insiders and outsiders, the two of them often reinforce each other (as when employers recruit favored workers exclusively from a single ethnic category), but emulation and adaptation lock either or both into place.

Governments involve themselves doubly in categorical inequality. First, they generally reinforce forms of exploitation and opportunity hoarding that manifestly benefit their dominant political actors. Not only do they enforce property laws and exclusive rights to niches, but also they support emulation and adaptation that sustain existing forms of exploitation and opportunity hoarding. Second, they themselves construct systems of exploitation and opportunity hoarding, for example, by conscripting young men for military service in wars that produce gains for rulers but not for soldiers and by establishing exclusive licenses to dispense religion or medicine.

Democracy is a special case of exploitation and opportunity hoarding, the case in which the bulk of a population belongs to the ruling classes, the government produces substantial collective goods, and categorical access to protected niches results from binding consultation of citizens. As the late Mancur Olson (1982) intuited but did not quite articulate, oligarchical ruling coalitions divert governmental activity and production in general from the common good. Olson saw most such coalition formation, including the creation of cartels and massive labor unions, as a hindrance to collective rationality because it kept free markets from adjudicating outcomes. Still he offered two insights that illuminate the process of democratization. First, coalitions approaching the whole population—democratic ruling classes—favor the production of genuinely collective goods (cf. Korpi 1983). Second, wars, revolutions, and other wholesale political housecleanings break up existing coalitions, thus providing unusual opportunities for political and economic reconstruction. We can use those insights.

Democratization entails dissolution or broadening of narrow coalitions among beneficiaries of exploitation and opportunity hoarding as well as creation of new, broad coalitions among beneficiaries. The presence of broad, relatively equal citizenship does not guarantee democratization, since it remains compatible with utter subjection to tyrannical and arbitrary authority; my earlier diagrams made just such an argument. But without substantial citizenship, formation of broad ruling coalitions faces insuperable obstacles.

What reduces the inscription of generalized categorical inequality into public politics? We have already discovered a few mechanisms that alter relations between governments and people living under their jurisdictions. Some of those mechanisms do their work through transformations of durable inequality; that is the case, for example, with central co-optation and elimination of previously autonomous political intermediaries. What additional mechanisms might dissolve, enlarge, or replace coalitions benefiting from government-backed exploitation and opportunity hoarding? Here are some candidates:

- Dissolution of coercive controls supporting current relations of exploitation and opportunity hoarding
- Education and communication that alter adaptations supporting current relations of exploitation and opportunity hoarding
- Education and communication that supplant existing models of organization, hence alter emulation in the production of new organizations
- Equalization of assets and/or well-being across categories within the population at large

More generally, changes that reduce benefits of exploitation and opportunity hoarding and/or increase the costs of their enforcement promote disintegration in existing systems of categorical inequality, and hence reduce obstacles to democratization in currently undemocratic regimes.

NETWORKS OF TRUST

The third arena that is crucial to democratization contains networks of trust. *Trust* is the knowing exposure of valued future outcomes to the risk of malfeasance by others. *Risk* is threat multiplied by uncertainty. People frequently confront short-term risk without creating elaborate social structure; on their own they leap raging rivers, engage in unsafe sex, drive while drunk, or bet a thousand dollars. When it comes to the long-term risks of reproduction, cohabitation, investment, migration, or agricultural enterprise, however, people generally embed those risks in durable, substantial social organization. To that extent, they trust others—they make the reduction of threat and/or uncertainty contingent on the performance of other people they cannot entirely control. Such sets of relations to others constitute networks of trust.

When people commit themselves to risky long-term enterprises whose outcomes depend significantly on the performances of other persons, they ordinarily embed those enterprises in interpersonal networks whose participants have strong incentives to meet their own commitments and encourage others to meet theirs. Such networks often pool risks and provide aid to unfortunate members. They commonly operate well, if and when they do, because members share extensive information about each other and about their social environment, because third parties monitor transactions among pairs of members, and because exclusion from the network inflicts serious harm on members who fail to meet their commitments (for more individualistic accounts of the same phenomena, see Besley 1995; Burt and Knez 1995; Burt 1998; Gambetta 1993; Granovetter 1995; Greif 1994; Landa 1994; Paxton 1999; Shapiro 1987; Warren 1999; Yamagishi and Yamagishi 1994). Trade diasporas, rotating credit circles, skilled crafts, professions, lineages, patron–client chains, and religious sects often exhibit these characteristics. They couple easily with control over systems of exploitation and, especially, opportunity hoarding.

Through most of human history, participants in networks of trust have guarded them jealously from governmental intervention. They have rightly feared that governmental agents would weaken them or divert them to less advantageous ends. Powerful participants who could not entirely escape governmental intervention have created partial immunities through such arrangements as indirect rule. Less powerful participants have characteristically adopted what James Scott calls weapons of the weak: concealment, foot-dragging, sabotage, and so on.

Democratization, however, entails a double shift of trust. First, within the political arena citizens trust the organization of consultation and protection sufficiently to wait out short-term losses of advantage instead of turning immediately to nongovernmental means of regaining lost advantages. Second, citizens build into risky long-term enterprises the assumption that government will endure and meet its commitments. Both are extremely rare circumstances over the long historical run. Within any regime that is not currently democratic, their realization faces enormous obstacles.

What mechanisms might reduce those obstacles? Here are some possibilities:

- Creation of external guarantees for government commitments
- Governmental incorporation and expansion of existing trust networks
- Governmental absorption or destruction of patron–client networks
- Disintegration of existing trust networks
- Expansion of the population lacking access to effective trust networks for their major long-term risky enterprises
- Appearance of new long-term risky opportunities that existing trust networks can't handle
- Substantial increase of the government's resources for risk reduction and/or compensation of loss
- Visible governmental meeting of commitments to the advantage of substantial new segments of the population

In general, these mechanisms promote acceptance of government and political participation as the least bad alternative.

CONQUEST, CONFRONTATION, COLONIZATION, AND REVOLUTION

Changes in public politics, inequality, and trust networks obviously interact. Most of the time they interact to block democratization. Under most circumstances, for example, increases in governmental capacity encourage those who already exercise considerable political power to divert governmental activity to their own advantage and incite participants in trust networks to reinforce those networks while shielding them more energetically from governmental intervention. Under what circumstances might we nevertheless expect government, inequality, and trust networks to move together toward democracy? Reflecting on European experience over the last three centuries, I see four recurrent circumstances that have sometimes activated multiple democracy-promoting mechanisms: conquest, confrontation, colonization, and revolution. All involve abrupt shocks to existing social arrangements.

Conquest is the forcible reorganization of existing systems of government, inequality, and trust by an external power. In the history of European democratization, the most famous example is no doubt conquest by French revolutionary and Napoleonic armies outside of France, which left governments on a semidemocratic French model in place through much of Western Europe after Napoleon's defeat. Reestablishment of France, Germany, Italy, and Japan on more or less democratic bases after World War II rivals French revolutionary exploits in this regard. Conquest probably promotes democratization when it does because it activates a whole series of the mechanisms enumerated earlier, notably including the destruction of old trust networks and the provision of external guarantees that the new government will meet its commitments.

Confrontation has provided the textbook cases of democratization, as existing oligarchies have responded to challenges by excluded political actors with broadening of citizenship, equalization of citizenship, increase of binding consultation and/or expansion of protection for citizens. Nineteenth-century British rulers' responses to large mobilizations by Protestant Dissenters, Catholics, merchants, and skilled workers fit the pattern approximately in Great Britain, but by no means always—and certainly not in Ireland. Confrontation probably promotes democratization, when it does, not only because it terminates a mobilization-repression-bargaining cycle but also because it generates new trust-bearing coalitions and weakens coercive controls supporting current relations of exploitation and opportunity hoarding.

Colonization with wholesale transplantation of population from mother country to colony has often promoted democratization, although frequently at the cost of destroying, expelling, or subordinating indigenous populations within the colonial territory. Thus, Canada, the United States, Australia, and New Zealand began

European settlement with coercive, oligarchic regimes, but rapidly moved some distance toward broad citizenship, equal citizenship, binding consultation, and protection. (Let us never forget how far short of theoretically possible maximum values in these four regards all really existing democracies have always fallen; by these demanding criteria, no near-democracy has ever existed on a large scale.) Colonization of this sort probably makes a difference not merely because it exports political institutions containing some rudiments of democracy but also because it promotes relative equality of material condition and weakens patron–client networks tied closely to the government of the colonizing power.

And revolution? As England's Glorious Revolution of 1688–1689 and the Russian revolution of 1905 illustrate, revolutions do not universally promote moves toward broad, equal citizenship, binding consultation, and protection. Let us take revolutions to be large splits in control over means of government followed by substantial transfers of power over government. As compared with previous regimes, the net effect of most revolutions over the last few centuries has been at least a modicum of democratization, as here defined. Why so? Probably because they typically activate even a wider range of democracy-promoting mechanisms than do conquest, colonization, and confrontation.

Revolutions rarely or never occur, for example, without coalition formation between segments of ruling classes and constituted political actors that are currently excluded from power. But they also commonly dissolve or incorporate nongovernmental patron–client networks, contain previously autonomous military forces, equalize assets and/or well-being across the population at large, and attack existing trust networks (for recent descriptions, reviews, and syntheses, see DeFronzo 1991; Foran 1997; Goldstone 1991; Goodwin 2001; Keddie 1995; Lupher 1996; Paige 1997; Selbin 1993; Tilly 1993). Thus, we arrive at an unexpected synthesis of Mancur Olson and Barrington Moore: Revolutions sometimes sweep away old networks that block democratization and promote the formation of governing coalitions far more general than those that preceded them. Any such conclusion will, of course, be intensely controversial in the present state of knowledge; a whole intellectual industry has grown up to challenge assessments in this vein of the French and Bolshevik revolutions (see, for example, Furet 1995; Malia 1998, 2001). All the more reason to take my arguments as an invitation to research and critical synthesis rather than as forgone conclusions.

Figure 14.1, with which we began, summarizes the research program that flows from these arguments. It consists of examining the following:

1. How environments of different sorts of regimes affect (a) their likelihood of experiencing different sorts of shocks, (b) the sorts of change mechanisms such shocks activate
2. How those change mechanisms and their interactions affect inequality, networks of trust, and public politics
3. How, when, and why alterations of this sort produce democratization

The program is vast but promising. It has powerful attractions: a focus on causal accounts, compatibility with highly variable causal processes, and an open invitation to proceed at many different scales, from a single crisis to continental history.

WHAT'S AT STAKE?

The inquiry has serious intellectual and political stakes. If the line of analysis I have recommended is roughly correct, scholars and political leaders who seek keys to democratization should stop looking for the elusive realm called "civil society" and abandon attempts to strengthen it—except insofar as the changes of public politics, categorical inequality, and networks of trust I have sketched actually identify what they have been looking for. Nor should they worry much about whether a given country has a previous history or collective memory of democracy. Instead they should be scrutinizing interactions among governmental institutions, trust-bearing networks, and systems of inequality.

The analysis raises doubts about the importance of generalized attitudes or political cultures, no matter what their content. It attributes far greater influence to understandings and commitments embedded in crucial social ties: culture, yes, but in daily practice and tight integration with social relations. It recommends converting current investigations of social capital into close studies of change in trust-bearing networks. It suggests that model democratic constitutions will make little difference to the actual content of politics without deep changes in categorical inequality and/or its insulation from public politics. It downgrades such differences as presidential versus parliamentary rule and two-party versus multiparty systems except as signs of prevailing power struggles. It singles out civilian control over military force and containment of material inequality as crucial steps toward democracy.

If this chapter's arguments are correct, monitoring of change should focus on democracy-promoting mechanisms rather than on public opinion or election results. The arguments challenge political designers to study those mechanisms and to invent devices that will activate them less brutally than conquest, confrontation, colonization, and revolution. Most of all, the analysis presented here gives reasons for mistrusting self-descriptions of political leaders in ostensibly democratizing countries. All the more reason for bringing systematic evidence to bear on its assertions—if only to prove them all wrong.

Where now for the work of explanation? A sixfold agenda flows from this chapter's observations.

1. Analysts of democratization must shift their gaze from necessary and sufficient conditions to causal sequences, from static comparisons of multiple cases to dynamic analyses of transformations, from epidemiology to physiology.
2. Researchers must sort out, cull, refine, augment, test, modify, and codify the miscellaneous democracy-promoting mechanisms so casually proposed here.

3. We must examine whether the three arenas of public politics, inequality, and trust-sustaining networks interact to promote democratization, if and when they do, in something like the manner sketched here.
4. The place of shocks associated with conquest, confrontation, colonization, and revolution deserves much more systematic attention.
5. Someone must synthesize these many elements into partial but verifiable causal models of concrete democratization processes.
6. At that point, researchers can reconsider such vexed questions as the relationship between democratization and interstate war by looking at causal mechanisms instead of elusive correlations (Mansfield and Snyder 1995; Ward and Gleditsch 1998).

If these lines goad a few bright researchers into reexamining democracy-promoting causal mechanisms, they will have served their purpose.

15

So What?

In my little corner of the intellectual world, "so what?" questions usually come up when a researcher has produced a reliable finding whose significance neighboring specialists can see. How does the researcher then explain to people outside that small circle why they should care about the finding? This book has not produced "findings" in any strong sense of the word, but its formulations, claims, assertions, and observations require some of the same justification. Do they provide a viable vision of anything important? Should readers who have not already spent their lives fixated by intersections of stories, identities, and political change care about what has happened in the previous fourteen chapters?

Yes, they should. At a minimum, anyone who cares about how what people loosely call "identity politics" works should care about the issues this book addresses. Many people regard identity claims primarily as a form of self-expression, or even of self-indulgence—what others do when they are too comfortable, too confused, or too distressed for serious politics. I have argued, on the contrary, that identity claims and their attendant stories constitute serious political business. Invention of the social movement, for instance, facilitated the staking of claims in the name of previously unrecognized political actors. At various points in U.S. history, for example, social movements helped establish opponents of slavery, enemies of alcohol, women, African Americans, gays, Vietnam veterans, and indigenous peoples as viable political actors.

Nationalism provides another example. During the nineteenth century, nationalist identity claims (whether bottom up or top down) began to make a serious difference to who would hold state power and who would not. Political

Original chapter written for this volume. I have also included a few paragraphs that I adapted from "How Do Relations Store Histories?" *Annual Review of Sociology* 26 (2000): 721–723.

rights and obligations themselves depend on negotiated claims linking members of established political categories, which means that they, too, involve identity claims. Battling out accepted answers to the questions "Who are you?" "Who are we?" and "Who are they?" with widely accepted stories to back those answers is no self-indulgence; it plays a consequential part in public politics. Available answers to the questions affect the very feasibility of democracy.

Or so I have claimed. This book falls far short of proving its claims. Its main contributions are to identify weaknesses in existing ideas about various forms of identity politics, then to present and illustrate a program for doing better. The program involves regarding transactions among social sites (including persons) as real and examining how such transactions actually work in a variety of political settings. It calls for the identification of robust causal mechanisms and processes that operate similarly in disparate circumstances but produce different large-scale outcomes depending on their combinations, sequences, and initial conditions.

If you have worked your way through this book chapter by chapter, you have seen the program in action repeatedly. You have seen analyses of transactions among major British political actors including government officials (chapters 4, 5, and 7), among French movement activists, government agents, and political parties (chapters 4 and 9), among nationalists, their rivals, national governments, and international agencies (chapters 7 and 12), among claimants to power in the collapsing Soviet Union (chapters 8 and 12), among Indian officials, local powerholders, and religious activists (chapter 9), among rulers, armies, and taxpayers (chapters 10 and 13), between state officials and ordinary citizens (chapters 11, 13, and 14). The cataloging of mechanisms and processes becomes most explicit in chapter 14's analysis of democratization. But throughout the book mechanisms and processes explicitly listed in that chapter—coalition formation, mobilization-repression-bargaining cycles, governmental absorption and destruction of patron–client networks, and so on—do a significant part of the explanatory work. The challenge is to pin down those mechanisms and processes, verify how they operate, and examine the effects they produce in different combinations, sequences, and initial conditions.

More specific agendas emerge for the study of stories, of political identities, of political change, and of their interactions. In each case, we need new work on two classes of problems: generation and constraint.

1. *Generation.* What causes the processes involved to (a) begin, (b) change? How, for example, did the identity "European" acquire sufficient force that old established states would dissolve national currencies in favor of the Euro and former socialist regimes would reshape themselves in the capitalist image as a step toward admission to the European Union?

2. *Constraint.* Once they are in operation, how do the processes affect social behavior (a) on the small scale, (b) on the large scale? For example, at what point and how should we expect participants in European social movements routinely to make claims on behalf of categories that span long-established national boundaries?

On the whole, my arguments in previous chapters have made do with an entrepreneurial-interactive account of generation and constraint: Political entrepreneurs draw together credible stories from available cultural materials, similarly create we–they boundaries, activate both stories and boundaries as a function of current political circumstances, and maneuver to suppress competing models, but interaction among parties to struggle alters stories, boundaries, and their social reinforcements. In this regard, my account resembles John Walton's conclusions concerning the narratives of public history:

> Public history is constructed, not, in the main, for the purposes of posterity or objectivity, but for the aims of present action (conquest, social reform, building, political reorganization, economic transformation). Narratives make claims for the virtues of their individual and institutional authors, often as counterpoint to rival claimants. They characterize the past in certain ways for the purpose of shaping the future. The ability of narratives to effect change depends in the first instance on their institutional power; whether they are produced by a powerful church, conquering state, fledgling town, or contending voluntary associations. (Walton 2001, 294)

Something like this process does often occur. But such an account has an excessively instrumental bias. It offers no explanation of the fact that most would-be political entrepreneurs fail most of the time. Nor does it provide a satisfactory explanation of day-to-day interactions around political identities, much less why people sometimes risk their lives in the course of those interactions. Clearly, we need more subtle and comprehensive explanations of generation and constraint.

In the case of stories, we have a few clues concerning generation. Although no one lives without stories, interacting people create new stories about their interaction after the fact, as they terminate sequences and seal agreements. In that regard, political stories resemble peace treaties, commencement addresses, memoirs, annual reports, and labor-management contracts. To be sure, materials for stories come largely from existing cultural repertoires. Viable new stories reassemble familiar elements. Certifying agents such as elders, peers, public authorities, and international organizations monitor stories and often provide models for their proper construction.

Nationalist stories, for example, bear striking resemblances from one part of the world to another. They speak of shared culture, longstanding tradition, connectedness, common geographic origin, and distinctness from others with whom the claimed nation might be confused. Those common properties do not spring from primordial consciousness, but from a body of nationalist models and practices that have spread through the world since 1789. Still we have no convincing general account of the process by which the specific contents of politically consequential stories—nationalist or otherwise—form and gain credibility. Nor do we have a persuasive account of change in prevailing stories. Similarly, we lack a compelling and comprehensive explanation for generation of the particular boundaries, relations, and stories that constitute political identities.

As for constraint, how do stories and identities produce their effects? In the construction and deployment of politically effective stories, what happens at the small scale of an individual or a pair of individuals, at the large scale of a state or a national movement, and in the interaction between those scales? Three bad answers readily spring to mind. The first is that stories directly alter individual consciousness in closely similar ways across individuals, before individual consciousness aggregates into collective consciousness. The answer is bad because it provides no account of how exposure to stories interacts with previous learning across individuals who have varied considerably in previous experience. We could, after all, plausibly expect such individuals to adopt different, even contradictory, stories. How does relative uniformity in public storytelling come about? Much less does the aggregation of individual consciousness explain how people who have their doubts about shared stories nevertheless cooperate in their public promulgation?

The second commonly proposed bad answer is that society does it: Those stories that serve society as a whole or (more likely) reinforce the interests of dominant groups come to prevail. This second answer is woefully inadequate because it invokes a dubious agent—society as a whole or a unified dominant group—and begs the question of how that agent does its work. Holistic ontologies keep returning to social science in such forms as evolutionary models and world-system analyses (see, for example, Sanderson 2001; Chase-Dunn 1998). But their vagueness with respect to agency—who does what to whom, why, and how—has greatly diminished their popularity among social scientists at large. That vagueness renders society-does-it answers as unhelpful explanations for the prominence of stories and identities in political change.

A third frequent bad answer credits culture, as the repository of collective experience, with the production of constraint. The answer is even worse than the first two because it combines their defects: It begs the question of how culture—that is, shared understandings and their representations in objects and practices— changes as it invokes a dubious agent. Like "society does it," the cultural answer fails to specify how that agent creates its effects in social life. Unquestionably, available culture figures importantly in political storytelling and identity politics. People undoubtedly draw on previously known representations and practices as they struggle with each other. But how? Since struggling people are constantly modifying their definitions of who they are and what they are fighting about, exactly how does culture constrain them?

Let me suggest three possible good answers as alternatives to the bad answers. Call them *entrepreneurship, creative interaction,* and *cultural ecology.* The three would take future work in somewhat different directions, but they would not necessarily yield incompatible results.

Entrepreneurship? We might improve the crude entrepreneurial account of previous chapters by following up analogies with intellectual, artistic, and religious schools. In those fields investigators usually discover strong network effects, polarization effects, and mutual reinforcement of common culture, with brokers both connecting and dividing crucial actors (see, for example, Abbott, 2001a; Collins 1998; Knoke 1990; White 1992, 1993). We have certainly seen glimmers of the same effects in our surveys of identity politics. In the British social movement politics on which previous chapters have repeatedly drawn, for example, offstage connections among such entrepreneurs as William Cobbett and Francis Place clearly affected which stories and identities became prominent in successive campaigns for parliamentary reform.

Creative interaction appears most visibly in such activities as jazz and soccer. In these cases, participants work within rough agreements on procedures and outcomes; arbiters set limits on performances; individual dexterity, knowledge, and disciplined preparation generally yield superior play; yet the rigid equivalent of military drill destroys the enterprise. Both jazz and soccer, when well executed, proceed through improvised interaction, surprise, incessant error and error correction, alternation between solo and ensemble action, and repeated responses to understandings shared by at least pairs of players. After the fact, participants and spectators create shared stories of what happened, and striking improvisations shape future performances. We have seen creative interaction at work, for example, in the process by which solemn processions and presentations of petitions evolved into street demonstrations. If we could explain how human beings bring off such improvisatory adventures, we could be well on our way to accounting for how sets of interacting people store histories in contentious repertoires, conversation, rights and obligations, war and peace, and similar phenomena.

Cultural ecology? Social life consists of transactions among social sites, some of them occupied by individual persons, but most of them occupied by shifting aspects or clusters of persons. None of the sites, goes the reasoning, contains all the culture—all the shared understandings or representations—on which transactions in its vicinity draw. But transactions among sites produce interdependence among extensively connected sites, deposit related cultural material in those sites, transform shared understandings in the process, and thus make large stores of culture available to any particular site through its connections with other sites. Thus, we might discover that identity politics creates its illusions of unity by means of incessantly negotiated interchange among distinct sites, then fixes its illusions by means of collectively produced stories. We have noticed signs of cultural ecology, for example, in James Scott's and Viviana Zelizer's documentation of dispersed local knowledge as a counter to uniform top-down templates.

Consider entrepreneurship, creative interaction, and cultural ecology to be three cloudy mirrors held up to narrative and identity processes from different angles. Analysts of stories, identities, and political change face the challenge of clearing the mirrors or creating better glasses. Improved vision should help us explain how the world's peoples are creating new identities, acting as if they believed their own shared answers to the question "Who are you?", and creating consequential stories about the past, present, and future of the world.

References

Abbott, Andrew. 1994. "History and Sociology: The Lost Synthesis." In Eric Monkkonen, ed., *Engaging the Past: The Uses of History across the Social Sciences*. Durham, N.C.: Duke University Press.

———. 2001a. *Chaos of Disciplines*. Chicago: University of Chicago Press.

———. 2001b. *Time Matters: On Theory and Method*. Chicago: University of Chicago Press.

Agre, Philip E. 1997. *Computation and Human Experience*. Cambridge, England: Cambridge University Press.

Alapuro, Risto. 1988. *State and Revolution in Finland*. Berkeley: University of California Press.

Alberoni, Francesco. 1968. *Statu nascenti*. Bologne: Il Mulino.

Alker, Hayward. 1992. "The Humanistic Moment in International Studies: Reflections on Machiavelli and las Casas." *International Studies Quarterly* 36: 347–372.

Alonso, William, and Paul Starr, eds. 1987. *The Politics of Numbers*. New York: Russell Sage Foundation.

Amenta, Edwin, Drew Halfmann, and Michael P. Young. 1999. "The Strategies and Contexts of Social Protest: Political Mediation and the Impact of the Townsend Movement in California." *Mobilization* 4: 1–24.

Aminzade, Ronald. 1992. "Historical Sociology and Time." *Sociological Methods & Research* 20: 456–480.

———. 2000. "The Politics of Race and Nation: Citizenship and Africanization in Tanzania." *Political Power and Social Theory* 14: 53–90.

Anderson, Benedict. 1991. *Imagined Communities: Reflections on the Origin and Spread of Nationalism*. London: Verso.

Anderson, James, ed. 1986. *The Rise of the Modern State*. Brighton, England: Wheatsheaf Books.

Anderson, M. S. 1988. *War and Society in Europe of the Old Regime, 1618–1789*. London: Fontana.

Appleby, Joyce, Lynn Hunt, and Margaret Jacob. 1994. *Telling the Truth about History*. New York: Norton.

Armstrong, John A. 1982. *Nations before Nationalism*. Chapel Hill: University of North Carolina Press.

Arnade, Peter. 1997. "City, State, and Public Ritual in the Late-Medieval Burgundian Netherlands." *Comparative Studies in Society and History* 39: 300–318.

Artéus, Gunnar, Ulf Olsson, and Kerstin Stromberg-Back. 1981. "The Influence of the Armed Forces on the Transformation of Society in Sweden, 1600–1945." *Kungl. Krigsvetenskaps akademiens Bihafte—Militarhistorisk Tidskrift*: 133–144.

Ashforth, Adam. 1990. *The Politics of Official Discourse in 20th-Century South Africa*. Oxford: Clarendon.

Ashley, David. 1997. *History without a Subject: The Postmodern Condition*. Boulder, Colo.: Westview.

Ashmore, Malcolm, Robin Wooffitt, and Stella Harding, eds. 1994. "Humans and Others: The Concept of 'Agency' and Its Attribution." *American Behavioral Scientist* 37 (special issue).

Auyero, Javier. 2000. *Poor People's Politics: Peronist Survival Networks and the Legacy of Evita*. Durham: Duke University Press.

Aya, Rod. 1990. *Rethinking Revolutions and Collective Violence: Studies on Concept, Theory, and Method*. Amsterdam: Het Spinhuis.

Aymes, Jean-René, Alberto Gil Novales, and Luis A. de Oliveira Ramos. 1989. *Les Révolutions dans le monde ibérique (1766–1834). I. La péninsule*. Bordeaux: Presses Universitaires de Bordeaux.

Ayres, Jeffrey M. 1998. *Defying Conventional Wisdom: Political Movements and Popular Contention against North American Free Trade*. Toronto: University of Toronto Press.

Baechler, Jean. 1970. *Les phénomènes révolutionnaires*. Paris: Presses Universitaires de France.

Barbalet, J. M. 1988. *Citizenship*. Minneapolis: University of Minnesota Press.

Barfield, Thomas J. 1989. *The Perilous Frontier: Nomadic Empires and China*. New York: Blackwell.

Barkey, Karen. 1994. *Bandits and Bureaucrats: The Ottoman Route of State Centralization*. Ithaca, N.Y.: Cornell University Press.

Barkey, Karen, and Sunita Parikh, 1991. "Comparative Perspectives on the State." *Annual Review of Sociology* 17: 523–549.

Barkey, Karen, and Mark von Hagen, eds. 1997. *After Empire: Multiethnic Societies and Nation-Building*. Boulder, Colo.: Westview.

Barnes, Jonathan, ed. 1984. *The Complete Works of Aristotle*. 2 vols. Princeton, N.J.: Princeton University Press.

Barnett, Michael, and Alexander Wendt. 1992. "The Systemic Sources of Dependent Militarization." In *The Insecurity Dilemma: National Security of Third World States*, ed. Brian L. Job. Boulder, Colo.: Lynne Rienner.

———. 1993. "Dependent State Formation and Third World Militarization." *Review of International Studies* 19: 321–347.

Baron, James N., and Michael T. Hannan. 1994. "The Impact of Economics on Contemporary Sociology." *Journal of Economic Literature* 32: 1111–1146.

Barth, Fredrik. 1981. *Process and Form in Social Life: Selected Essays of Fredrik Barth: Volume I*. London: Routledge and Kegan Paul.

Bearman, Peter S., and Glenn Deane. 1992. "The Structure of Opportunity: Middle-Class Mobility in England, 1548–1689." *American Journal of Sociology* 98: 30–66.

Beissinger, Mark R. 1996. "How Nationalisms Spread: Eastern Europe Adrift in the Tides and Cycles of Nationalist Contention." *Social Research* 63: 97–146.

Belchem, John. 1990. *Industrialization and the Working Class: The English Experience, 1750–1900*. Aldershot, England: Scolar Press.

Bender, John, and David E. Wellbery, eds. 1991. *Chronotypes: The Construction of Time*. Stanford, Calif.: Stanford University Press.

Bendix, Reinhard. 1964. *Nation-Building and Citizenship*. New York: Wiley.

Benford, Robert D., and Scott A. Hunt. 1992. "Dramaturgy and Social Movements: The Social Construction and Communication of Power." *Sociological Inquiry* 62: 35–55.

Benton, Lauren. 1996. "From the World-Systems Perspective to Institutional World History: Culture and Economy in Global Theory." *Journal of World History* 7: 261–295.

Beramendi, Justo G., Ramón Máiz, and Xosé M. Núñez, eds. 1994. *Nationalism in Europe, Past and Present*. 2 vols. Santiago: Universidade de Santiago de Compostela.

Berejikian, Jeffrey. 1992. "Revolutionary Collective Action and the Agent-Structure Problem." *American Political Science Review* 86: 647–657.

Bergesen, Albert. 1993. "The Rise of Semiotic Marxism." *Sociological Perspectives* 36: 1–22.

Berlanstein, Lenard R., ed. 1993. *Rethinking Labor History*. Urbana: University of Illinois Press.

Bermeo, Nancy, and Philip Nord, eds. 2000. *Civil Society before Democracy: Lessons from Nineteenth-Century Europe*. Lanham, Md.: Rowman & Littlefield.

Besley, Timothy. 1995. "Nonmarket Institutions for Credit and Risk Sharing in Low-Income Countries." *Journal of Economic Perspectives* 9: 169–188.

Best, G.F.A. 1958. "The Protestant Constitution and Its Supporters, 1800–1829." *Transactions of the Royal Historical Society*, 5th series. 8: 105–127.

———. 1967. "Popular Protestantism in Victorian Britain." In *Ideas and Institutions of Victorian Britain*, ed. Robert Robson. London: G. Bell and Sons.

Best, Geoffrey. 1982. *War and Society in Revolutionary Europe, 1770–1870*. London: Fontana.

Bhargava, Rajeev. 1992. *Individualism in Social Science: Forms and Limits of a Methodology*. Oxford, England: Clarendon.

Birkbeck, Christopher. 1991. "Latin American Banditry as Peasant Resistance: A Dead-End Trail?" *Latin American Research Review* 26: 155–160.

Birnbaum, Pierre. 1982. *La logique de l'État*. Paris: Fayard.

———. 1988. *States and Collective Action: The European Experience*. Cambridge, England: Cambridge University Press.

———. 1993. *"La France aux Français." Histoire des haines nationalistes*. Paris: Seuil.

———. 1998. *La France imaginée. Déclin des rêves unitaires?* Paris: Fayard.

Bjørn, Claus, Alexander Grant, and Keith J. Stringer, eds. 1994a. *Nations, Nationalism and Patriotism in the European Past*. Copenhagen: Academic.

———. 1994b. *Social and Political Identities in Western History*. Copenhagen: Academic.

Black, Jeremy. 1997. *Maps and Politics*. Chicago: University of Chicago Press.

———. 1998. *War and the World: Military Power and the Fate of Continents 1450–2000*. New Haven, Conn.: Yale University Press.

Blickle, Peter, ed. 1997. *Resistance, Representation, and Community*. Oxford, England: Clarendon.

Blockmans, Wim P. 1997. *A History of Power in Europe: People, Markets, States*. Antwerp: Fonds Mercator.

Blondel, Jean, et al. 1994. "Où en est la politique comparée?" *Revue Internationale de Politique Comparée* 1: 3–132.

Boggs, Carl. 1986. *Social Movements and Political Power: Emerging Forms of Radicalism in the West*. Philadelphia: Temple University Press.

Boli-Bennett, John. 1979. "The Ideology of Expanding State Authority in National Constitutions, 1870–1970." In *National Development and the World System: Educational, Economic, and Political Change, 1950–1970,* ed. John W. Meyer and Michael T. Hannan. Chicago: University of Chicago Press.

Bollen, Kenneth A., Barbara Entwisle, and Arthur S. Alderson. 1993. "Macrocomparative Research Methods." *Annual Review of Sociology* 19: 321–351.

Bonnell, Victoria. 1980. "The Uses of Theory, Concepts and Comparisons in Historical Sociology." *Comparative Studies in Society and History* 22 (April): 156–173.

Booth, John A., and Mitchell Seligson. 1983. "Peasants as Activists: A Reevaluation of Political Participation in the Countryside." *Comparative Political Studies* 12: 29–59.

Borst, Arno. 1993. *The Ordering of Time: From the Ancient Computus to the Modern Computer.* Chicago: University of Chicago Press.

Bose, Sugata, and Ayesha Jalal. 1998. *Modern South Asia: History, Culture, Political Economy.* London: Routledge.

Boswell, Terry, ed. 1989. *Revolution in the World System.* New York: Greenwood.

Brady, Thomas A., Jr. 1985. *Turning Swiss: Cities and Empire, 1450–1550.* Cambridge, England: Cambridge University Press.

Brake, Wayne 1998. *Shaping History. Ordinary People in European Politics 1500–1700.* Berkeley: University of California Press.

Brass, Paul R. te. 1994. *The Politics of India Since Independence.* Part IV, vol. 1 of *The New Cambridge History of India,* 2d ed. Cambridge: Cambridge University Press.

———. 1996. Introduction to *Riots and Pogroms,* ed. Paul R. Brass. New York: New York University Press.

Brass, Tom. 1991. "Moral Economists, Subalterns, New Social Movements, and the (Re-)Emergence of a (Post-)Modernized (Middle) Peasant." *Journal of Peasant Studies* 18: 173–205.

Bratton, Michael. 1989. "Beyond the State: Civil Society and Associational Life in Africa." *World Politics* 41: 407–430.

Breuer, Stefan, and Hubert Treiber, eds. 1982. *Entstehung und Strukturwandel des Staates.* Opladen: Westdeutscher Verlag.

Brewer, John. 1976. *Party Ideology and Popular Politics at the Accession of George III.* Cambridge, England: Cambridge University Press.

———. 1979–80. "Theater and Counter-Theater in Georgian Politics: The Mock Elections at Garrat." *Radical History Review* 22: 7–40.

———. 1980. "The Wilkites and the Law, 1763–74: A Study of Radical Notions of Governance." In *An Ungovernable People: The English and Their Law in the 17th and 18th Centuries,* ed. John Brewer and John Styles. New Brunswick, N.J.: Rutgers University Press.

———. 1989. *The Sinews of Power: War, Money, and the English State, 1688–1783.* New York: Knopf.

Brian, Eric. 1992. "Histoire de chiffres. Note sur la renaissance de l'arithmétique politique." *Genèses* 9: 107–113.

Bright, Charles, and Susan Harding, eds. 1984. *Statemaking and Social Movements.* Ann Arbor: University of Michigan Press.

Brinton, Crane. 1938. *The Anatomy of Revolution.* New York: Norton.

Brock, Michael. 1974. *The Great Reform Act.* New York: Humanities Press.

Brubaker, Rogers. 1992. *Citizenship and Nationhood in France and Germany.* Cambridge, Mass.: Harvard University Press.

———. 1993. "East European, Soviet, and Post-Soviet Nationalisms: A Framework for Analysis." *Research on Democracy and Society* 1: 353–378.

――――. 1996. *Nationalism Reframed: Nationhood and the National Question in the New Europe.* Cambridge, England: Cambridge University Press.

Brubaker, Rogers, and Frederick Cooper. 2000. "Beyond 'Identity.'" *Theory and Society* 29: 1–47.

Bruckmüller, Ernst. 1990. "Ein 'deutsches' Bürgertum? Zu Fragen nationaler Differenzierung der bürgerlichen Schichten in der Habsburgermonarchie vom Vormärz bis um 1860." *Geschichte und Gesellschaft* 16: 343–354.

Bruner, Jerome. 1996. *The Culture of Education.* Cambridge, Mass.: Harvard University Press.

Bulst, Neithard, and Jean-Philippe Genet, eds. 1988. *La ville, la bourgeoisie et la genèse de l'Etat moderne (XIIe–XVIIIe siècles).* Paris: Editions du Centre National de la Recherche Scientifique.

Bunge, Mario. 1996. *Finding Philosophy in Social Science.* New Haven, Conn.: Yale University Press.

Burawoy, Michael. 1990. "Marxism as Science: Historical Challenges and Theoretical Growth." *American Sociological Review* 55: 775–793.

Burguière, André, and Raymond Grew, eds. 2001. *The Construction of Minorities: Cases for Comparison across Time and around the World.* Ann Arbor: University of Michigan Press.

Burke, Edmund, III, ed. 1988. *Global Crises and Social Movements: Artisans, Peasants, Populists, and the World Economy.* Boulder, Colo.: Westview.

Burke, Peter. 1992. *History and Social Theory.* Ithaca, N.Y.: Cornell University Press.

――――. 1993. *The Art of Conversation.* Ithaca, N.Y.: Cornell University Press.

Burke, Victor Lee. 1997. *The Clash of Civilizations: War-Making and State Formation in Europe.* Cambridge, England: Polity.

Burt, Ronald S. 1992. *Structural Holes: The Social Structure of Competition.* Cambridge, Mass.: Harvard University Press.

――――. 1998. "The Gender of Social Capital." *Rationality and Society* 10: 5–46.

Burt, Ronald S., and Marc Knez. 1995. "Kinds of Third-Party Effects on Trust." *Rationality and Society* 7: 255–292.

Busch, Otto. 1962. *Militärsystem und Sozialleben im alten Preussen 1713–1807: Die Anfänge der sozialen Militarisierung der preussisch-deutschen Gesellschaft.* Berlin: de Gruyter.

Calhoun, Craig. 1991. "The Problem of Identity in Collective Action." In *Macro-Micro Linkages in Sociology,* ed. Joan Huber. Newbury Park, Calif.: Sage.

――――. 1993a. "Nationalism and Ethnicity." *Annual Review of Sociology* 19: 211–239.

――――. 1993b. "New Social Movements of the Early 19th Century." *Social Science History* 17: 385–428.

Cannon, John. 1973. *Parliamentary Reform, 1640–1832.* Cambridge, England: Cambridge University Press.

Caporaso, James A., ed. 1989. *The Elusive State: International and Comparative Perspectives.* Newbury Park, Calif.: Sage.

Casanova, Julián. 1991. *La Historia Social y los Historiadores.* Barcelona: Editorial Crítica.

Casquette, Jesús. 1998. *Política, cultura y movimientos sociales.* Bilbao: Bakeaz.

Castells, Manuel. 1983. *The City and the Grassroots: A Cross-Cultural Theory of Urban Social Movements.* Berkeley: University of California Press.

――――. 1997. *The Power of Identity.* Vol. 2 of *The Information Age: Economy, Society, and Culture.* Oxford, England: Blackwell.

Cattacin, Sandro, and Florence Passy. 1993. "Der Niedergang von Bewegungsorganisationen. Zur Analyse von organisatorischen Laufbahnen." *Kölner Zeitschrift für Soziologie un Sozialpsychologie* 45: 419–438.

Centeno, Miguel. 2002. *Blood and Debt: War and the Nation-State in Latin America*. University Park: Penn State University Press.

Cerulo, Karen A. 1997. "Identity Construction: New Issues, New Directions." *Annual Review of Sociology* 23: 385–409.

Chamberlayne, Prue, Joanna Bornat, and Tom Wengraf, eds. 2000. *The Turn to Biographical Methods in Social Science: Comparative Issues and Examples*. London: Routledge.

Charlesworth, Andrew, ed. 1983. *An Atlas of Rural Protest in Britain, 1548–1900*. London: Croom Helm.

Chase-Dunn, Christopher. 1998. *Global Formation: Structures of the World-Economy*. Rev. ed. Lanham, Md.: Rowman & Littlefield. Originally published in 1989.

Chaturvedi, Jayati, and Gyaneshwar Chaturvedi. 1996. "*Dharma Yudh:* Communal Violence, Riots, and Public Space in Ayodhya and Agra City: 1990 and 1992." In *Riots and Pogroms*, ed. Paul R. Brass. New York: New York University Press.

Chazel, François, ed. 1993. *Action collective et mouvements sociaux*. Paris: Presses Universitaires de France.

Chirot, Daniel, and Karen Barkey. 1983. "States in Search of Legitimacy: Was There Nationalism in the Balkans of the Early 19th Century?" *International Journal of Comparative Sociology* 24: 30–45.

Clark, Andy. 1997. *Being There: Putting Brain, Body, and World Together Again*. Cambridge, Mass.: MIT Press.

Clark, J. C. D. 1985. *English Society 1688–1832*. Cambridge, England: Cambridge University Press.

———. 1986. *Revolution and Rebellion: State and Society in England in the 17th and 18th Centuries*. Cambridge, England: Cambridge University Press.

———. 1989. "English History's Forgotten Context: Scotland, Ireland, Wales." *Historical Journal* 32: 211–228.

———. 1990. "Revolution in the English Atlantic Empire, 1660–1800." In *Revolution and Counter-Revolution*, ed. E. E. Rice. Oxford, England: Basil Blackwell.

———. 1991. "Sovereignty: The British Experience." *Times Literary Supplement*, 29 November 1991: 15–16.

———. 1994. *The Language of Liberty, 1660–1832: Political Discourse and Social Dynamics in the Anglo-American World*. Cambridge, England: Cambridge University Press.

Clark, S. D. 1959. *Movements of Social Protest in Canada, 1640–1840*. Toronto: University of Toronto Press.

Clemens, Elisabeth S. 1993. "Organizational Repertoires and Institutional Change: Women's Groups and the Transformation of U.S. Politics, 1890–1920." *American Journal of Sociology* 98: 755–798.

Cobban, Alfred. 1969. *The Nation State and National Self-Determination*. London: Collins. First published in Fontana Library, 1945.

Cobbett, William. [1829] 1977. *The Poor Man's Friend, or Essays on the Rights and Duties of the Poor*. Reprint, Fairfield, N.J.: Augustus M. Kelley.

———. [1830] 1967. *Rural Rides*, ed. George Woodcock. Reprint, Harmondsworth, England: Penguin.

———. 1933. *The Autobiography of William Cobbett: The Progress of a Plough-boy to a Seat in Parliament*, ed. William Reitzel. London: Faber and Faber.

Cohen, Anthony Paul. 1985. *The Symbolic Construction of Community*. Chichester, England: Ellis Horwood.

Cohen, David William. 1994. *The Combing of History*. Chicago: University of Chicago Press.

Cohen, Jean. 1985. "Strategy or Identity: New Theoretical Paradigms and Contemporary Social Movements." *Social Research* 52: 663–716.

Cohen, Jean L., and Andrew Arato. 1992. *Civil Society and Political Theory*. Cambridge, Mass.: MIT Press.

Cohen, Miriam, and Michael P. Hanagan. 1995. "Politics, Industrialization, and Citizenship: Unemployment Policy in England, France, and the United States, 1890–1950." *International Review of Social History* Supplement 3: 91–130.

Coleman, James S. 1990. *Foundations of Social Theory*. Cambridge, Mass.: Harvard University Press.

Collier, David, and Steven Levitsky. 1997. "Democracy with Adjectives: Conceptual Innovation in Comparative Research." *World Politics* 49: 430–451.

Collier, Ruth Berins. 1999. *Paths toward Democracy: The Working Class and Elites in Western Europe and South America*. New York: Cambridge University Press.

Collins, Randall. 1998. *The Sociology of Philosophies: A Global Theory of Intellectual Change*. Cambridge, Mass.: Harvard University Press.

Comaroff, John. 1991. "Humanity, Ethnicity, Nationality: Conceptual and Comparative Perspectives on the U.S.S.R." *Theory and Society* 20: 661–688.

Comaroff, John, and Jean Comaroff. 1992. *Ethnography and the Historical Imagination*. Boulder, Colo.: Westview.

Conell, Carol, and Kim Voss. 1990. "Formal Organization and the Fate of Social Movements: Craft Association and Class Alliance in the Knights of Labor." *American Sociological Review* 55: 255–269.

Connell, R. W. 1990. "The State, Gender, and Sexual Politics: Theory and Appraisal." *Theory and Society* 19: 507–544.

———. 1995. *Masculinities*. Berkeley: University of California Press.

Connor, Walker. 1994. *Ethnonationalism: The Quest for Understanding*. Princeton, N.J.: Princeton University Press.

Conville, Richard L. 1997. "Between Spearheads: *Bricolage* and Relationships." *Journal of Social and Personal Relationships* 14: 373–386.

Cooper, Frederick. 1994. "Conflict and Connection: Rethinking Colonial African History." *American Historical Review* 99: 1516–1545.

Cooper, Frederick, and Ann Laura Stoler, eds. 1997. *Tensions of Empire: Colonial Cultures in a Bourgeois World*. Berkeley: University of California Press.

Corrigan, Philip, and Derek Sayer. 1985. *The Great Arch: English State Formation as Cultural Revolution*. Oxford, England: Blackwell.

Coser, Lewis A., and Otto N. Larsen, eds. 1976. *The Uses of Controversy in Sociology*. New York: Free Press.

Cronin, James E. 1993. "Neither Exceptional nor Peculiar: Towards the Comparative Study of Labor in Advanced Society." Part 1. *International Review of Social History* 38: 59–75.

Crosby, Alfred W. 1997. *The Measure of Reality: Quantification and Western Society, 1250–1600*. Cambridge, England: Cambridge University Press.

Cultures et Conflits. 1993. "Identité et Action Collective." *Cultures et Conflits* 12: 3–7.

Curtis, Bruce. 2001. *The Politics of Population: State Formation, Statistics, and the Census of Canada, 1840–1875*. Toronto: University of Toronto Press.

Cuzan, Alfred. 1991. "Resource Mobilization and Political Opportunity in the Nicaraguan Revolution: The Praxis." *American Journal of Economics and Sociology* 50: 71–83.

Dahl, Robert. 1989. *Democracy and Its Critics.* New Haven, Conn.: Yale University Press.

———. 1998. *On Democracy.* New Haven, Conn.: Yale University Press.

Dahles, H., and A. Trouwborst. 1993. "Visies op de Staat. Beschouwingen naar Aanleiding van een interdisciplinaire Studiedag." *Antropologische Verkenningen* 12 (special issue).

Dalton, Russell J., ed. 1993. "Citizens, Protest, and Democracy." *Annals of the American Academy of Political and Social Science* 528 (July).

Daniel, E. Valentine. 1996. *Charred Lullabies: Chapters in an Anthropography of Violence.* Princeton, N.J.: Princeton University Press.

Dann, Otto, and John Dinwiddy. 1988. *Nationalism in the Age of the French Revolution.* London: Hambledon.

Davis, John. 1992. *Exchange.* Minneapolis: University of Minnesota Press.

Davis, Richard H. 1996. "The Iconography of Rama's Chariot." In *Contesting the Nation: Religion, Community, and the Politics of Democracy in India,* ed. David Ludden. Philadelphia: University of Pennsylvania Press.

Davis, Richard W. 1966. "The Strategy of 'Dissent' in the Repeal Campaign, 1820–1828." *Journal of Modern History* 38: 374–406.

———. 1971. *Dissent in Politics 1780–1830: The Political Life of William Smith MP.* London: Epworth.

Dawisha, Karen. 1997. "Democratization and Political Participation: Research Concepts and Methodologies." In *The Consolidation of Democracy in East-Central Europe,* ed. Karen Dawisha and Bruce Parrott. Vol. 1 of *Authoritarianism and Democratization in Postcommunist Societies.* Cambridge, England: Cambridge University Press.

DeFronzo, James. 1991. *Revolutions and Revolutionary Movements.* Boulder, Colo.: Westview.

della Porta, Donatella. 1995. *Social Movements, Political Violence, and the State: A Comparative Analysis of Italy and Germany.* Cambridge, England: Cambridge University Press.

della Porta, Donatella, and Mario Diani. 1999. *Social Movements: An Introduction.* Oxford: Blackwell.

della Porta, Donatella, and Herbert Reiter, eds. 1998. *Policing Protest: The Control of Mass Demonstrations in Western Democracies.* Minneapolis: University of Minnesota Press.

Deneckere, Gita. 1990. "Norm en deviantie. Een bijdrage over diagnoses van collectieve populaire actie in de Nieuwste Geschiedenis." *Tijdschrift voor Sociale Geschiedenis* 16: 105–127.

———. 1997. *Sire, het volk mort. Sociaal protest in België (1831–1918).* Antwerp: Baarn, Ghent: Amsab.

Desrosières, Alain. 1998. *The Politics of Large Numbers: A History of Statistical Reasoning.* Cambridge, Mass.: Harvard University Press.

de Waal, Alex. 1997. "Group Identity, Rationality, and the State." *Critical Review* 11: 279–289.

Diani, Mario. 1988. *Isole nell'arcipelago. Il movimento ecologista in Italia.* Bologna: Il Mulino.

———. 1990. "The Network Structure of the Italian Ecology Movement." *Social Science Information* 29: 5–31.

———. 1992. "The Concept of Social Movement." *Sociological Review* 40: 1–25.

Dickinson, Harry T. 1989. "Counter-Revolution in Britain in the 1790s." *Tijdschrift voor Geschiedenis* 102: 354–367.

Ditchfield, G. M. 1978. "Dissent and Toleration: Lord Stanhope's Bill of 1789." *Journal of Ecclesiastical History* 29: 51–73.

Dodgshon, Robert A. 1998. *Society in Time and Space: A Geographical Perspective on Change.* Cambridge, England: Cambridge University Press.

Douglas, Mary, and Steven Ney. 1998. *Missing Persons: A Critique of the Social Sciences.* Berkeley: University of California Press.

Downing, Brian M. 1992. *The Military Revolution and Political Change: Origins of Democracy and Autocracy in Early Modern Europe.* Princeton, N.J.: Princeton University Press.

Drescher, Seymour. 1994. "Whose Abolition? Popular Pressure and the Ending of the British Slave Trade." *Past & Present* 143: 136–166.

Drew, Paul, and John Heritage. 1992. "Analyzing Talk at Work: An Introduction." In *Talk at Work,* ed. Paul Drew and John Heritage. Cambridge, England: Cambridge University Press.

Druckman, Daniel. 1994. "Nationalism, Patriotism, and Group Loyalty: A Social Psychological Perspective." *Mershon International Studies Review* 38: 43–68.

Duffy, Michael, ed. 1980. *The Military Revolution and the State, 1500–1800.* Exeter Studies in History, vol. 1. Exeter: University of Exeter.

Durandin, Catherine. 1989. *Révolution à la Française ou à la Russe. Polonais Roumains, et Russes au XIXème siècle.* Paris: Presses Universitaires de France.

Duyvendak, Jan Willem. 1994. *Le poids du politique. Nouveaux mouvements sociaux en France.* Paris: L'Harmattan.

Duyvendak, Jan Willem, Hein-Anton van der Heijden, Ruud Koopmans, and Luuk Wijmans, eds. 1992. *Tussen Verbeelding en Macht. 25 jaar nieuwe social bewegingen in Nederland.* Amsterdam: Sua.

Dyck, Ian. 1992. *William Cobbett and Rural Popular Culture.* Cambridge, England: Cambridge University Press.

———. 1993. "William Cobbett and the Rural Radical Platform." *Social History* 18: 185–204.

Eden, Lynn, and Steven E. Miller, eds. 1989. *Nuclear Arguments: Understanding the Strategic Nuclear Arms and Arms Control Debates.* Ithaca, N.Y.: Cornell University Press.

Edney, Matthew H. 1997. *Mapping an Empire: The Geographical Construction of British India, 1765–1843.* Chicago: University of Chicago Press.

Edwards, Bob, Michael W. Foley, and Mario Diani, eds. 2001. *Beyond Tocqueville: Civiil Society and the Social Capital Debate in Comparative Perspective.* Hanover, N.H.: University Press of New England.

Eliasoph, Nina. 1997. "'Close to Home': The Work of Avoiding Politics." *Theory and Society* 26: 605–647.

———. 1998. *Avoiding Politics: How Americans Produce Apathy in Everyday Life.* Cambridge, England: Cambridge University Press.

Elster, Jon. 1977. "Ulysses and the Sirens: A Theory of Imperfect Rationality." *Social Science Information* 16: 469–526.

Emirbayer, Mustafa. 1997. "Manifesto for a Relational Sociology." *American Journal of Sociology* 103: 281–317.

Emirbayer, Mustafa, and Jeff Goodwin. 1994. "Network Analysis, Culture, and the Problem of Agency." *American Journal of Sociology* 99: 1411–1454.

Emirbayer, Mustafa, and Ann Mische. 1998. "What Is Agency?" *American Journal of Sociology* 103: 962–1023.

Ennis, James G. 1987. "Fields of Action: Structure in Movements' Tactical Repertoires." *Sociological Forum* 2: 520–533.

Epstein, James. 1990. "The Constitutional Idiom: Radical Reasoning, Rhetoric, and Action in Early Nineteenth Century England." *Journal of Social History* 23: 553–574.

Ertman, Thomas. 1997. *Birth of the Leviathan: Building States and Regimes in Medieval and Early Modern Europe.* Cambridge, England: Cambridge University Press.

Esherick, Joseph W., and Jeffrey N. Wasserstrom. 1990. "Acting Out Democracy: Political Theater in Modern China." *Journal of Asian Studies* 49: 835–865.

Espeland, Wendy Nelson, and Mitchell L. Stevens. 1998. "Commensuration as a Social Process." *Annual Review of Sociology* 24: 313–343.

Etzioni, Amitai. 1968. *The Active Society*. New York: Free Press.

Eyerman, Ron, and Andrew Jamison. 1991. *Social Movements: A Cognitive Approach*. University Park: Pennsylvania State University Press.

Farrell, Sean. 2000. *Rituals and Riots: Sectarian Violence and Political Culture in Ulster, 1784–1886*. Lexington: University Press of Kentucky.

Fatton, Robert. 1992. *Predatory Rule: State and Civil Society in Africa*. Boulder, Colo.: Lynne Rienner.

Favre Pierre, ed. 1990. *La manifestation*. Paris: Presses de la Fondation Nationale des Sciences Politiques.

Feige, Edgar. 1998. "Underground Activity and Institutional Change: Productive, Protective, and Predatory Behavior in Transition Economies." In *Transforming Post-Communist Political Economies*, ed. Joan Nelson, Charles Tilly, and Lee Walker. Washington D.C.: National Academy Press.

Fein, Helen. 1993a. "Accounting for Genocide after 1945: Theories and Some Findings." *International Journal on Group Rights* 1: 79–106.

———. 1993b. "Revolutionary and Antirevolutionary Genocides: A Comparison of State Murders in Democratic Kampuchea, 1975 to 1979, and in Indonesia, 1965 to 1966." *Comparative Studies in Society and History* 35: 796–823.

Fernandez, Roberto, and Doug McAdam. 1988. "Social Networks and Social Movements: Multiorganizational Fields and Recruitment to Mississippi Freedom Summer." *Sociological Forum* 3: 357–382.

Feshbach, Seymour. 1987. "Individual Aggression, National Attachment, and the Search for Peace: Psychological Perspectives." *Aggressive Behavior* 13: 315–325.

Feuer, Lewis S. 1969. *The Conflict of Generations: The Character and Significance of Student Movements*. New York: Basic.

Fillieule, Olivier. 1997. *Stratégies de la rue. Les manifestations en France*. Paris: Presses de Sciences Po.

Finer, S. E. 1997. *The History of Government from the Earliest Times*. 3 vols. Oxford: Oxford University Press.

Fischer-Galati, Stephen. 1969. "Romanian Nationalism." In *Nationalism in Eastern Europe*, ed. Peter F. Sugar and Ivo J. Lederer. Seattle: University of Washington Press.

Fitch, Kristine L. 1998. *Speaking Relationally: Culture, Communication, and Interpersonal Connection*. New York: Guilford.

Flacks, Richard. 1993. "The Party's Over—So What Is To Be Done?" *Social Research* 60: 445–470.

Fogel, Robert W., and Dora L. Costa. 1997. "A Theory of Technophysio Evolution, with Some Implications for Forecasting Population, Health Care Costs, and Pension Costs." *Demography* 34: 49–66.

Foran, John. 1997. "The Future of Revolutions at the *fin-de-siècle*." *Third World Quarterly* 18: 791–820.

Fredrickson, George M. 1997. *The Comparative Imagination: On the History of Racism, Nationalism, and Social Movements*. Berkeley: University of California Press.

Freitag, Sandria B. 1996. "Contesting in Public: Colonial Legacies and Contemporary Communalism." In *Contesting the Nation: Religion, Community, and the Politics of Democracy in India,* ed. David Ludden. Philadelphia: University of Pennsylvania Press.

Friedman, Jeffrey, ed. 1996. *The Rational Choice Controversy: Economic Models of Politics Reconsidered.* New Haven, Conn.: Yale University Press.

Fuentes, Marta, and André Gunder Frank. 1989. "Ten Theses on Social Movements." *World Development* 17: 179–192.

Fullbrook, Mary. 1993. *National Histories and European History.* Boulder, Colo.: Westview.

Furet, François. 1995. *Le passé d'une illusion. Essai sur l'idée communiste au xxe siècle.* Paris: Robert Laffont.

Gal, Susan. 1987. "Codeswitching and Consciousness in the European Periphery." *American Ethnologist* 14: 637–653.

———. 1989. "Language and Political Economy." *Annual Review of Anthropology* 18: 345–369.

Gallant, Thomas W. 1994. "Turning the Horns: Cultural Metaphors, Material Conditions, and the Peasant Language of Resistance in Ionian Islands (Greece) during the 19th Century." *Comparative Studies in Society and History* 36: 702–719.

Gambetta, Diego. 1993. *The Sicilian Mafia: The Business of Private Protection.* Cambridge, Mass.: Harvard University Press.

Gamson, William A. 1989. *Power and Discontent.* Homewood, Ill.: Dorsey, 1968. Revised edition, Homewood, Ill.: Dorsey.

———. 1990. *The Strategy of Social Protest.* 2d ed. Belmont, Calif.: Wadsworth. First published in 1975.

———. 1992. *Talking Politics.* Cambridge, England: Cambridge University Press.

Gamson, William A., Bruce Fireman, and Steven Rytina. 1982. *Encounters with Unjust Authority.* Homewood, Ill.: Dorsey.

Garfinkel, Michelle R. 1994. "Domestic Politics and International Conflict." *American Economic Review* 84: 1294–1309.

Gauthier, Florence. 1989. "Le droit naturel en révolution." In *Permanances de la Révolution. Pour un autre bicentenaire,* Etienne Balibar et al. Montreuil: La Brèche.

Geertz, Clifford, ed. 1963. *Old Societies and New States.* New York: Free Press.

Gellner, Ernest. 1983. *Nations and Nationalism.* Ithaca, N.Y.: Cornell University Press.

———. 1992. *Reason and Culture: The Historic Role of Rationality and Rationalism.* Oxford: Blackwell.

———. 1994. *Conditions of Liberty: Civil Society and Its Rivals.* London: Allen Lane The Penguin Press.

Genet, Jean-Philippe, ed. 1990. *L'Etat moderne: Genèse.* Paris: Editions du Centre National de la Recherche Scientifique.

Genet, Jean-Philippe, and Michel Le Mené, eds. 1987. *Genèse de l'état moderne. Prélèvement et Redistribution.* Paris: Editions du Centre National de la Recherche Scientifique.

George, Alexander L. 1991. "The Transition in US–Soviet Relations, 1985–1990: An Interpretation from the Perspectives of International Relations Theory and Political Psychology." *Political Psychology* 12: 469–486.

Gerstenberger, Heide. 1990. *Die subjektlose Gewalt. Theorie der Entstehung bürgerlicher Staatsgewalt.* Münster: Westfälisches Dampfboot.

Ghosh, Amitav. 1992. *In an Antique Land: History in the Guise of a Traveler's Tale.* New York: Vintage.

Giddens, Anthony. 1985. *The Nation-State and Violence.* Berkeley: University of California Press.

Ginzburg, Carlo. 1986. *Clues, Myths, and the Historical Method.* Baltimore: Johns Hopkins University Press.

Ginzburg, Carlo, and Carlo Poni. 1991. "The Name and the Game: Unequal Exchange and the Historiographic Marketplace." In *Microhistory and the Lost Peoples of Europe,* ed. Edward Muir and Guido Ruggiero. Baltimore: Johns Hopkins University Press.

Giugni, Marco. 1995. *Entre stratégie et opportunité. Les nouveaux mouvements sociaux en Suisse.* Zürich: Seismo.

Giugni, Marco G., and Hanspeter Kriesi. 1990. "Nouveaux mouvements sociaux dans les années '80: Evolution et perspectives." *Annuaire suisse de science politique* 30: 79–100.

Giugni, Marco G., and Florence Passy. 1993. "Etat et nouveaux mouvements sociaux, comparaison de deux cas contrastés: la France et la Suisse." *Revue Suisse de Sociologie* 19: 545–570.

———, eds. 2001. *Political Altruism? The Solidarity Movement in International Perspective.* Lanham, Md.: Rowman & Littlefield.

Giugni, Marco G., Doug McAdam, and Charles Tilly, eds. 1998. *From Contention to Democracy.* Lanham, Md.: Rowman & Littlefield.

Glassie, Henry. 1982. *Passing the Time in Ballymenone: Culture and History of an Ulster Community.* Philadelphia: University of Pennsylvania Press.

Goffman, Erving. 1971. *Relations in Public: Microstudies of the Public Order.* New York: Basic.

Goldstone, Jack A. 1991. *Revolution and Rebellion in the Early Modern World.* Berkeley: University of California Press.

Goodwin, Jeff. 2001. *No Other Way Out: States and Revolutionary Movements, 1945–1991.* Cambridge, England: Cambridge University Press.

Goodwin, Jeff, and Theda Skocpol. 1989. "Explaining Revolutions in the Contemporary Third World." *Politics and Society* 17: 489–509.

Gorski, Philip S. 1993. "The Protestant Ethic Revisited: Disciplinary Revolution and State Formation in Holland and Prussia." *American Journal of Sociology* 99: 265–316.

Gould, Roger V. 1995. *Insurgent Identities: Class, Community, and Protest in Paris from 1848 to the Commune.* Chicago: University of Chicago Press.

———, ed. 2001. *General History and Historical Sociology.* Chicago: University of Chicago Press.

Granovetter, Mark. 1995. "The Economic Sociology of Firms and Entrepreneurs." In *The Economic Sociology of Immigration: Essays on Networks, Ethnicity, and Entrepreneurship,* ed. Alejandro Portes. New York: Russell Sage Foundation.

Graubard, Stephen, ed. 1993. "Reconstructing Nations and States." *Daedalus* 122.

Green, Donald P., and Ian Shapiro. 1994. *Pathologies of Rational Choice Theory: A Critique of Applications in Political Science.* New Haven, Conn.: Yale University Press.

Greenfeld, Liah. 1990. "The Formation of the Russian National Identity: The Role of Status Insecurity and *Ressentiment.*" *Comparative Studies in Society and History* 32: 549–591.

———. 1992. *Nationalism: Five Roads to Modernity.* Cambridge, Mass.: Harvard University Press.

Greengrass, Mark, ed. 1991. *Conquest and Coalescence: The Shaping of the State in Early Modern Europe.* London: Edward Arnold.

Greif, Avner. 1994. "Cultural Beliefs and the Organization of Society: A Historical and Theoretical Reflection on Collectivist and Individualist Societies." *Journal of Political Economy* 102: 912–950.

Grillo, R. D. 1980. *"Nation" and "State" in Europe: Anthropological Perspectives.* New York: Academic.

Guardino, Peter. 1994. "Identity and Nationalism in Mexico: Guerrero, 1780–1840." *Journal of Historical Sociology* 7: 314–342.

Gurr, Ted Robert. 1992. "The Internationalization of Protracted Communal Conflicts since 1945: Which Groups, Where, and How." In *The Internationalization of Communal Conflict,* ed. Manus I. Midlarsky. London: Routledge.

———. 1993a. *Minorities at Risk: A Global View of Ethnopolitical Conflicts.* Washington, D.C.: United States Institute of Peace Press.

———. 1993b. "Why Minorities Rebel: A Global Analysis of Communal Mobilization and Conflict since 1945." *International Political Science Review* 14: 157–197.

———. 1994. "Peoples against States: Ethnopolitical Conflict and the Changing World System." *International Studies Quarterly* 38: 347–377.

———. 2000. *Peoples versus States: Minorities at Risk in the New Century.* Washington, D.C.: United States Institute of Peace Press.

Gurr, Ted Robert, and Barbara Harff. 1994. *Ethnic Conflict in World Politics.* Boulder, Colo.: Westview.

Gurr, Ted Robert, Keith Jaggers, and Will H. Moore. 1990. "The Transformation of the Western State: The Growth of Democracy, Autocracy, and State Power since 1800." *Studies in Comparative International Development* 25: 73– 108.

Gusterson, Hugh. 1993. "Realism and the International Order after the Cold War." *Social Research* 60: 279–300.

Haas, Ernst. 1986. "What Is Nationalism and Why Should We Study It?" *International Organization* 40: 707–744.

Haimson, Leopold, and Charles Tilly, eds. 1989. *Strikes, Wars, and Revolutions in an International Perspective: Strike Waves in the Late 19th and Early 20th Centuries.* Cambridge, England: Cambridge University Press.

Halebsky, Sandor. 1976. *Mass Society and Political Conflict: Toward a Reconstruction of Theory.* Cambridge, England: Cambridge University Press.

Hall, John A., ed. 1986. *States in History.* Oxford: Blackwell.

Hall, John A., and G. John Ikenberry. 1989. *The State.* Minneapolis: University of Minnesota Press.

Hall, Peter. 1981. *Great Planning Disasters.* Rev. ed. Berkeley: University of California Press. First published in 1980.

Hamilton, Richard F. 1996. *The Social Misconstruction of Reality: Validity and Verification in the Scholarly Community.* New Haven, Conn.: Yale University Press.

Hanagan, Michael P. 1994. "New Perspectives on Class Formation: Culture, Reproduction, and Agency." *Social Science History* 18: 77–94.

———. 1998. "Irish Transnational Social Movements, Deterritorialized Migrants, and the State System: The Last One Hundred and Forty Years." *Mobilization* 13: 107–126.

Hanagan, Michael P., Leslie Page Moch, and Wayne te Brake, eds. 1998. *Challenging Authority: The Historical Study of Contentious Politics.* Minneapolis: University of Minnesota Press.

Hardin, Russell. 1983. *Collective Action.* Baltimore: Johns Hopkins University Press for Resources for the Future.

Harff, Barbara, and Ted Robert Gurr. 1990. "Victims of the State: Genocides, Politicides, and Group Repression since 1945." *International Review of Victimology* 1: 23–41.

Harper, Douglas A. 1987. *Working Knowledge: Skill and Community in a Small Shop.* Chicago: University of Chicago Press.

Hawthorn, Geoffrey. 1991. *Plausible Worlds: Possibility and Understanding in History and the Social Sciences.* Cambridge, England: Cambridge University Press.

Heberle, Rudolf. 1951. *Social Movements: An Introduction to Political Sociology.* New York: Appleton-Century-Crofts.

Hechter, Michael. 1987. *Principles of Group Solidaritiy.* Berkeley: University of California Press.

——. 2000. *Containing Nationalism.* New York: Oxford University Press.

Heilbroner, Robert. 1990. "Analysis and Vision in the History of Modern Economic Thought." *Journal of Economic Literature* 28: 1097–1114.

Heller, Patrick. 2000. "Degrees of Democracy: Some Comparative Lessons from India." *World Politics* 52: 484–519.

Hermant, Daniel, ed. 1992. "Nationalismes et Construction Européenne." *Cultures et Conflits* 7.

Hernes, Helga. 1988. "Scandinavian Citizenship." *Acta Sociologica* 31: 199–215.

Hibbert, Christopher. 1958. *King Mob: The Story of Lord George Gordon and the London Riots of 1780.* Cleveland: World.

Hinde, Wendy. 1992. *Catholic Emancipation: A Shake to Men's Minds.* Oxford: Blackwell.

Hirsch, Eric L. 1990. "Sacrifice for the Cause: Group Processes, Recruitment, and Commitment in a Student Social Movement." *American Sociological Review* 55: 243–254.

Hobsbawm, E. J. 1990. *Nations and Nationalism since 1789: Programme, Myth, Reality.* Cambridge, England: Cambridge University Press.

——. 1994. "What Is Ethnic Conflict and How Does It Differ from Other Conflicts?" In *Ethnic Conflict and International Security,* ed. Anthony McDermott. Oslo: Norwegian Institute of International Affairs.

——. 1997. *On History.* New York: New Press.

Hobson, John M. 1997. *The Wealth of States: A Comparative Sociology of International Economic and Political Change.* Cambridge, England: Cambridge University Press.

Hochschild, Arlie Russell. 1983. *The Managed Heart: Commercialization of Human Feeling.* Berkeley: University of California Press.

Hochstadt, Steve. 1982. "Social History and Politics: A Materialist View." *Social History* 7: 75–83.

Hofstadter, Dan. 1996. *The Love Affair as a Work of Art.* New York: Noonday Press/Farrar, Straus and Giroux.

Hohenberg, Paul M., and Lynn Hollen Lees. 1985. *The Making of Urban Europe, 1000–1950.* Cambridge, Mass.: Harvard University Press.

Holsti, K. J. 1985. *The Dividing Discipline: Hegemony and Diversity in International Theory.* Boston: Allen and Unwin.

——. 1991. *Peace and War: Armed Conflicts and International Order 1648–1989.* Cambridge, England: Cambridge University Press.

——. 1996. *The State, War, and the State of War.* Cambridge, England: Cambridge University Press.

Hont, Istvan. 1994. "The Permanent Crisis of a Divided Mankind: 'Contemporary Crisis of the Nation State' in Historical Perspective." *Political Studies* 42: 166–231.

Horowitz, Donald. 1985. *Ethnic Groups in Conflict.* Berkeley: University of California Press.

——. 2001. *The Deadly Ethnic Riot.* Berkeley: University of California Press.

Hroch, Miroslav. 1985. *Social Preconditions of National Revival in Europe: A Comparative Analysis of the Social Composition of Patriotic Groups among the Smaller European Nations.* Cambridge, England: Cambridge University Press.

Huggins, Martha Knisely. 1985. *From Slavery to Vagrancy in Brazil.* New Brunswick, N.J.: Rutgers University Press.

——. 1998. *Policing The United States and Latin America.* Durham, N.C.: Duke University Press.

Ibarra, Pedro, and Benjamín Tejerina, eds. 1998. *Los movimientos socials: Transformaciones políticas y cambio cultural.* Madrid: Trotta.

Ikegami, Eiko. 1995. "Nationhood and Citizenship in Early Meiji Japan 1868–1900: A Comparative Assessment." *International Review of Social History* Supplement 3: 185–222.

Immerfall, Stefan. 1992. "Macrohistorical Models in Historical-Electoral Research: A Fresh Look at the Stein-Rokkan-Tradition." *Historical Social Research* 17: 103–116.

Jacobs, Ronald N. 1996. "Civil Society and Crisis: Culture, Discourse, and the Rodney King Beating." *American Journal of Sociology* 101: 1238–1272.

Janoski, Thomas. 1998. *Citizenship and Civil Society: A Framework of Rights and Obligations in Liberal, Traditional, and Social Democratic Regimes.* Cambridge, England: Cambridge University Press.

Jelavich, Barbara. 1983. *History of the Balkans.* 2 vols. Cambridge, England: Cambridge University Press.

Jelavich, Charles, and Barbara Jelavich. 1977. *The Establishment of the Balkan National States, 1804–1920.* Seattle: University of Washington Press.

Jenkins, J. Craig. 1983. "Resource Mobilization Theory and the Study of Social Movements." *Annual Review of Sociology* 9: 527–553.

———. 1985. *The Politics of Insurgency: The Farm Worker Movement in the 1960s.* New York: Columbia University Press.

Jenkins, J. Craig, and Kurt Schock. 1992. "Global Structures and Political Processes in the Study of Domestic Political Conflict." *Annual Review of Sociology* 18: 161–185.

Johnson, Chalmers. 1966. *Revolutionary Change.* Boston: Little, Brown.

Johnston, Hank. 1991. *Tales of Nationalism: Catalonia, 1939–1979.* New Brunswick, N.J.: Rutgers University of Press.

Joppke, Christian. 1991. "Social Movements during Cycles of Issue Attention: The Decline of the Anti-Nuclear Energy Movements in West Germany and the USA." *British Journal of Sociology* 42: 43–60.

Joyce, Patrick. 1991. *Visions of the People: Industrial England and the Question of Class, 1848–1914.* Cambridge, England: Cambridge University Press.

———. 1995. "The End of Social History?" *Social History* 20: 73–92.

Kakar, Sudhir. 1996. *The Colors of Violence: Cultural Identities, Religion, and Conflict.* Chicago: University of Chicago Press.

Kalb, Don. 1993. "Frameworks of Culture and Class in Historical Research." *Theory and Society* 22: 513–537.

Kaplan, Temma. 1992. *Red City, Blue Period: Social Movements in Picasso's Barcelona.* Berkeley: University of California Press.

Karakasidou, Anastasia N. 1997. *Fields of Wheat, Hills of Blood: Passages to Nationhood in Greek Macedonia, 1870–1990.* Chicago: University of Chicago Press.

Karpat, Kemal H. 1993. "Gli stati balcanici e il nazionalismo: l'immagine e la realtà." *Quaderni Storici* 84: 679–718.

Kearney, Michael. 1991. "Borders and Boundaries of State and Self at the End of Empire." *Journal of Historical Sociology* 4: 52–72.

Keddie, Nikki R., ed. 1995. *Debating Revolutions.* New York: New York University Press.

Keeney, Barnaby C. 1947. "Military Service and the Development of Nationalism in England, 1272–1327" *Speculum* 4: 534–549.

Kerbo, Harold R. 1982. "Movements of 'Crisis' and Movements of 'Affluence': A Critique of Deprivation and Resource Mobilization Theories." *Journal of Conflict Resolution* 26: 645–663.

Kessler, Suzanne J., and Wendy McKenna. 1985. *Gender: An Ethnomethodological Approach.* 2d ed. Chicago: University of Chicago Press. First published by Wiley in 1978.

Keyssar, Alexander. 1986. *Out of Work: The First Century of Unemployment in Massachusetts.* Cambridge, England: Cambridge University Press.

Kiernan, V. G. 1973. "Conscription and Society in Europe before the War of 1914–18." In *War and Society: Historical Essays in Honour and Memory of J. R. Western, 1928–1971,* ed. M.R.D. Foot. London: Elek Books.

————. 1980. *State and Society in Europe, 1550–1650.* Oxford: Blackwell.

Kim, Quee-Young, ed. 1991. *Revolutions in the Third World.* Leiden, the Netherlands: Brill.

Kimmel, Michael. 1990. *Revolution: A Sociological Interpretation,* Philadelphia: Temple University Press.

Kiser, Edgar, and Michael Hechter. 1991. "The Role of General Theory in Comparative-Historical Sociology." *American Journal of Sociology* 97: 1–30.

Kitschelt, Herbert. 1986. "Political Opportunity Structures and Political Protest: Anti-Nuclear Movements in Four Democracies." *British Journal of Political Science* 16: 57–85.

————. 1993. "Social Movements, Political Parties, and Democratic Theory." *Annals of the American Academy of Political and Social Science* 528: 13–29.

Klandermans, Bert. 1993. "A Theoretical Framework for Comparisons of Social Movement Participation." *Sociological Forum* 8: 383–402.

————, ed. 1989. *Organizing for Change: Social Movement Organizations in Europe and the United States.* International Social Movement Research, vol. II. Greenwich, Conn.: JAI Press.

Klandermans, Bert, Hanspeter Kriesi, and Sidney Tarrow, eds. 1988. *From Structure to Action: Comparing Social Movement Research across Cultures.* International Social Movement Research, vol. I. Greenwich, Conn.: JAI Press.

Klausen, Jytte, and Louise A. Tilly, eds. 1997. *European Integration in Social and Historical Perspective, 1850 to the Present.* Lanham, Md.: Rowman & Littlefield.

Klausen, Kurt Klaudi. 1988. *Konflikter, Kollektive Aktioner og Protestbevaegelser i Danmark.* Copenhagen: Samfunds Fagsnyt.

Klima, Arnost. 1986. "The Bourgeois Revolution of 1848–49 in Central Europe." In *Revolution in History,* ed. Roy Porter and Mikulas Teich. Cambridge, England: Cambridge University Press.

Knoke, David. 1990. *Political Networks: The Structural Perspective.* Cambridge, England: Cambridge University Press.

Kocka, Jürgen. 1977. *Sozialgeschichte. Begriffe—Entwicklungen—Probleme.* Göttingen: Vandenhoeck and Ruprecht.

Kontopoulos, Kyriakos M. 1993. *The Logics of Social Structure.* Cambridge, England: Cambridge University Press.

Koopmans, Ruud. 1993. "The Dynamics of Protest Waves: West Germany, 1965 to 1989." *American Sociological Review* 58: 637–658.

Korpi, Walter. 1983. *The Democratic Class Struggle.* London: Routledge and Kegan Paul.

Kossmann, E. H. 1990. "Liep de Nederlandse Patriottenbeweging op de Franse vooruit?" In *De Franse Revolutie en Vlaanderen,* ed. J. Craeybeckx and F. Scheelings. Brussels: VUB Press.

Kosterman, Rick, and Seymour Feshbach. 1989. "Toward a Measure of Patriotic and Nationalistic Attitudes." *Political Psychology* 10: 257–274.

Krasner, Steven. 1984. "Approaches to the State: Alternative Conceptions and Historical Dynamics." *Comparative Politics* 16: 223–246.

Krieger, Joel. 1999. "Egalitarian Social Movements in Western Europe: Can They Survive Globalization and the EMU?" *International Studies Review* 3: 69–86.

Kriesi, Hanspeter. 1993. *Political Mobilization and Social Change: The Dutch Case in Comparative Perspective.* Aldershot, England: Avebury.

Kriesi, Hanspeter, René Levy, Gilbert Ganguillet, and Heinz Zwicky. 1981. *Politische Aktivierung in der Schweiz, 1945–1978.* Diessenhofen: Verlag Ruegger.

Kristeva, Julia. 1993. *Nations without Nationalism.* New York: Columbia University Press.

Kula, Witold. 1986. *Measures and Men.* Princeton, N.J.: Princeton University Press.

Kushner, Harvey W., ed. 2001. "Terrorism in the 21st Century." *American Behavioral Scientist* 44, no. 6.

Lachmann, Richard. 1987. *From Manor to Market: Structural Change in England, 1536–1640.* Madison: University of Wisconsin Press.

———. 1989a. "Elite Conflict and State Formation in 16th and 17th Century England and France." *American Sociological Review* 54: 141–162.

———. 1989b. "Origins of Capitalism in Western Europe: Economic and Political Aspects." *Annual Review of Sociology* 15: 47–72.

Lafargue, Jérôme. 1996. *Contestations démocratiques en Afrique.* Paris: Karthala and IFRA.

Laitin, David D. 1991. "The National Uprisings in the Soviet Union." *World Politics* 44: 139–177.

———. 1998. *Identity in Formation: The Russian-Speaking Populations in the Near Abroad.* Ithaca, N.Y.: Cornell University Press.

Landa, Janet Tai. 1994. *Trust, Ethnicity, and Identity: Beyond the New Institutional Economics of Ethnic Trading Networks, Contract Law, and Gift-Exchange.* Ann Arbor: University of Michigan Press.

Landes, David S. 1998. *The Wealth and Poverty of Nations: Why Some Are So Rich and Some So Poor.* New York: Norton.

Lang, James. 1988. *Inside Development in Latin America.* Chapel Hill: University of North Carolina Press.

Laqueur, Thomas. 1989. "Crowds, Carnival, and the State in English Executions, 1604–1868." In *The First Modern Society,* ed. A. L. Beier, David Cannadine, and James M. Rosenhelm. Cambridge, England: Cambridge University Press.

Laslett, Barbara. 1980. "Beyond Methodology: The Place of Theory in Quantitative Historical Research." *American Sociological Review* 45: 214–228.

Leacock, Stephen B. 1957. *Literary Lapses.* Toronto/Montreal: McClelland and Stewart. First published in 1910.

———. 1970. *Sunshine Sketches of a Little Town.* Toronto: McClelland and Stewart. First published in 1931.

Ledeneva, Alena V. 1998. *Russia's Economy of Favours: Blat, Networking, and Informal Exchange.* Cambridge, England: Cambridge University Press.

Lempert, David. 1993. "Changing Russian Political Culture in the 1990s: Parasites, Paradigms, and Perestroika." *Comparative Studies in Society and History* 35: 628–646.

Lepetit, Bernard. 1993. "Architecture, géographie, histoire: usages de l'échelle." *Genèses* 13: 118–138.

Lerner, Adam J., ed. 1991. "Reimagining the Nation." *Millennium* 20.

Lewis, Martin W., and Kären W. Wigen. 1997. *The Myth of Continents: A Critique of Metageography.* Berkeley: University of California Press.

Lichbach, Mark Irving, and Alan S. Zuckerman, eds. 1997. *Comparative Politics: Rationality, Culture, and Structure.* Cambridge, England: Cambridge University Press.

Lindegren, Jan. 1985. "The Swedish 'Military State,' 1560–1720." *Scandinavian Journal of History* 10: 305–336.

Linder, Marc. 1994. *Labor Statistics and Class Struggle.* New York: International Publishers.

Lindert, Peter H., and Jeffrey G. Williamson. 1983. "English Workers' Living Standards during the Industrial Revolution: A New Look." *Economic History Review,* 2d series, 36: 1–25.

Linebaugh, Peter. 1992. *The London Hanged: Crime and Civil Society in the Eighteenth Century.* Cambridge, England: Cambridge University Press.

Lis, Catharina, and Hugo Soly. 1996. *Disordered Lives: 18th-Century Families and Their Unruly Relatives.* Oxford: Polity Press.

Little, Daniel. 1989. "Marxism and Popular Politics: The Microfoundations of Class Conflict." In *Marx Analyzed: New Essays in Analytical Marxism, Canadian Journal of Philosophy,* ed. Kai Nielsen and Robert Ware. Supplementary vol. 15: 163–204.

———. 1991. *Varieties of Social Explanation: An Introduction to the Philosophy of Social Science.* Boulder, Colo.: Westview.

———. 1993. "Evidence and Objectivity in the Social Sciences." *Social Research* 60: 363–396.

Lloyd, Christopher. 1993. *The Structures of History.* Oxford: Blackwell.

Lorwin, Val, and Jacob M. Price, eds. 1972. *The Dimensions of the Past.* New Haven, Conn.: Yale University Press.

Lowi, Theodore J. 1992. "The State in Political Science: How We Became What We Study." *American Political Science Review* 86: 1–7.

Löwy, Michael. 1989. "Internationalisme, nationalisme et anti-impérialisme." *Critique Communiste* 87: 31–42.

Luard, Evan. 1986. *War in International Society: A Study in International Sociology.* New Haven, Conn.: Yale University Press.

Lucassen, Leo. 1996. *Zigeuner: Die Geschichte eines polizeilichen Ordnungsbegriffes in Deutschland 1700–1945.* Cologne: Böhlau.

Lüdtke, Alf. 1980. "Genesis und Durchsetzung des 'modernen Staates': Zur Analyse von Herrschaft und Verwaltung." *Archiv für Sozialgeschichte* 20: 470–491.

———. 1997. *Was bleibt von marxistischen Perspektiven in der Geschichtsforschung?* Göttingen: Wallstein Verlag.

Lupher, Mark. 1996. *Power Restructuring in China and Russia.* Boulder, Colo.: Westview.

Lynn, John. 1993. "The Evolution of Armies 800–2000." Unpublished tables, University of Illinois. Cited by permission.

Macartney, C. A. 1962. *Hungary: A Short History.* Edinburgh: Edinburgh University Press.

Machin, G.I.T. 1963. "The No-Popery Movement in Britain in 1828–29." *Historical Journal* 6: 193–211.

———. 1964. *The Catholic Question in English Politics 1820 to 1830.* Oxford: Clarendon Press.

———. 1979. "Resistance to Repeal of the Test and Corporation Acts, 1828." *Historical Journal* 22: 115–139.

Mack, Arien, ed. 1997. "Technology and the Rest of Culture." *Social Research* 64, no. 3.

Macy, Michael W. 1990. "Learning Theory and the Logic of Critical Mass." *American Sociological Review* 55: 809–826.

Madan, T. N. 1997. "Religion, Ethnicity, and Nationalism in India." In *Religion, Ethnicity, and Self-Identity: Nations in Turmoil,* ed. Martin E. Marty and R. Scott Appleby. Hanover, N.H.: University Press of New England/Salzburg Seminar.

Malia, Martin. 1998. "The Lesser Evil?" *Times Literary Supplement,* March 27, 1998, 3–4.

———. 2001. "Revolution Fulfilled." *Times Literary Supplement,* June 15, 2001, 3–4.

Mamdani, Mahmood. 1996. *Citizen and Subject: Contemporary Africa and the Legacy of Late Colonialism.* Princeton, N.J.: Princeton University Press.

———. 2001. *When Victims Turn Killers: A Political Analysis of the Origins and Consequences of the Rwanda Genocide*. Princeton, N.J.: Princeton University Press.

Mann, Michael. 1986, 1993. *The Sources of Social Power, I. A History of Power from the Beginning to A.D. 1760; II. The Rise of Classes and Nation-States, 1760–1914*. Cambridge, England: Cambridge University Press.

———. 1988. *States, War and Capitalism*. Oxford: Blackwell.

———, ed. 1990. *The Rise and Decline of the Nation State*. Oxford: Blackwell.

Mansfield, Edward D., and Jack Snyder. 1995. "Democratization and the Danger of War." *International Security* 20: 5–38

Maravall, Jose Antonio. 1972. *Estado Moderno y mentalidad social siglos XV a XVII*. 2 vols. Madrid: Ediciones de la Revista de Occidente.

Margadant, Ted. 1992. *Urban Rivalries in the French Revolution*. Princeton, N.J.: Princeton University Press.

Marini, Margaret Mooney. 1992. "The Role of Models of Purposive Action in Sociology." In *Rational Choice Theory: Advocacy and Critique*, ed. James S. Coleman and Thomas J. Fararo. Newbury Park, Calif.: Sage.

Marini, Margaret Mooney, and Burton Singer. 1988. "Causality in the Social Sciences." *Sociological Methodology* 347–409.

Markoff, John. 1990. "Peasants Protest: The Claims of Lord, Church, and State in the *Cahiers de doléances* of 1789." *Comparative Studies in Society and History* 32: 413–454.

Marshall, T. H. 1965. *Class, Citizenship, and Social Development*. Garden City, N.Y.: Doubleday. First published in 1964.

Marston, Sallie A. 1989. "Public Rituals and Community Power: St. Patrick's Day Parades in Lowell, Massachusetts, 1841–1874." *Political Geography Quarterly* 8: 255–269.

Marwell, Gerald, and Pamela Oliver. 1993. *The Critical Mass in Collective Action: A Micro-Social Theory*. Cambridge, England: Cambridge University Press.

Marx, Anthony W. 1998. *Making Race and Nation: A Comparison of the United States, South Africa, and Brazil*. Cambridge, England: Cambridge University Press.

Mastnak, Tomaz. 1990. "Civil Society in Slovenia: From Opposition to Power." *Studies in Comparative Communism* 23: 305–317.

Mayer, Margit. 1991. "Social Movement Research and Social Movement Practice: The U.S. Pattern." In *Research on Social Movements: The State of the Art in Western Europe and the USA*, ed. Dieter Rucht. Frankfurt: Campus/Westview.

McAdam, Doug, and Ronnelle Paulsen. 1993. "Specifying the Relationship between Social Ties and Activism." *American Journal of Sociology* 99: 640–667.

McAdam, Doug, John D. McCarthy, and Mayer N. Zald. 1988. "Social Movements." In *Handbook of Sociology*, ed. Neil J. Smelser. Newbury Park, Calif.: Sage.

McAdam, Doug, Sidney Tarrow, and Charles Tilly. 2001. *Dynamics of Contention*. Cambridge, England: Cambridge University Press.

McCammon, Holly J., Karen E. Campbell, Ellen M. Granberg, and Christine Mowery. 2001. "How Movements Win: Gendered Opportunity Structures and U.S. Women's Suffrage Movements, 1866 to 1919." *American Sociological Review* 66: 49–70.

McCarthy, John D., David W. Britt, and Mark Wolfson. 1991. "The Institutional Channeling of Social Movements by the State in the United States." *Research in Social Movements, Conflicts and Change* 13: 45–76.

McClelland, Peter D. 1975. *Causal Explanation and Model Building in History, Economics, and the New Economic History*. Ithaca, N.Y.: Cornell University Press.

McMichael, Philip. 1990. "Incorporating Comparison within a World-Historical Perspective." *American Sociological Review* 55: 385–397.

McNeill, William H. 1982. *The Pursuit of Power: Technology, Armed Force and Society since A.D. 1000.* Chicago: University of Chicago Press.

McPhail, Clark. 1991. *The Myth of the Madding Crowd.* Hawthorne, N.Y: Aldine de Gruyter.

McWilliams, Wayne C., and Harry Piotrowski. 1990. *The World since 1945: A History of International Relations.* Boulder, Colo.: Lynne Rienner.

Meier, Richard L. 1962. *A Communications Theory of Urban Growth.* Cambridge, Mass.: MIT Press.

Meinzer, Michael. 1992. *Der französische Revolutionskalendar (1792–1805). Planung, Durchführung und Scheitern einer politischen Zeitrechnung.* Munich: Oldenbourg.

Mellor, Roy E. H. 1989. *Nation, State, and Territory: A Political Geography.* London: Routledge.

Melucci, Alberto. 1989. *Nomads of the Present: Social Movements and Individual Need in Contemporary Society.* Philadelphia: Temple University Press.

———. 1992. "Liberation or Meaning? Social Movements, Culture and Democracy." *Development and Change* 23: 43–77.

Merton, Robert K. 1984. "Socially Expected Durations: A Case Study of Concept Formation in Sociology." In *Conflict and Consensus: A Festschrift for Lewis A. Coser,* ed. W. W. Powell and Richard Robbins. New York: Free Press.

Messick, David M., and Diane M. Mackie. 1989. "Intergroup Relations." *Annual Review of Psychology* 40: 45–81.

Meyer, David S. 1993a. "Institutionalizing Dissent: The United States Structure of Political Opportunity and the End of the Nuclear Freeze Movement." *Sociological Forum* 8: 157–179.

———. 1993b. "Protest Cycles and Political Process: American Peace Movements in the Nuclear Age." *Political Research Quarterly* 47: 451–479.

———. 1994. "Political Opportunity After the Cold War." *Peace & Change* 19: 114–140.

Meyer, David S., and Douglas R. Imig. 1993. "Political Opportunity and the Rise and Decline of Interest Group Sectors;" *Social Science Journal* 30: 253–270.

Meyer, David S., and Nancy Whittier. 1994. "Social Movement Spillover." *Social Problems* 41: 277–298.

Mills, C. Wright. 1959. *The Sociological Imagination.* New York: Oxford University Press.

Mische, Ann. 1995. "Projecting Democracy: The Formation of Citizenship across Youth Networks in Brazil." *International Review of Social History,* Supplement 3, 131–158.

Mitchell, B. R., and Phyllis Deane. 1971. *Abstract of British Historical Statistics.* Cambridge, England: Cambridge University Press.

Mohr, John W., and Roberto Franzosi, eds. 1997. "Special Double Issue on New Directions in Formalization and Historical Analysis." *Theory and Society* 28, no. 2–3.

Mols, Roger. 1954–56. *Introduction à la démographie historique des villes d'Europe du XIVe au XVIIIe siècle.* 3 vols. Louvain: Université de Louvain.

Mondonico-Torri, Cécile. 1995. "Aux origines du Code de la nationalité en France." *Le Mouvement Social* 171: 31–46.

de Montlibert, Christian. 1997. *La Domination Politique.* Strasbourg: Presses Universitaires de Strasbourg.

Moore, Barrington, Jr. 1966. *Social Origins of Dictatorship and Democracy.* Boston: Beacon.

Morawska, Ewa, and Willfried Spohn. 1994. "'Cultural Pluralism' in Historical Sociology: Recent Theoretical Directions." In *The Sociology of Culture: Emerging Theoretical Perspectives,* ed. Diana Crane. Oxford: Blackwell.

Morgenstern, Oskar. 1963. *On the Accuracy of Economic Observations.* 2d ed. Princeton, N.J.: Princeton University Press. First published in 1950.

Morris, Aldon D. 1984. *The Origins of the Civil Rights Movement: Black Communities Organizing for Change.* New York: Free Press.

———. 1993. "Birmingham Confrontation Reconsidered: An Analysis of the Dynamics and Tactics of Mobilization." *American Sociological Review* 58: 621–636.

Morris, Aldon, and Cedric Herring. 1987. "Theory and Research in Social Movements: A Critical Review." *Annual Review of Political Science* 2: 137–195.

Morris, Aldon D., and Carol McClurg Mueller, eds. 1992. *Frontiers in Social Movement Theory.* New Haven, Conn.: Yale University Press.

Motyl, Alexander J., ed. 1992a. "From Imperial Decay to Imperial Collapse: The Fall of the Soviet Empire in Comparative Perspective." In *Nationalism and Empire: The Habsburg Empire and the Soviet Union,* ed. Richard J. Rudolph and David F. Good. New York: St. Martin's.

———. 1992b. *Thinking Theoretically about Soviet Nationalities: History and Comparison in the Study of the USSR.* New York: Columbia University Press.

———. 1999. *Revolutions, Nations, Empires.* New York: Columbia University Press.

Mumford, Lewis. 1961. *The City in History: Its Origins, Its Transformations, and Its Prospects.* New York: Harcourt, Brace and World.

Nagi, Saad Z. 1992. "Ethnic Identification and Nationalist Movements." *Human Organization* 51: 307–317.

Nilsson, Sven A. 1988. "Imperial Sweden: Nation-Building, War and Social Change." In *The Age of New Sweden,* ed. Sven A. Nilsson et al. Stockholm: Livrustkammaren.

Noiriel, Gérard. 1988. *Le Creuset français: Histoire de l'Immigration xixe-xxe siècles.* Paris: Le Seuil.

———. 1991. *La tyrannie du National. Le droit d'asile en Europe 1793–1993.* Paris: Calmann-Lévy.

———. 1993. "L'identification des citoyens. Naissance de l'état civil républicain." *Genèses* 13: 3–28.

———. 1996. *Sur la "crise" de l'histoire.* Paris: Belin.

North, Douglass C. 1990. *Institutions, Institutional Change, and Economic Performance.* Cambridge: Cambridge University Press.

Oberschall, Anthony. 1973. *Social Conflict and Social Movements.* Englewood Cliffs, N.J.: Prentice Hall.

———. 1993. *Social Movements.* New Brunswick, N.J.: Transaction.

O'Donnell, Guillermo. 1998. "Polyarchies and the (Un)rule of Law in Latin America." Working Paper 1998/125, Instituto Juan March de Estudios e Investigaciones, Madrid.

Oegema, Dirk, and Bert Klandermans. 1994. "Why Social Movement Sympathizers Don't Participate: Erosion and Nonconversion of Support." *American Sociological Review* 59: 703–722.

O'Ferrall, Fergus. 1985. *Catholic Emancipation: Daniel O'Connell and the Birth of Irish Democracy 1820–30.* Dublin: Gill and Macmillan.

O'Gorman, Frank. 1982. *The Emergence of the British Two-Party System 1760–1832.* London: Arnold.

———. 1984. "Electoral Deference in 'Unreformed' England: 1760–1832." *Journal of Modern History* 56: 391–429.

———. 1989. *Voters, Patrons, and Parties: The Unreformed Electoral System of Hanoverian England 1734–1832.* Oxford: Clarendon.

234   *References*

References

———. 1992. "Campaign Rituals and Ceremonies: The Social Meanings of Elections in England, 1780–1860." *Past and Present* 135: 79–115.

Ohlemacher, Thomas. 1993. *Brücken der Mobilisierung. Soziale Relais und persönliche Netzwerke in Bürgerinitiativen gegen militärischen Tiefflug.* Wiesbaden: Deutscher Universitäts Verlag.

Olick, Jeffrey K., ed. 1998. "Memory and the Nation." *Social Science History* 22, no. 4.

Oliver, Pamela E. 1993. "Formal Models of Collective Action." *Annual Review of Sociology* 19: 271–300.

Olson, Mancur, Jr. 1965. *The Logic of Collective Action.* Cambridge, Mass.: Harvard University Press.

———. 1982. *The Rise and Decline of Nations: Economic Growth, Stagflation, and Social Rigidities.* New Haven, Conn.: Yale University Press.

Opp, Karl-Dieter. 1989. *The Rationality of Political Protest: A Comparative Analysis of Rational Choice Theory.* Boulder, Colo.: Westview.

———. 1992. "Spontaneous Revolutions: The Case of East Germany in 1989." In *German Unification and European Integration,* ed. Heinz Kurz. London: Edward Elgar.

Opp, Karl-Dieter, and Christiane Gern. 1993. "Dissident Groups, Personal Networks, and Spontaneous Cooperation: The East German Revolution of 1989." *American Sociological Review* 58: 659–680.

Orbuch, Terri L. 1997. "The People's Accounts Count: The Sociology of Accounts." *Annual Review of Sociology* 23: 455–478.

Orloff, Ann Shola. 1993. "Gender and the Social Rights of Citizenship: The Comparative Analysis of Gender Relations and Welfare States." *American Sociological Review* 58: 303–328.

Østergard, Uffe. 1991. "'Denationalizing' National History. The Comparative Study of Nation-States." *Culture and History* 9/10: 9–41.

———. 1992. "Peasants and Danes: The Danish National Identity and Political Culture." *Comparative Studies in Society and History* 34: 3–27.

Outram, Dorinda. 1992. "Revolution and Repression." *Comparative Studies in Society and History* 34: 58–67.

Padgett, John F., and Christopher K. Ansell. 1993. "Robust Action and the Rise of the Medici, 1400–1434." *American Journal of Sociology* 98: 1259–1319.

Paige, Jeffery M. 1997. *Coffee and Power: Revolution and the Rise of Democracy in Central America.* Cambridge, Mass.: Harvard University Press.

Paige, Karen, and Jeffery Paige. 1981. *The Politics of Reproductive Ritual.* Berkeley: University of California Press.

Palmer, Bryan D. 1990. *Descent into Discourse: The Reification of Language and the Writing of Social History.* Philadelphia: Temple University Press.

———. 1993. "Critical Theory, Historical Materialism, and the Ostensible End of Marxism: The Poverty of Theory Revisited." *International Review of Social History* 38, part 2: 133–162.

Palmer, Stanley H. 1988. *Police and Protest in England and Ireland 1780–1850.* Cambridge, England: Cambridge University Press.

Passy, Florence. 1998. *L'Action altruiste. Contraintes et opportunités de l'engagement dans les mouvements sociaux.* Geneva: Droz.

Patterson, Molly, and Kristen Renwick Monroe. 1998. "Narrative in Political Science." *Annual Review of Political Science* 1: 315–331.

Pauly, Louis W. 1997. *Who Elected the Bankers? Surveillance and Control in the World Economy.* Ithaca, N.Y.: Cornell University Press.

Paxton, Pamela. 1999. "Is Social Capital Declining in the United States? A Multiple Indicator Assessment." *American Journal of Sociology* 108: 88–127.

Peattie, Lisa, and Martin Rein. 1983. *Women's Claims: A Study in Political Economy.* Oxford: Oxford University Press.

Peled, Yoav. 1992. "Ethnic Democracy and the Legal Construction of Citizenship: Arab Citizens of the Jewish State." *American Political Science Review* 86: 432–443.

Phillips, John A. 1982. *Electoral Behavior in Unreformed England: Plumpers, Splitters, and Straights.* Princeton, N.J.: Princeton University Press.

———. 1990. "Municipal Politics in Later 18th-Century Maidstone: Electoral Polarization in the Reign of George III." In *The Transformation of Political Culture: England and Germany in the Late 18th Century,* ed. Eckhart Hellmuth. London: German Historical Institute and Oxford University Press.

———. 1992. *The Great Reform Bill in the Boroughs: English Electoral Behaviour, 1818–1841.* Oxford: Clarendon.

Phillips, John A., and Charles Wetherell. 1991. "The Great Reform Bill of 1832 and the Rise of Partisanship." *Journal of Modern History* 63: 621–646.

Piven, Frances Fox, and Richard A. Cloward. 1979. *Poor Peoples Movements: Why They Succeed, How They Fail.* New York: Vintage.

———. 1991. "Collective Protest: A Critique of Resource Mobilization Theory." *International Journal of Politics, Culture and Society* 4: 435–458.

Plotz, John M. 2000. *The Crowd: British Literature and Public Politics.* Berkeley: University of California Press.

Poggi, Gianfranco. 1990. *The State: Its Nature, Development and Prospects.* Stanford, Calif.: Stanford University Press.

Pomeranz, Kenneth. 2000. *The Great Divergence: China, Europe, and the Making of the Modern World Economy.* Princeton, N.J.: Princeton University Press.

Powers, Denise V., and James H. Cox. 1997. "Echoes from the Past: The Relationship between Satisfaction with Economic Reforms and Voting Behavior in Poland." *American Political Science Review* 91: 617–633.

Prak, Maarten. 1991. "Citizen Radicalism and Democracy in the Dutch Republic: The Patriot Movement of the 1780s." *Theory and Society* 20: 73–102.

Pred, Allan. 1990. *Making Histories and Constructing Human Geographies: The Local Transformation of Practice, Power Relations, and Consciousness.* Boulder, Colo.: Westview.

Pro Ruiz, Juan. 1992. *Estado, geometría y propriedad. Les orígenes del catastro en España, 1715–1941.* Madrid: Ministerio de Economia y Hacienda.

Puchala, Donald J. 1995. "The Pragmatics of International History." *Mershon International Studies Review* [supplement to *International Studies Quarterly*] 39: 1–18.

Puhle, Hans-Jürgen, ed. 1994. "Nationalismen und Regionalismen in Westeuropa." *Geschichte und Gesellschaft* 20, Heft 3.

Quadagno, Jill. 1992. "Social Movements and State Transformation: Labor Unions and Racial Conflict in the War on Poverty." *American Sociological Review* 57: 616–634.

Ragin, Charles C. 1994. *Constructing Social Research: The Unity and Diversity of Method.* Thousand Oaks, Calif.: Pine Forge.

———. 2000. *Fuzzy-Set Social Science.* Chicago: University of Chicago Press.

Ragin, Charles C., and Howard S. Becker, eds. 1992. *What Is a Case? Exploring the Foundations of Social Inquiry.* Cambridge, England: Cambridge University Press.

Rancière, Jacques. 1992. *Les mots de l'histoire. Essai de poétique du savoir.* Paris: Seuil.

Rasler, Karen A., and William R. Thompson. 1990. *War and State Making: The Shaping of the Global Powers*. Boston: Unwin Hyman.

Ray, Raka, and A. C. Korteweg. 1999. "Women's Movements in the Third World: Identity, Mobilization, and Autonomy." *Annual Review of Sociology* 25: 47–71.

Rian, Oystein. 1985. "State and Society in 17th-Century Norway." *Scandinavian Journal of History* 10: 337–363.

Rice E. E., ed. 1990. *Revolution and Counter-Revolution*. Oxford: Blackwell.

Ringmar, Erik. 1996. *Identity, Interest and Action: A Cultural Explanation of Sweden's Intervention in the Thirty Years War*. Cambridge, England: Cambridge University Press.

Rokkan, Stein. 1969. "Models and Methods in the Comparative Study of Nation Building." *Acta Sociologica* 12: 52–73.

———. 1970. *Citizens Elections Parties: Approaches to the Comparative Study of the Processes of Development*. Oslo: Universitets-forlaget.

———. 1974. "Macro-Histoire et Analyse Comparative des Processus de Développement Politique: Note Introductive." Unpublished report to *la journée d'études de l'Association Française de Science Politique*.

———. 1976. "Une Famille de Modèles pour l'Histoire Comparée de l'Europe Occidentale." Unpublished report to *la journée d'études de Association Française de Science Politique*.

———. 1979. "Economy, Territory, Identity: The Politics of the European Peripheries." Unpublished paper.

———. 1980. "Territories, Centres, and Peripheries: Toward a Geoethnic-Geoeconomic-Geopolitical Model of Differentiation Within Western Europe." In *Centre and Periphery: Spatial Variation in Politics*, ed. Jean Gottmann. Beverly Hills: Sage.

———, ed. 1968. *Comparative Research across Cultures and Nations*. Paris: Mouton.

Rokkan, Stein, and Derek W. Urwin, eds. 1982. *The Politics of Territorial Identity: Studies in European Regionalism*. Beverly Hills: Sage.

Rosanvallon, Pierre. 1992. *Le sacre du citoyen. Histoire du suffrage universel en France*. Paris: Gallimard.

Ross, John, et al., eds. and trans. 1995. *Shadows of Tender Fury: The Letters and Communiqués of Subcomandante Marcos and the Zapatista Army of National Liberation*. New York: Monthly Review Press.

Roy, Beth. 1994. *Some Trouble with Cows: Making Sense of Social Conflict*. Berkeley: University of California Press.

Rudé, George. 1959. *The Crowd in the French Revolution*. Oxford: Oxford University Press.

Rueschemeyer, Dietrich, Evelyne Huber Stephens, and John D. Stephens. 1992. *Capitalist Development and Democracy*. Chicago: University of Chicago Press.

Ruggie, John Gerard. 1993. "Territoriality and Beyond: Problematizing Modernity in International Relations." *International Organization* 47: 139–174.

Rule, James. 1988. *Theories of Civil Violence*. Berkeley: University of California Press.

Sacks, Oliver. 1985. *Migraine: Understanding a Common Disorder*. Berkeley: University of California Press.

Sahlins, Peter. 1989. *Boundaries: The Making of France and Spain in the Pyrenees*. Berkeley: University of California Press.

Salais, Robert, Nicolas Baverez, and Bénédicte Reynaud. 1986. *L'Invention du chômage. Histoire et transformations d'une catégorie en France des années 1890 aux années 1980*. Paris: Presses Universitaires de France.

Sanderson, Stephen K. 2001. *The Evolution of Human Sociality: A Darwinian Conflict Perspective*. Lanham, Md.: Rowman & Littlefield.

Schaffer, Frederic C. 1998. *Democracy in Translation: Understanding Politics in an Unfamiliar Culture.* Ithaca, N.Y.: Cornell University Press.

Schieder, Theodor. 1969. *Zum Problem des Staatenpluralismus in der modernen Welt.* Cologne: Westdeutscher Verlag.

Schlumbohm, Jürgen, ed. 1998. *Mikrogeschichte—Makrogeschichte: komplementär oder inkommensurabel?* Göttingen: Wallstein.

Schneider, Mark A. 1993. *Culture and Enchantment.* Chicago: University of Chicago Press.

Schneider, Robert A. 1995. *The Ceremonial City: Toulouse Observed 1738–1780.* Princeton, N.J.: Princeton University Press.

Schram, Stuart, ed. 1985. *The Scope of State Power in China.* London: European Science Foundation by School of Oriental and African Studies, University of London and the Chinese University Press of Hong Kong.

———. 1987. *Foundations and Limits of State Power in China.* London: European Science Foundation by School of Oriental and African Studies, University of London and the Chinese University Press of Hong Kong.

Schröder, Wilhelm Heinz. 1994. *Historische Sozialforschung: Identifikation, Organisation, Institution.* Historical Social Research series, Supplement no. 6. Köln: Zentrum für Historische Sozialforschung.

Schulze, Hagen, ed. 1987. *Nation-Building in Central Europe.* Leamington Spa, U.K.: Berg.

Schwartz, Mildred A. 1974. *Politics and Territory: The Sociology of Regional Persistence in Canada.* Montreal: McGill-Queens University Press.

Scott, James C. 1985. *Weapons of the Weak: Everyday Forms of Peasant Resistance.* New Haven, Conn.: Yale University Press.

———. 1990. *Domination and the Arts of Resistance: Hidden Transcripts.* New Haven, Conn.: Yale University Press.

———. 1998. *Seeing Like a State: How Certain Schemes to Improve the Human Condition Have Failed.* New Haven, Conn.: Yale University Press.

Searle, John R. 1993. "Rationality and Realism, What Is at Stake?" *Daedalus* 122: 55–84.

———. 1995. *The Construction of Social Reality.* New York: Free Press.

Sedaitis, Judith B., and Jim Butterfield, eds. 1991. *Perestroika from Below: Social Movements in the Soviet Union.* Boulder, Colo.: Westview.

Segal, Daniel A. 1988. "Nationalism, Comparatively Speaking." *Journal of Historical Sociology* 1: 301–321.

Selbin, Eric. 1993. *Modern Latin American Revolutions.* Boulder, Colo.: Westview.

Seligman, Adam. 1992. *The Idea of Civil Society.* New York: Free Press.

Sen, Amartya K. 1977. "Rational Fools: A Critique of the Behavioral Foundations of Economic Theory." *Philosophy and Public Affairs* 6: 317–344.

———. 1981. *Poverty and Famines: An Essay on Entitlement and Deprivation.* Oxford: Clarendon.

Sewell, William H., Jr. 1992. "A Theory of Structure: Duality, Agency, and Transformation." *American Journal of Sociology* 98: 1–29.

Shapiro, Gilbert, and John Markoff. 1998. *Revolutionary Demands: A Content Analysis of the Cahiers de Doléances of 1789.* Stanford, Calif.: Stanford University Press.

Shapiro, Susan P. 1987. "The Social Control of Impersonal Trust." *American Journal of Sociology* 93: 623–658.

Shell, Marc. 1993. *Children of the Earth: Literature, Politics and Nationhood.* New York: Oxford University Press.

Sheller, Mimi. 2000. *Democracy after Slavery: Black Publics and Peasant Radicalism in Haiti and Jamaica.* London: Macmillan (Warwick University Caribbean Studies).

References

Shennan, J. H. 1974. *The Origins of the Modern European State, 1450–1725*. London: Hutchinson University Library.

Shue, Vivienne. 1988. *The Reach of the State: Sketches of the Chinese Body Politic*. Stanford, Calif.: Stanford University Press.

Sider, Gerald. 1997. "The Making of Peculiar Local Cultures." In *Was bleibt von marxistischen Perspektiven in der Geschichtsforschung?* ed. Alf Lüdtke. Göttingen: Wallstein Verlag.

Sider, Gerald, and Gavin Smith, eds. 1997. *Between History and Histories: The Making of Silences and Commemorations*. Toronto: University of Toronto Press.

Simon, Herbert A. 1993. "Altruism and Economics." *American Economic Review. Papers and Proceedings* 83: 156–161.

Skinner, G. William. 1964. "Marketing and Social Structure in Rural China." *Journal of Asian Studies* 24: 3–43.

———. 1985. "The Structure of Chinese History." *Journal of Asian Studies* 44: 271–292.

Skocpol, Theda. 1979. *States and Social Revolutions: A Comparative Analysis of France, Russia, and China*. Cambridge, England: Cambridge University Press.

———, ed. 1998. *Democracy, Revolution, and History*. Ithaca, N.Y.: Cornell University Press.

Smelser, Neil J. 1963. *Theory of Collective Behavior*. New York: Free Press.

Smith, Anthony D. 1981. *The Ethnic Revival*. Cambridge, England: Cambridge University Press.

———. 1990. "The Supersession of Nationalism?" *International Journal of Comparative Sociology* 31: 1–31.

Smith, Dennis. 1991. *The Rise of Historical Sociology*. Philadelphia: Temple University Press.

Smith, Michael Peter, ed. 1991. *Breaking Chains: Social Movements and Collective Action*. Comparative Urban and Community Research, vol. 3. New Brunswick, N.J.: Transaction.

Snow, David A., E. Burke Rochford Jr., Steven K. Worden, and Robert D. Benford. 1986. "Frame Alignment and Mobilization." *American Sociological Review* 51: 464–481.

Solnick, Steven L. 1998. *Stealing the State: Control and Collapse in Soviet Institutions*. Cambridge, Mass.: Harvard University Press.

Somers, Margaret R. 1992. "Narrativity, Narrative Identity, and Social Action: Rethinking English Working-Class Formation." *Social Science History* 16: 591–630.

———. 1993. "Citizenship and the Place of the Public Sphere: Law, Community, and Political Culture in the Transition to Democracy." *American Sociological Review* 58: 587–620.

Sørensen, Georg. 1998. *Democracy and Democratization: Processes and Prospects in a Changing World*. Boulder, Colo.: Westview.

Spater, George. 1982. *William Cobbett: The Poor Man's Friend*. 2 vols. Cambridge, England: Cambridge University Press.

Sperber, Dan. 1996. *Explaining Culture: A Naturalistic Approach*. Oxford: Blackwell.

Stanley, William. 1996. *The Protection Racket State: Elite Politics, Military Extortion, and Civil War in El Salvador*. Philadelphia: Temple University Press.

Stark, David, and László Brust. 1998. *Postsocialist Pathways: Transforming Politics and Property in East Central Europe*. Cambridge, England: Cambridge University Press.

Starr, Harvey. 1994. "Revolution and War: Rethinking the Linkage between Internal and External Conflict." *Political Research Quarterly* 47: 481–507.

Steinberg, Marc. 1993. "New Canons or Loose Cannons? The Post-Marxist Challenge to Neo-Marxism as Represented in the Work of Calhoun and Reddy." *Political Power and Social Theory* 8: 221–270.

———. 1995. "'The Great End of All Government . . .': Working Peoples' Construction of Citizenship Claims in Early 19th-Century England and the Matter of Class." *International Review of Social History,* Supplement 3, 19–50.

———. 1999a. *Fighting Words: Working-Class Formation, Collective Action, and Discourse in Early 19th-Century England.* Ithaca, N.Y.: Cornell University Press.

———. 1999b. "The Talk and Back Talk of Collective Action: A Dialogic Analysis of Repertoires of Discourse among 19th-Century English Cotton Spinners." *American Journal of Sociology* 105: 736–780.

Steinmetz, George. 1993. *Regulating the Social: The Welfare State and Local Politics in Imperial Germany.* Princeton, N.J.: Princeton University Press.

Stevenson, John. 1992. *Popular Disturbances in England, 1700–1832.* 2d ed. London: Longman.

Stinchcombe, Arthur L. 1968. *Constructing Social Theories.* New York: Harcourt, Brace and World.

———. 1978. *Theoretical Methods in Social History.* New York: Academic.

———. 1996. *Sugar Island Slavery in the Age of Enlightenment: The Political Economy of the Caribbean World.* Princeton, N.J.: Princeton University Press.

Stoianovitch, Traian. 1976. *French Historical Method: The Annales Paradigm.* Ithaca, N.Y.: Cornell University Press.

———. 1994. *Balkan Worlds: The First and Last Europe.* Armonk, N.Y.: M. E. Sharpe.

Stoler, Ann Laura. 1989. "Rethinking Colonial Categories: European Communities and the Boundaries of Rule." *Comparative Studies in Society and History* 31: 134–161.

Sztompka, Piotr. 1996. "Trust and Emerging Democracy: Lessons from Poland." *International Sociology* 11: 37–62.

Taagepera, Rein. 1997. "Expansion and Contraction Patterns of Large Polities: Context for Russia." *International Studies Quarterly* 41: 475–504.

Tacke, Charlotte. 1993. "Les lieux de mémoire et la mémoire des lieux: Mythes et monuments entre nation et région en France et en Allemagne au XIXe siècle." In *Culture et Société dans l'Europe moderne et contemporaine,* ed. Dominique Julia. Florence: European University Institute.

Tambiah, Stanley J. 1996. *Leveling Crowds. Ethnonationalist Conflicts and Collective Violence in South Asia.* Berkeley: University of California Press.

———. 1997. "Friends, Neighbors, Enemies, Strangers: Aggressor and Victim in Civilian Ethnic Riots." *Social Science and Medicine* 45: 1177–1188.

Tarrow, Sidney. 1988. "National Politics and Collective Action: Recent Theory and Research in Western Europe and the United States." *Annual Review of Sociology:* 421–440.

———. 1989a. *Democracy and Disorder: Social Conflict, Political Protest and Democracy in Italy, 1966–1973.* New York: Oxford University Press.

———. 1989b. *Struggle, Politics, and Reform: Collective Action, Social Movements, and Cycles of Protest.* Western Societies Program, Occasional Paper No. 21. Ithaca, N.Y.: Center for International Studies, Cornell University.

———. 1993a. "La mondialisation des conflits: encore un siècle de rébellion?" *Etudes Internationales* 24: 513–532.

———. 1993b. "Modular Collective Action and the Rise of the Social Movement: Why the French Revolution Was Not Enough." *Politics and Society* 21: 69–90.

———. 1998. *Power in Movement: Social Movements, Collective Action and Revolution in the Modern World.* 2d ed. Cambridge, England: Cambridge University Press.

Taylor, Verta, and Nancy Whittier, eds. 1998. "Gender and Social Movements, Part I." *Gender & Society* 12 (special issue): 622–756.

Tetlock, Philip E. 1998. "Close-Call Counterfactuals and Belief-System Defenses: I Was Not Almost Wrong, But I Was Almost Right." *Journal of Personality and Social Psychology* 75: 639–652.

Thomas, Robert J. 1985. *Citizenship, Gender, and Work: Social Organization of Industrial Agriculture.* Berkeley: University of California Press.

Thompson, E. P. 1963. *The Making of the English Working Class.* London: Gollancz.

———. 1991. *Customs in Common.* London: Merlin.

Thompson, Richard H. 1989. *Theories of Ethnicity: A Critical Appraisal.* New York: Greenwood.

Tilly, Charles. 1964. *The Vendée.* Cambridge, Mass.: Harvard University Press.

———. 1978a. "Anthropology, History, and the *Annales.*" *Review* 1: 207–213.

———. 1978b. *From Mobilization to Revolution.* Reading, Mass.: Addison-Wesley.

———. 1982. "Britain Creates the Social Movement." In *Social Conflict and the Political Order in Modern Britain,* ed. James Cronin and Jonathan Schneer. London: Croom Helm.

———. 1983. "Speaking Your Mind Without Elections, Surveys, or Social Movements." *Public Opinion Quarterly* 47: 461–478.

———. 1987a. "Action collective et mobilisation individuelle." In *Sur l'individualisme,* ed. Pierre Birnbaum and Jean Leca. Paris: Presses de la Fondation nationale des sciences politiques

———. 1987b. "Formalization and Quantification in Historical Analysis." In *Quantitative History of Society and Economy: Some International Studies,* ed. Konrad H. Jarausch and Wilhelm Schröder. St. Katharinen: Scripta Mercaturae Verlag.

———. 1993. *European Revolutions, 1492–1992.* Oxford: Blackwell.

———. 1993–1994. "Social Movements as Historically Specific Clusters of Political Performances." *Berkeley Journal of Sociology* 38: 1–30.

———. 1995a. "Democracy Is a Lake." In *The Social Construction of Democracy,* ed. George Reid Andrews and Herrick Chapman. New York: New York University Press.

———. 1995b. "The Emergence of Citizenship in France and Elsewhere." In *Citizenship, Identity and Social History,* ed. Charles Tilly. Cambridge, England: Cambridge University Press.

———. 1995c. "To Explain Political Processes." *American Journal of Sociology* 100: 1594–1610.

———. 1995d. *Popular Contention in Great Britain, 1758–1834.* Cambridge, Mass.: Harvard University Press.

———. 1996. "Invisible Elbow." *Sociological Forum* 11: 589–601.

———. 1997a. "Parliamentarization of Popular Contention in Great Britain, 1758–1834." *Theory and Society* 26: 245–273.

———. 1997b. *Roads from Past to Future.* Lanham, Md.: Rowman & Littlefield.

———. 1998. *Durable Inequality.* Berkeley: University of California Press.

Tilly, Charles, and Wim P. Blockmans. 1994. *Cities and the Rise of States in Europe, AD 1000–1800.* Boulder, Colo.: Westview.

Tishkov, Valery. 1997. *Ethnicity, Nationalism and Conflict in and after the Soviet Union: The Mind Aflame.* London: Sage.

Topalov, Christian. 1991. "Patriotismes et citoyennetés." *Genèses* 3: 162–176.

———. 1994. *Naissance du chômeur, 1880–1910.* Paris: Albin Michel.

Torsvik, Per, ed. 1981. *Mobilization, Center-Periphery Structures and Nation-Building.* Bergen: Universitetsforlaget.

Touraine, Alain. 1981. *The Voice and the Eye: An Analysis of Social Movements.* Cambridge, England: Cambridge University Press.

———. 1985. "An Introduction to the Study of Social Movements." *Social Research* 52: 749–788.

——. 1994. "La Crise de l'Etat-Nation." *Revue Internationale de Politique Comparée* 1: 341–350.

Traugott, Mark, ed. 1995. *Repertoires and Cycles of Collective Action*. Durham, N.C.: Duke University Press.

Trexler, Richard C. 1981. *Public Life in Renaissance Florence*. New York: Academic.

Turner, Bryan S. 1988. "Religion and State Formation: A Commentary on Recent Debates." *Journal of Historical Sociology* 1: 322–333.

——. 1990. "Outline of a Theory of Citizenship." *Sociology* 24: 189–218.

——. 1993. *Citizenship and Social Theory*. Newbury Park, Calif.: Sage.

Turner, Ralph. 1986. *Collective Behavior*. 3d ed. Englewood Cliffs, N.J.: Prentice Hall.

Udehn, Lars. 1996. *The Limits of Public Choice: A Sociological Critique of the Economic Theory of Politics*. London: Routledge.

Vail, Leroy, ed. 1989. *The Creation of Tribalism in Africa*. London: James Curry.

Van Den Braembussche, A. A. 1989. "Historical Explanation and Comparative Method: Towards a Theory of the History of Society." *History and Theory* 28: 1–24.

van der Veer, Peter. 1996. "Riots and Rituals: The Construction of Violence and Public Space in Hindu Nationalism." In *Riots and Pogroms*, ed. Paul R. Brass. New York: New York University Press.

Verdery, Katherine. 1983. *Transylvanian Villagers*. Berkeley: University of California Press.

Vernon, James. 1993. *Politics and the People: A Study in English Political Culture c. 1815–1867*. Cambridge, England: Cambridge University Press.

Von Eckhardt, Barbara. 1993. *What Is Cognitive Science?* Cambridge, Mass.: MIT Press.

Wachter, Kenneth W. 1988. "Statistics in Historical Studies." *Kotz-Johnson Encyclopedia of Statistical Sciences*. New York: Wiley. Pp. 732–738.

Waldmann, Peter. 1989. *Ethnischer Radikalismus. Ursachen und Folgen gewaltsamer Minderheitenkonflikte*. Opladen: Westdeutscher Verlag.

Walicki Adam. 1991. "From Stalinism to Post-Communist Pluralism: The Case of Poland." *New Left Review* 185: 93–121.

Walker, Jack L. 1991. *Mobilizing Interest Groups in America: Patrons, Professions, and Social Movements*. Ann Arbor: University of Michigan Press.

Walton, John. 2001. *Storied Land: Community and Memory in Monterey*. Berkeley: University of California Press.

Walton, John, and Charles Ragin. 1990. "Global and National Sources of Political Protest: Third World Responses to the Debt Crisis." *American Sociological Review* 55: 876–890.

Ward, Bernard. 1912. *The Eve of Catholic Emancipation, 1803–1829*. London: Longman.

Ward, Michael D., and Kristian S. Gleditsch. 1998. "Democratizing for Peace." *American Political Science Review* 92: 51–61.

Warren, Mark E., ed. 1999. *Democracy and Trust*. Cambridge, England: Cambridge University Press.

Watkins, Susan Cotts. 1990. *From Provinces into Nations*. Princeton, N.J.: Princeton University Press.

Weil, Patrick. 1994. "Immigration, nation et nationalité: regards comparatifs et croisés." *Revue Française de Science Politique* 44: 308–326.

Wellman, Barry. 1971. "Social Identities in Black and White." *Sociological Inquiry* 41: 57–66.

——. 1988. "Structural Analysis: From Method and Metaphor to Theory and Substance." In *Social Structures: A Network Approach*, ed. Barry Wellman and S. D. Berkowitz. Cambridge, England: Cambridge University Press.

Wendorff, Rudolf. 1985. *Zeit und Kultur. Geschichte des Zeitbewusstseins in Europa.* Opladen: Westdeutscher Verlag.

Wendt, Alexander E. 1987. "The Agent-Structure Problem in International Relations Theory." *International Organization* 41: 335–370.

———. 1994. "Collective Identity Formation and the International State." *American Political Science Review* 88: 384–398.

White, Harrison. 1992. *Identity and Control: A Structural Theory of Social Action.* Princeton, N.J.: Princeton University Press.

———. 1993. *Careers and Creativity: Social Forces in the Arts.* Boulder, Colo.: Westview.

Whitney, Joseph B. R. 1970. *China: Area, Administration, and Nation Building.* Research Paper 123. Chicago: Department of Geography, University of Chicago.

Wilder, D. A. 1986. "Social Categorization: Implications for Creation and Reduction of Intergroup Bias." In *Advances in Experimental Social Psychology,* ed. Leonard Berkowitz. New York: Academic.

Will, Pierre-Étienne. 1994. "Chine moderne et sinologie." *Annales: Histoire, Sciences Sociales* 49: 7–26.

Williams, Brackette F. 1989. "A Class Act: Anthropology and the Race to Nation across Ethnic Terrain." *Annual Review of Anthropology* 18: 401–444.

Williams, Robin. 1994. "The Sociology of Ethnic Conflicts: Comparative International Perspectives." *Annual Review of Sociology* 20: 49–79.

Willigan, J. Dennis, and Katherine A. Lynch. 1982. *Sources and Methods of Historical Demography.* New York: Academic.

Wilson, Charles, and Geoffrey Parker, eds. 1977. *An Introduction to the Sources of European Economic History, 1500–1800.* London: Weidenfeld and Nicolson.

Wirtschafter, Elise Kimerling. 1997. *Social Identity in Imperial Russia.* DeKalb: Northern Illinois University Press.

Wolf, Eric R. 1969. *Peasant Wars of the 20th Century.* New York: Harper and Row.

———. 1999. *Envisioning Power: Ideologies of Dominance and Crisis.* Berkeley: University of California Press.

Woloch, Isser. 1994. *The New Regime: Transformations of the French Civic Order, 1789–1820s.* New York: Norton.

Wong, R. Bin. 1997. *China Transformed: Historical Change and the Limits of European Experience.* Ithaca, N.Y.: Cornell University Press.

Wood, Elisabeth Jean. 2000. *Forging Democracy from Below: Insurgent Transitions in South Africa and El Salvador.* Cambridge, England: Cambridge University Press.

Woolcock, Michael. 1998. "Social Capital and Economic Development: Toward a Theoretical Synthesis and Policy Framework." *Theory and Society* 27: 151–208.

World Bank. 1997. *The State in a Changing World: World Development Report.* Oxford: Oxford University Press.

Wrigley, E. A., ed. 1972. *Identifying People of the Past.* London: Edward Arnold.

Wrigley, E. A., and R. S. Schofield. 1981. *The Population History of England, 1541–1871: A Reconstruction.* Cambridge, Mass.: Harvard University Press.

Yamagishi, Toshio, and Midori Yamagishi. 1994. "Trust and Commitment in the United States and Japan." *Motivation and Emotion* 18: 129–166.

Yashar, Deborah J. 1997. *Demanding Democracy: Reform and Reaction in Costa Rica and Guatemala, 1870s–1950s.* Stanford, Calif.: Stanford University Press.

———. 1999. "Democracy, Indigenous Movements, and the Postliberal Challenge in Latin America." *World Politics* 52: 76–104.

Zald, Mayer N., and John D. McCarthy, eds. 1979. *The Dynamics of Social Movements: Resource Mobilization, Social Control, and Tactics.* Cambridge, Mass.: Winthrop.

———. 1987. *Social Movements in an Organizational Society.* New Brunswick, N.J.: Transaction.

Zaslavsky, Victor. 1992. "Nationalism and Democratic Transition in Postcommunist Societies." *Daedalus* 121, no. 2: 97–122.

Zdravom'islova, E. A. 1993. *Paradigm'i Zapadnoi Sotsiologii obschestvenn'ix dvizhenii.* St. Petersburg: Nauka.

Zelizer, Viviana. 1979. *Morals and Markets: The Development of Life Insurance in the United States.* New York: Columbia University Press.

———. 1985. *Pricing the Priceless Child: The Changing Social Value of Children.* New York: Basic.

———. 1994. *The Social Meaning of Money.* New York: Basic.

Zunz, Olivier, ed. 1985. *Reliving the Past: The Worlds of Social History.* Chapel Hill: University of North Carolina Press.

Index

245

Naples, kingdom of, 108
nationalism, 55–56, 94–95; bottom-up, 68,
 96, 163; citizenship rights and, 163–64;
 comparison to social movements, 97;
 European Union and, 168–69; identity
 and, 68, 95, 96, 207–8; stories of, 209;
 top-down, 68, 95–96, 163, 166, 167;
 war and, 164
nation-states, 163–64, 178; certification of,
 96–97. *See also* states
Nazi Germany, 146, 196
networks: social, 48, 79, 80; trust, 190,
 197–98, 201, 202–3
New Social Movements, 67
New Zealand, 203–4
Noiriel, Gérard, 95, 163
Nord, Philip, 192
North, Douglass, 173–74
Norway, 163
Nunavut, ix

oath of supremacy, 58, 82
Oberschall, Anthony, 79
O'Connell, Daniel, xiii–xiv, 53, 84–85, 87,
 89
O'Ferrall, Fergus, 92
O'Gorman, Frank, 59, 62, 63
Ohlemacher, Thomas, 50, 79
Olson, Mancur, 103, 200
On the Accuracy of Economic Observations
 (Morgenstern), 149
ontology, relational, 46–48
Opp, Karl-Dieter, 50
opportunity hoarding, mechanism of
 categorical inequality, 200
organizations, 54–55, 63, 80, 105. *See also*
 associations; social movements
Østergard, Uffe, 95
Ottoman Empire, 55, 107, 179

Paige, Jeffery M., 204; and Karen Paige,
 62
Palmer, Stanley H., 52
Parker, Geoffrey, 148
parliamentary time, 185
particularized time, 175–76

parties, political, 23, 63; Bharatiya Janata
 Party (India), 111–12; Peasant Party
 (Poland), 102; ties to social movements,
 54
Passy, Florence, 50, 54, 79
path-dependency, 172
Paulsen, Ronnelle, 50
Paxton, Pamela, 202
peace movement, 54
Peasant Wars of the 20th Century (Wolf), 145
Peel, Robert, 92, 93
petitions, 52, 61, 65, 90, 118
Phillips, John A., 93
Pitt the Younger, William, xiii–xiv, 84
Place, Francis, 91
Plotz, John M., 52
Poland, 102, 109, 195
political center, 45
political opportunity structures, 50, 54–55,
 79, 109
political participation, 22–23, 60–61, 66
political performances, 118, 153–54. *See
 also* repertoires of contention
Political Register (Cobbett), 57, 60
political rights, 126
Politics (Aristotle), 189
Politics and the People (Vernon), 16
The Politics of Large Numbers (Desrosières),
 145, 146–50
polity, 67
polyvalent performances, 153–54
Pomeranz, Kenneth, 142
Portugal, 163
power, political, 145–46; causal processes
 of, 153–58; dangers of top-down, 140,
 144; negotiation of, 152–53
Preston (Lancashire), 58–60
Price, Jacob M., 148
processes, causal, xii; of power, 153–58;
 stories and, 28–29, 35. *See also*
 mechanisms, causal
processes, social: explanation of, ix–x, xii,
 4–5, 9–10, 33–35; stories and, 9–10,
 73–75
prohibition of alcohol movement, 107
property rights, 173–74
Pro Ruiz, Juan, 174

social movement cycles, 105–8

social movements, 53–54, 207; comparison to nationalism, 97; defined, 88–91; factors determining success of, 88, 89–90; identity assertion of, 121; legitimacy of, 63; mystification in, 89–90; origins of simultaneity in, 109; repertoires of contention, 54, 90, 110; stories and, 40; study of, 77–81, 90; time and, 184–86; transformation of, 65–66, 104–5; WUNC and, 88–89, 120–21. *See also* countermovements; *specific movements*

Social Origins of Dictatorship and Democracy (Moore), 123–24

The Social Relations of Money (Zelizer), 150–51

social rights, 126

social sites, xi, 11

societies. *See* associations

solidarity movement, 54

solipsism, 16, 17

Solnick, Steven L., 151

Soly, Hugo, 143

Somers, Margaret R., 125

Some Trouble with Cows (Roy), 114

South Africa, 67–68

Soviet Union, 79, 97; centralized planning of, 151; collectivized agriculture of, 156–57; decline in central power of, 168; demilitarization of, 101–2, 109

Spain, 163

Spater, George, 58, 59

standardization, 139–40

Stanley, E. G., 58

Stanley, William, 154

Starr, Harvey, 148

states: circumscription of, 165, 166, 182–84; consolidated, 178, 179, 181; dangers of standardization by, 139–40; defined, 61, 177; legitimacy of, 137; pursuit of homogeneity, 162–66; segmented, 177; shaping of time, 175, 176–77, 182–86; threats to interventions of time by, 184, 186–87; time of, 172, 176–79; transformations of, 124–25, 141–43; transition from indirect to

direct rule, 127–30. *See also* armies; citizenship, rights of; nation-states; revolutions

statistics, 146–50, 154

Steinmetz, George, 135

Stevenson, John, 52

Stinchcombe, Arthur, 153

stories: boundary, 11–12; constraint and, 209–10; contextualized, 41; enlightenment and, 39–40, *40;* explanation of social processes, ix–x; generated, 41; generation and, 209; inferior, 40; problems of, x–xi; superior, xiii–xiv, 39–40, 41

stories, standard, 26, 29; causal mechanisms and, 30–32; function of, 8–9, 27; interviewing and, 27–28; overcoming limitations of, 35–39; representation of causal processes, 28–29, 35; social processes and, 9–10, 73–75. *See also* construction, social

The Story of Canada (Lunn and Moore), viii–ix

The Story of the Atom (Hakim), 29

strikes, 23, 51, 57, 61, 65, 68

Stringer, Keith J., 95

strong time, 175

Sunshine Sketches of a Little Town (Leacock), viii

Sweden, 130–31, 163

Switzerland, 128, 180, 196

Tambiah, Stanley J., 111, 112

Tarkhania, Kumar, 114, 116

Tarrow, Sidney, 50, 53, 79, 90, 104; on boundary stories, 12; on protest cycles, 68, 105–8; on repertoires of contention, 110, 118

taxation, 184; funding of standing armies, 129; resistance against, 132

Taylor, Verta, 53

Taylorism, 182

techne (theoretical knowledge), 143–44

Tejerina, Benjamín, 53

Test and Corporation Acts, 85

Therry, John Joseph, 77

Thirty Years War (1618–1648), 130

About the Author

Charles Tilly teaches social sciences at Columbia University. His recently completed books include *Dynamics of Contention* (with Doug McAdam and Sidney Tarrow, 2001), *The Politics of Collective Violence* (forthcoming), and *Contention and Democracy in Europe, 1650–2000* (forthcoming). He is currently co-authoring a college world history textbook.